THE HISTORIC GARDENS OF
OXFORD & CAMBRIDGE

THE HISTORIC GARDENS OF
OXFORD & CAMBRIDGE

Mavis Batey

With photographs by
Hugh Palmer

MACMILLAN
LONDON

© Antler Books Ltd 1989
First published in 1989 by
MACMILLAN LONDON LTD
4 Little Essex Street
London WC2R 3LF
and Basingstoke
Associated companies in Auckland, Delhi, Dublin, Gaborone, Hamburg,
Harare, Hong Kong, Johannesburg, Kuala Lumpur, Lagos, Manzini,
Melbourne, Mexico City, Nairobi, New York, Singapore and Tokyo.

Produced by John Stidolph
Editor Peter Fitzmaurice
Additional Research Charles Jacoby
Designed by Peter Hedges

British Library Cataloguing in Publication Data

Batey, Mavis
    The Historic Gardens of Oxford and Cambridge
    I. University of Cambridge
    II. Historic gardens—England—Cambridge—(Cambridgeshire)
    III. University of Oxford
    IV. Historic gardens—England—Oxford—(Oxfordshire)
    I. Title
    712′.7′0942659   SB466.G75C3

    ISBN 0–333–44680–1

Typesetting by TJB Photosetting Ltd., Grantham, Lincs.
Origination by BBE Colour Ltd.
Printed by Graficromo S.A., Cordoba, Spain

*Frontispiece: A view from the garden at Christ Church looking towards
Merton and Magdalen Tower*

Contents

1	Introduction	7
2	Mediaeval Origins	14
3	St Frideswide's Cloister Garden	27
4	Profit and Pleasure in the College Gardens	34
5	Elizabethan Oxford and Cambridge	43
6	Botanical Gardening	55
7	The Restoration	67
8	The Grand Manner	82
9	The Glorious Revolution and Dutch Gardening	95
10	The Pleasure of the Imagination	103
11	Landscaping in the Age of Taste	115
12	The Picturesque	127
13	Horticulture in Victorian Oxford and Cambridge	143
14	Arts and Crafts	155
15	Modern Oxford and Cambridge	167
	Notes and References	183
	Acknowledgements	187
	Index	189

1 Introduction

Oxford and Cambridge colleges with their quadrangles, courts, gardens and groves are renowned throughout the world. Here, in the words of a foreign Regency visitor,[1] can be seen a 'living spring of antiquity' and it is this that attracts the thousands of tourists today. Castles and ruined abbeys abound as ancient monuments in Britain, but the ideas of feudalism and monasticism which these embody are only to be found in history books and novels. The pursuit of learning, which was the inspiration of the mediaeval universities, is still the motivation for Oxford and Cambridge, so that there is a continuity of life and purpose in their cloisters, chapels, libraries, halls, gardens and bustling streets which links us visibly and emotionally with the past. For Henry James this seemed to embody 'with undreamed completeness a kind of dim and sacred ideal of the Western intellect'. It was often in the gardens that such passionate pilgrims found what they were seeking.

'We repaired in turn to a series of gardens and spent long hours sitting in their greenest places. They struck us as the fairest things in England and the ripest and sweetest fruit of the English system. Locked in their antique verdure...filled with nightingales and memories, a sort of chorus of tradition.'[2]

Lord Kames, writing in the eighteenth century, saw the college gardens as a necessary part of a training for excellence: 'Good professors are not more essential to a college than a spacious garden sweetly ornamented, but without anything staring or fantastic, so as upon the whole to inspire our youth with a taste no less for simplicity than for elegance'.[3] Later romantics dreamed dreams under the shadow of pinnacles and buttresses in 'gardens spreading to the moonlight'[4] and, like Arnold Toynbee, saw

Spring on the Backs.
The 'college groves and
tributary walks' that
inspired Wordsworth

7

Christ Church, the Deanery garden, a watercolour by William Turner c.1790. A secret garden that later became the scene for many of Lewis Carroll's Alice stories

the college garden as a place where 'one walks at night and listens to the wind in the trees, and weaves the stars into the web of one's thoughts'.[5]

The college gardens form a distinctive and unique part of the history of gardens. Monastery gardens disappeared at the Dissolution and only here and there in castles and cathedral precincts does the atmosphere of mediaeval enclosed gardens persist. The Oxford and Cambridge gardens, surrounded by ancient walls and buildings, present an overall collegiate layout unrivalled in the world. Many of the enclosed gardens are private or fellows' gardens, only open to the public on special occasions, but they can still be glimpsed magically through grilles or ancient doorways, in the spirit of mediaeval secret gardens. The planting has, of course, changed but there still remains the feeling of the original meaning of the word garden as a garth or piece of enclosed ground, a Chaucerian 'yarde'. As with the buildings, a complete history of gardens is there to be discovered with many rare historic features such as mounts, raised terraces, baroque quadrangles and a moated wilderness, now recorded in the English Heritage Register of Historic Parks and Gardens.[6]

Oxford and Cambridge are distinguished from other universities by the dominance of the colleges, each individually founded and with its own statutes, buildings and gardens. They are widely spread throughout the town and only in the Backs at Cambridge is there any attempt to create a unifying landscape. The gardens, orchards, groves and meadow walks were an important and necessary part of collegiate life and each college appointed its own garden master or equivalent from among its fellows. Although by the sixteenth century Oxford and Cambridge were seen as university towns, they were not planned as such, but were universities planted as cuckoos in the nests of flourishing market towns.

The differences in the character and outlook of the mediaeval towns of Oxford and Cambridge have affected the ways in which the universities gradually dominated the two cities, and their topography today. Oxford developed more compactly within its town walls while Cambridge followed the river. Both are now about an hour and a half's journey from London by motorway, but in the Middle Ages, Cambridge's links were mainly with the fens and by waterway with Kings Lynn. Oxford, however, was linked with London by the royal river and had easy connection with the Court and the city. It had developed commercially, while Cambridge was mainly agricultural. Farms were actually to be found within Cambridge and when the colleges along the Backs wanted to landscape the ground across the Cam, it was necessary to enclose the town's common fields. The resulting compensation of land within the town has, however, given Cambridge an advantage not enjoyed by today's citizens of Oxford, where no such enclosure had occurred. Open spaces such as Parker's Piece, exchanged by Trinity College in 1613, are public places, thronged with cyclists and football players, open to all and sundry at all times. Oxford's major open space, Christ Church meadow is owned by the college and, although open in daylight hours, is not a public open space, nor is it possible to cycle to work through it. Ironically, in view of Cambridge's agricultural origins, it is in Oxford that cows still graze in Chrish Church meadow in the heart of the city; and college and

The much admired garden at Worcester College, Oxford's only true landscaped garden, was planned by the Bursar, Richard Greswell

9

The Magdalen deer park to which public access is of necessity restricted

citizens have been united in opposing threats of a road through their *rus in urbe*. The pressures on Cambridge, in terms of housing development and servicing, are far less than on Oxford, since it remains the market town for an agricultural hinterland, whereas Oxford, having begun in a commercial way with such easy communications, was to become swamped by industry. Many still remember the sign at one of the roundabout approaches to the city: Welcome to Oxford, the home of the Motor Car.

The student of Oxford and Cambridge garden history is fortunate in having well-preserved college accounts, the Agas map of 1578 for Oxford and Hamond's map of Cambridge of 1592 showing their Elizabethan gardens. Loggan's *Oxonia Illustrata* of 1675 and *Cantabrigia Illustrata* of 1690 give remarkable details of garden features, while Williams's *Oxonia Depicta* of 1733 shows the lengths to which Dutch gardening had been taken by the colleges. There were great men and great events in the university towns and visitors frequently recorded their impressions, some of which, like those of the German Zacharias von Uffenbach,[8] were not always favourable. Many famous sons, including poets, have written

King's College bridge over the Cam. The citizens of Cambridge for historical reasons, have had easier access across college grounds

about their colleges and the gardens, which have been painted by Turner, Le Keux, Malchair and Delamotte. Excellent colour plates were made for Ackermann's histories showing the setting of the colleges in Regency times. The Oxford Almanacks[9] which began in the seventeenth century and continue today show the changing scenes in college gardens. The gossipy seventeenth-century antiquary, Anthony Wood, recorded day by day events in Oxford, slating town and gown alike, but giving interesting accounts of the making of the New College parterre with its royal coat of arms at the Restoration and how the Warden's wife spied on the Merton fellows from the summerhouse. In Cambridge George Dyer, the poet and gardenist, has much to say about eighteenth-century college gardening, which is relevant to the history of landscaping as a whole. Architectural historians usually only refer to gardens in footnotes but the monumental *Architectural History of the University of Cambridge* by R. Willis and J.W. Clark, published in 1886, is a mine of information about college records concerning gardens.

The best architects and garden designers of the calibre of Bridgeman, Brown and Repton were consulted by the colleges, but their plans were

*The woodland garden at
St John's College, Oxford*

seldom carried out. Most colleges have piles of rejected plans in their
archives; indeed Howard Colvin has written a fascinating book, *Unbuilt
Oxford*, using this material. Capability Brown was given an inscribed
silver tray by the University of Cambridge as a token of gratitude for his
plan to landscape the Backs, but nothing came of his proposal. Humphry
Repton's account for his magnificent Red Book for Magdalen College,
Oxford was settled but his suggested improvements were ignored.
Designing a building or a garden for an academic body has special
difficulties as there are so many different 'wisdomes' to be consulted, as
Hawksmoor found to his chagrin in Oxford and Cambridge. When
Professor Willmer, a fellow of Clare, designed the post-war garden across
the Cam for his college, he found that he had to accommodate his
colleagues' different preferences and interests into his design.
Remarkably he has succeeded in providing both the element of formality
favoured by the theatrical society supporters and the natural setting
urged by the solitary muses.

Fellows have always been widely travelled and brought back plants
and ideas from abroad and many were themselves foresters, ecologists or
botanists who influenced the planting of their college gardens. The much
admired landscaped garden at Worcester College, Oxford was laid out by
the Bursar, as was the rock garden at St John's. More recently, when the
eminent plant physiologist Professor Geoffrey Blackman was Keeper of
the Groves at St John's, he imported cartloads of leaf mould from Bagley
Wood and transformed the lime-soaked Oxford soil of his college garden

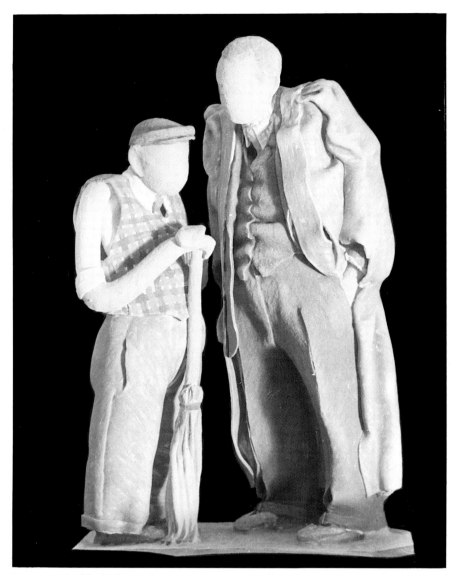

*'A Study in Persuasion',
a ceramic by Audrey
Blackman. The* Custos
Silvarum *and the head
gardener at St John's
College, Oxford*

into a suitable habitat for ericaceous woodland gardening, although the
head gardener, Mr Mundy, needed gentle persuading about the wisdom
of the idea.

Architecture, in Pugin's words, represents 'the history of the world'.
Gardens can go even deeper in reflecting the spirit of the age, not only
because more people can actually participate in the art of gardening than
in building, but because it involves man's changing attitudes to the
natural world. There is no better place than Oxford and Cambridge in
which to study this history of gardens and environmental attitudes. From
early times scholars had believed that botany was fundamental to the
study of life as a whole and, in seventeenth-century Oxford and
Cambridge, gardening became part of natural philosophy. The college
gardens can be seen as reflections of monastic and Renaissance ideas,
Puritan good husbandry, the exuberance of the Restoration and baroque
ideas of grandeur, classical philosophy, eighteenth-century taste,
romanticism, Arts and Crafts principles and modernism.

2   Mediaeval Origins

Oxford and Cambridge were flourishing towns long before the universities gave them their special character and claim to fame. Both appeared in the Anglo-Saxon Chronicles as important crossing places; Cambridge, Grantabrycge, with its great bridge across the Granta or Cam, had probably already been fortified by the Romans while Oxnaforde, which marked the division between Mercia and Wessex, was fortified as a stronghold against the Danes at its vulnerable fording place. Both Oxford and Cambridge had a castle and a mint in the Domesday Survey, Oxford having already been styled a *civitas* on its tenth-century coins. Oxford received its charter in 1191, Cambridge in 1201, but the development and growth of the mediaeval boroughs with their guilds were thereafter to be restricted by the rise of the universities.

It has always been said that Oxford grew up round the Saxon priory of St Frideswide situated above the ford where the oxen crossed the Thames. The only illumination of Oxford shows its patron saint standing by the river with an ox at her feet. These myths were challenged by twentieth-century historians but recently archaeological investigations have proved that St Frideswide's priory did stand on the site of the later Christ Church[1] and that the Oxford ford really was at the present Folly Bridge crossing, just as the myths had said.[2] The castle mound is clearly visible, sandwiched between the prison and the Oxfordshire County Council offices. In Saxon Cambridge there were communities on both sides of the Cam, but after the building of the Norman castle and fortifications, the emphasis shifted to the south bank where there were good wharfing facilities. The Cam was extensively used for transport, the river, being navigable from Kings Lynn by way of the Ouse, made it remarkably accessible as an inland port. The mediaeval Stourbridge Fair, held just outside the town, was world famous,[3] but it declined in the eighteenth century leaving only street names such as Mercers Row, Cheddars Lane and Garlic Row as reminders of its existence. The prosperity of Norman Oxford and Cambridge is seen in the number of their religious foundations. The son of Robert D'Oilly, King William's baron who built Oxford Castle, founded the great Abbey of Osney in 1129. Seven years before St Frideswide's priory, also Augustinian, had been refounded, and in 1133 the Benedictine nunnery at Godstow was founded. As early as 1112 an important Augustinian monastery had been established at Barnwell outside Cambridge, to be followed by the nunnery of St Radegund (later to become Jesus College). Monastic hospitals of St John were set up, in Cambridge on the site of the present college, and in Oxford where Magdalen College now stands.

The conversion of Oxford and Cambridge into seats of learning was a gradual process. It is not known exactly when Chaucer's 'sely clerks' of Oxenford and Canterbrigge had begun to change the character of the thriving towns, but by the end of the twelfth century, Oxford had been accorded a *studium generale* and in 1303 the University of Cambridge was publishing its own statutes. Henry I was said to have enjoyed conversation with the clerks when in Oxford and European scholars are known to have visited the town in the early part of the twelfth century. There were also scholars attached to Cambridge religious foundations and several teaching communities long before the Pope proclaimed a *studium generale* in 1318. The number of scholars was greatly increased by the arrival of the thirteenth-century friars – Carmelites, Franciscans, Dominicans, Austin Friars and some short-lived sects.[4]

The monasteries were founded in rural secluded areas, but the friars went out into the world and settled in populous towns to minister to their needs. They espoused poverty and relied on gifts of goods and land for their communities. In Oxford they were chiefly to be found between the old St Ebbes and the river. The Grey Friars' garden was still referred to as the 'Graye Fryars Paradise' in the seventeenth century, when the friary garden had become a flourishing market garden.[5] Paradise Square now stands incongruously in the middle of the Westgate development. Another reminder of the days of the friars is the narrow passage at the side of Debenhams, still called Friars' Entry, which once led to the settlements of the White Friars, the Carmelites, on land which had belonged to Beaumont Palace. In Cambridge the White Friars settled at Newnham; Peterhouse is on the site of the buildings belonging to the Brothers of the Sack; Sidney Sussex has replaced the house of the Grey Friars, the Franciscans; and Emmanuel that of the Black Friars, the Dominicans. It is in the gardens of these colleges, where some of the old boundary walls remain, that we may feel some continuity between the friars and the fellows. There is a garden at Sidney Sussex which was made in the friars' churchyard and on the wall is a memorial to the famous Franciscan Duns Scotus (who actually did his duncing in Oxford). The Franciscan system of piped water from the river to the friary still supplies the fountain in Trinity Great Court; at Emmanuel a pool in the peaceful paddock was probably the fishpond of the Black Friars.

A continuity with pre-Dissolution monastic life is also felt in the gardens of Worcester College, Oxford and Magdalene College, Cambridge. These were originally colleges of student monks from Benedictine abbeys, which were set up in the hope of regaining for the Order the intellectual leadership it had lost to the Friars. The first cell was founded in Oxford in 1283 by the Abbey of St Peter's, Gloucester, in surviving buildings of the present Worcester College. The camerae in

The New College cloister. The idea of the monastic cloister was adapted for college use in Oxford

which the various cells which followed Gloucester lived can be seen on the south side of the quadrangle with the shields of their abbeys over the doors. An arch from the monastic buildings resited by the landscaped lake, which was originally the Benedictine fishpond, adds a romantic touch of history to one of Oxford's most picturesque scenes. The original name of the college is perpetuated by nearby Gloucester Green, where the coach from Cambridge used to arrive. Gloucester College was founded for abbeys in the south but was followed by Durham College (later to become Trinity College) three years later for student monks from the north. It was not until the fifteenth century that the Augustinians and the Cistercians followed suit by founding in Oxford, St Mary's College (now Frewin Hall) and St Bernard's College (to become St John's College at the Reformation) respectively.

The monasteries were largely self-sufficient and the Rule of Benedict obliged the order to undertake manual work in the garden. Their diet was vegetarian and consisted of thick starchy pottage made of leeks, peas, beans, and onions, which were grown near the kitchen. Herbs were needed in the making of beer and ale and were also dried as 'drugs' for use in the infirmary; these included comfrey, cumin, sage, clary, hyssop, rue, camomile, betony, dittany, dill, borage, elecampane, southernwood and fennel. Even those who had been sent to the universities to study would have been required to take up their share of productive 'swink' in the long parallel beds in the monastery's vegetable and herb gardens. Cambridge did not receive a monks' hostel until 1428, when a site was acquired north of the Cam to provide accommodation for students from the Benedictine Abbeys of Ely, Crowland, Ramsey and Walden with separate chambers similar to those built at Gloucester College, Oxford. Here too in the gardens of its successor, Magdalene College, a monastic feeling still prevails as at Worcester College in Oxford. The boundaries of the fellows' garden have remained unchanged from the original grant of land to the Benedictines. The northern yew-clad terrace is still known as Monks Walk. As well as the vegetable and herb gardens there were riverside walks amongst orchards and groves which must have been pleasant places for quiet contemplation. Part of the Magdalene garden was once called pond-yards in reference to its seven fish ponds now filled in. The word yard, meaning a garth or enclosure, was used for garden even in the great houses and still is in some parts of America today.

Chaucer, who visited both Oxford and Cambridge, tells us much about the conduct of affairs in the fourteenth-century universities in two of his most bawdy tales. The Miller's Tale for Oxford and The Reeve's Tale for Cambridge. There was also on the Canterbury pilgrimage a 'clerk of Oxenford', a sober modest man, steeped in Aristotle and logic, and 'gladly wolde he lerne and gladly teche'.[6] The university from which Chaucer's well-read scholar had obtained his degree was in reality, as in Cambridge, a guild of teachers, who could sanction others to teach by licence. In both towns traders set up nearby, – book binders, parchmenters and illuminators – to meet the new demands of scholarship. In Oxford, illuminators, who set up in Catte Street and Schools Street, had migrated from places such as Winchester, Dorchester and Christchurch, where they would have learned their skills from the monasteries.[7]

We do not know whether Chaucer's clerk of Oxenford was attached to one of the eight colleges which existed then, but we are told that the poor scholar Nicholas in The Miller's Tale boarded with an Oxford carpenter who worked for nearby Osney Abbey. He too had many books as well as calculating devices and herbs to sweeten his room, but also musical instruments spurned by the more sober teaching clerk.[8] His friends who had lent him money for his studies would hardly have approved of his goings-on described by Chaucer. In the Middle Ages students either found their own accommodation, like Nicholas, or stayed within an approved hall. It was the need for the supervision of the likes of Nicholas that led the University of Oxford to decree in 1410 that all students must live in recognized halls of residence. St Edmund Hall still keeps the name, and until this century had the status of such an institution.[9]

The endowed colleges were for graduate or special category students and it was from one of these that the two young students set forth in The Reeve's Tale to take the manciple's corn to be ground at the Trumpington Mill outside Cambridge. In Chaucer's time there were nine colleges in Cambridge, mostly situated between the High Street and the river, and, as in Oxford, a number of hostels rented by graduates to keep students as

The Magdalen cloister with its allegorical figures and chambers on the upper storey

19

lodgers. As John and Aleyn were young but from 'a greet college, men clepen the Soler-halle at Cantebregge',[10] this probably meant that they were 'King's childer', from King's Hall, (later to become Trinity College) which was founded in 1317 for training young students of well-connected families for service in administration.

As early as 1249 William of Durham bequeathed money to the University of Oxford for the maintenance of ten Masters of Arts. This became the first corporate body or *collegium*, and in 1280 became University College. In 1255 John Balliol, condemned to do penance for misconduct, founded a small community of scholars in Oxford, which was first mentioned in 1266. Care for souls was a major concern of the early foundations, where poor scholars prayed daily for their benefactors. Walter de Merton at the same time set about building a college better endowed and planned than any other. Preference was to be given to 'Founder's Kin', and in fact the first fellows of Merton were the eight nephews of Walter de Merton. He sought to strengthen the secular priesthood and forbade scholars to enter monasteries. Peterhouse,

Queens' College, the most domestic looking of the early Cambridge colleges

Cambridge's first college, was founded in 1284 by the Bishop of Ely, when his plan to introduce scholars into the monastic hospital of St John's misfired. Some colleges were founded with a regional bias, such as Exeter in 1314 whose fellows were to come from the diocese of Exeter.

The Black Death wreaked havoc in all sections of society. Trinity Hall was founded in Cambridge by the Bishop of Norwich to produce a supply of clergy to compensate for the loss suffered in the pestilence. Corpus was founded by two Cambridge guilds, Corpus Christi and the Blessed Virgin, to train priests to celebrate masses for the souls of the departed of their guilds. This explains why Corpus is the only college to be sited in the civic heart of old Cambridge. Oxford suffered severely in the economic depression following the Black Death and there were many empty spaces within the town walls, so that New College in 1369 was able to acquire the land for its unusually large garden. New College, which was being built when Chaucer visited Oxford, was, as its name suggests, an innovation. Its foundation of a society of students and teachers living together set the pattern for future colleges. The collegiate system later died out in Paris and other European universities, but it gathered strength in Oxford and Cambridge with the universities emerging as federations of their colleges.

A *collegium* was, like a monastery, a community living under a rule, but its way of life was more secular and provisions were made not only for devotions and studies, but for the domestic comforts, exercises and amusements of members, which included bowling greens and ball courts. The colleges specifically disassociated themselves from the monastic concept, by stipulating that their members were training as secular priests, teachers or civil servants. Many of the colleges which, like New College, were purpose built did take much from traditional monastic layouts, which had proved their use for community living. The cloister was the most striking feature of monastic inheritance. Chaucer calls monks 'cloisterers' and it was the symbol of the enclosed monastic life. The monastic cloister was probably derived from the colonnaded courtyards of Graeco-Roman houses. The earliest cloister known in this country is that discovered at St Augustine's Abbey at Canterbury, which is believed to date from the tenth century. It had the obvious advantage of providing shelter in bad weather when walking from one monastic building to another. Jesus College in Cambridge and Christ Church in Oxford both inherited cloisters from dissolved monasteries, which they retained in their colleges, but New College, All Souls and Magdalen actually planned cloistered walks in their new foundations.

New College was founded in 1379 by William of Wykeham, Bishop of Winchester, who would have recognized the usefulness of the covered cloister leading from cathedral to chapter house as well as in the monastery. At New College the cloister was intended for sheltered perambulation rather than as a means of communication, as there were no buildings on three sides of it. The blackened wall along the north side of New College Lane is, in fact, the back of the cloister and is a good example of how collegiate architecture dictates the shape and character of the town lanes. The cloister garden was consecrated in 1400 for a

Jesus College, Cambridge, the cloister of the former priory of St Radegund

private college burial ground, which may have been a combined orchard and graveyard as at the Abbey of St Gall.[11] William of Wykeham also provided his purpose built school at Winchester, where boys were prepared for New College, with cloisters for perambulation. All Souls later copied the idea of a detached cloister for sheltered walks, looking on to a tree-planted garden. Magdalen College's cloister, built in 1474, was also a covered perambulation looking onto a green open space but having chambers built as an upper storey. In 1508 allegorical figures were set up to adorn the buttresses on three sides of the garden cloister, representing arts, divinity, law and medicine and heraldic emblems. The greatest cloistered quadrangle in Oxford was planned by Wolsey for his Cardinal College, but although three of the ranges of buildings were finished, only the shafts of the cloisters, which can still be seen in Tom Quad, were begun before his fall.

Cambridge colleges built no true cloisters in the monastic tradition. Relatively few of their founders were ecclesiastical like William of Wykeham or a later Bishop of Winchester, William of Waynflete, the builder of Magdalen College or Archbishop Chichele, the founder of All Souls or the great Cardinal Wolsey in Oxford. Cambridge colleges were founded mainly by monarchs, noble ladies, merchants and guilds, and had many of the architectural features, such as solars, oriels, galleries and garden staircases of the courtyard manor houses. Cotehele in Cornwall, which still survives as an unchanged late mediaeval manor house, bears a striking resemblance to Cambridge colleges of the period. Queens' College is the most noticeably domestic looking of all the colleges and its Old Court with its fine mediaeval brickwork remains almost untouched. It contained all the essential requirements of a college, a gate-house, chapel, hall, library, kitchen and chambers. It seems, however, that when a second court was needed the advantage of covered walks had been realized, so that Cloister Court was planned, with its brick arcades, although it was not fully enclosed until about 1495 when the arcades on the north and south sides were built. Old Court at Corpus Christi is also an outstanding example of an early mediaeval college layout, particularly as through its guild origins it is an integral part of the town, being sited between the two ancient churches of St Bene't's and St Botolph. The guild was housed near the churchyard of St Bene't's church which served as the college chapel, a gallery being built to link them. Entering from St Benet Street, rather than through the main college entrance in Trumpington Street, this long-standing connection between church, guild and college is recalled by the small garden in its mediaeval plot surrounded by old walls, uniting the Saxon church with the Old Court of Corpus.

The layout of the Cambridge college is always associated with the court: the Old Court, the Front Court, the Tree Court, the New Court or those named after benefactors, Nevile's Court, Cripps Court etc. The more institutional and less domestic sounding Oxford equivalent is the quadrangle: Mob Quad, Fellows' Quadrangle, Canterbury Quadrangle, Pump Quad, the Garden Quad. Architecturally it is the court or quadrangle which gives a college its special character, but the regularity that we associate with it only began with New College in 1379. Previous arrangements were haphazard and irregular as the buildings developed with the growing needs of the scholars. Merton's influential Mob Quad had only evolved gradually over a hundred years.

Walter de Merton also owned manors near Cambridge and the college rolls show that there was frequent communication with the other up-and-coming university. Merton Hall at St John's College, Cambridge, still owned by Merton College until 1959, and the new Merton Court recall the Oxford connection. Walter de Merton, who was well versed in administration, set the pattern of individual statutes which provided the impetus for college autonomy in both places. The monastic hostels were answerable to their order and the principal of an unendowed hall was responsible to the university, but the head of a college was to be bound by the founder's statutes and only responsible to his appointed visitor. The colleges attracted benefactors in a way that the corporate university could not and the individually endowed colleges prospered. Often, as at Merton, town houses and halls provided the nucleus of the college in its early days. The name Peterhouse reminds us of its origins as a citizen's house. The royally endowed King's Hall started life as the timber town house of Robert de Croyland, to which additions were made and adjoining plots bought up until finally, along with Michaelhouse opposite, it was absorbed into Henry VIII's Trinity College. To begin with the halls and endowed colleges fitted in behind the shops and houses of the two towns without dominating them. At the end of the fourteenth century, in the economic depression, it could be said that New College rendered Oxford a service by taking up some of the wasteland and agreeing for all time to keep up that section of the town walls. The college has always carried out its obligations and they remain today as one of Oxford's most historic features. The city fathers still inspect the walls periodically according to tradition although the city has long since knocked down practically all the rest of its defensive walls in development schemes.

The ambitious schemes of Henry VI did radically change the face of Cambridge. There had been a lull of nearly a century since the first colleges, Peterhouse(1284), Michaelhouse(1324), University Hall(1326), King's Hall(1337), Clare Hall(1338), Pembroke Hall(1347), Gonville Hall(1348), Trinity Hall(1350) and Corpus Christi(1352) had been built. King's College, the foundation stone of whose famous chapel was laid in 1446, was planned on a totally different scale. Whole streets of shops, hostels, houses and gardens and a church were obliterated and access to the river docks removed. Despite this great clearance it was to be another 400 years before the college occupied more than a corner of the site. The town council was not entirely satisfied by the compensation received for the loss of their commonland and thoroughfares,[12] and there was fear for the town's future prosperity if the self-supporting colleges continued to expand.

The next major expansion and seizure of land in Cambridge, however, after a lull in college founding during the Wars of the Roses, was to be at the expense of the monasteries rather than the town. Jesus College was founded in 1496 after the abolition of the priory of St Radegund by the Bishop of Ely, when it was discovered that there were reports of scandalous conduct by the nuns, two only being left in the nunnery.[13] Their church is the present college chapel and other features of the priory can be seen round the Cloister Court, which is the only true cloister in Cambridge. The original pentice-type cloister with simple windows, which can still be seen on the seventeenth-century Loggan drawing, was replaced by arches in the eighteenth century and is now covered with vines and adorned with hanging baskets. For Christ's College the Lady Margaret Beaufort took over the small Godshouse for training schoolmasters and enlarged its buildings. In 1511 St John's College was built on the site of the decaying monastic hospital, the foundations of which are exposed in the First Court planted up with flowers. Other colleges later to benefit from monastic land after the Dissolution in 1538 were Magdalene, founded on the site of the Benedictine monks hostel in 1542, Emmanuel in 1584 on the site of the house of the Black Friars and Sidney Sussex in 1596 on the site of the Franciscan friary, Henry VIII having used the building stone for his own Trinity College, founded in 1546. After the sixteenth-century post-Dissolution colleges no other college was founded in Cambridge until Downing in 1800.

In Oxford it was the same story. Some monastic land was acquired for colleges even before the 1538 suppression. Magdalen was able to take over the decaying St John's hospital and Wolsey dissolved St Frideswide's priory and absorbed its buildings into his Cardinal College. The monastic colleges fell at the Dissolution with their abbeys; Gloucester College passed eventually to St John's and evolved into Worcester College, Durham College was absorbed into Trinity College, St Bernard's into St John's and Canterbury College into Christ Church and the house of the Austin Friars into Wadham. One intended monastic college was saved by a premonition of the impending disaster. In 1513 Bishop Fox was planning a college for monks from St Swithin's but was advised by the Bishop of Exeter to change his plan. Holinshead reports him as saying, 'Shall we build houses and provide livelihoods for a company of bussing monks, whose end and fall we may ourselves see?' His advice was taken and Corpus Christi College was founded as a secular college in 1517. It was the first true Renaissance college in England, whose progressive curriculum was described by its founder in horticultural terms. 'The bees make not honey of all flowers without choice, but from those of all the sweetest and best scents and savours, which are tasted and distinguishable in the honey itself. We therefore are resolved to constitute within our bee-garden for ever three right skilful herbalists, therein to plant and sow stocks, herbs and flowers of the choicest, as well for fruit as thrift, that ingenious bees swarming hitherward from the whole gymnasium of Oxford, may thereout suck and cull matter convertible not so much into food for themselves, as to the behoof, grace and honour of the whole English name.'[14]

The fate of all colleges in Oxford and Cambridge did in fact hang in the balance, when in 1544, following the Dissolution of the Monasteries, an Act was passed enabling the King to dissolve any chantry, college or hospital. Greedy courtiers encouraged him to use these powers on the two universities so that their properties could be acquired at the same easy prices as the monastic spoils. Fortunately Queen Katherine Parr, Henry VIII's last wife, was acting as Regent in 1544 while her husband was out of the country and she consulted with her well trusted clerk Dr Thomas Smith of Queens'. The Cambridge Vice-Chancellor was instructed to draw up an account of the activities and finances of the colleges which so impressed the King that he thought 'he had not in his realm so many persons so honestly maintained in living by so little land and rent'.[15] He then turned on his courtiers accusing them that 'whereas we had regard only to pull down sin by defacing the monasteries, you have a desire also to overthrow all goodness by subversion of colleges. I tell you sirs, that I judge no land in England better bestowed than that which is given to our universities, for by their maintenance our realm shall be well governed when we be dead and rotten.'[16] To show that he meant what he said he then used the Act to dissolve two secular colleges Michaelhouse and King's Hall to found, with some of the monastic wealth, his great Trinity College, whose Master should be appointed by the Crown. In Oxford Henry VIII refounded Wolsey's great college as the cathedral college of Christ Church, whose Dean should also be appointed by the Crown. The foundation of these two great colleges was virtually the last act before his death.

F R
T

Qu
in
ric[t]

enim qui seipsum
ille probatus est: se[d]
v s commendat. V[-]

3 St Frideswide's Cloister Garden

Mediaeval buildings can still be seen and experienced as part of Matthew Arnold's 'enchantments of the Middle Age', but of the gardens only old walls, raised terraces or rare ancient yews survive. Vanished gardens can be recreated, however, where these historic enclosures exist, whereas buildings can only be restored when some of the original structure remains. When authentic plants are used in recreated gardens there is a living, inherited continuity with the past. An instruction in an old document to John the gardener to grow saffron crocus, rosemary, leeks or lilies can provide the starting point for the recreation of a mediaeval garden. Through the plants and the way they are used associative links can also be made with the history contained in these gardens.

A mediaeval garden has been created at Winchester outside the Great Hall, which is all that remains of the old castle. The garden,[1] designed by Dr Sylvia Landsberg for the Hampshire Gardens Trust, is known as Queen Eleanor's garden, in memory of the two gardening queens, Queen Eleanor of Provence and her daughter-in-law Eleanor of Castile, wife of Edward I. Nothing of the actual thirteenth-century gardens is known except for the command. 'Let three herbaria be made', but fragmentary descriptions of other royal residences of the time have been pieced together, so that what today's visitor sees, the Queen's herber, the fountain and channel, the tunnel arbour, the Glastonbury thorn, roses, lillies, hollyhocks and herbs, would all have been familiar to the two queens at Winchester.

The Christ Church mediaeval garden was begun in 1985 after the cleaning of the stone in the old priory cloister. The central space had become an eyesore, and the Dean and Chapter felt that a sympathetic garden would enhance the newly restored cloister. The garden is known as St Frideswide's garden, after Oxford's patron saint who founded her monastery on the site and whose shrine is in the cathedral. It is in no way considered as a restoration of a garden which was known through documentary or archaeological investigations to have existed, but as an authentically planted mediaeval garden which commemorates the remarkable span of history which still links St Frideswide's priory with Christ Church, the cathedral college, founded by Henry VIII to replace Wolsey's ill-fated Cardinal College.

St Frideswide, patron saint of Oxford, an illumination from Wolsey's Epistle Book at Christ Church

27

St Frideswide's garden showing trellised railing and raised bed

The first task was to ascertain the nature of the broken footings in the centre of the cloister garth and to record them before grassing the area. It was known that during the Gilbert Scott restoration of the cathedral the level of the garden was lowered to expose the cloister plinths and the foundation of an unknown building was discovered. In true Victorian style, with the idea of enhancing antiquity, the cloister arcade was covered with creepers and the mysterious footings, in the shape of the Cross of Lorraine, were capped and covered with ivy to form a garden feature. This was later removed and the rubble footings broke up giving the cloister garth a most unkempt appearance. The Oxford Archaeological Unit excavated beneath the exposed foundation and produced evidence that the structure had been a temporary belfry which housed the bells that Wolsey had removed from the steeple of the priory church before their installation in an intended new bell tower. The belfry and bells were scrapped when, in 1546, the bells from dissolved Osney Abbey, including Great Tom (later to be removed to Wren's Tom Tower), were brought to Christ Church and hoisted into the restored priory church steeple. Having duly recorded the building, it was not thought to have been significant enough to take into account when planning the garden; the footings could therefore be lowered and covered up before grassing the area. As the site is such an historic one, however, the archaeologists were asked to make a thorough investigation before the garden was laid out. The extended excavations revealed evidence of the burial ground of the Saxon minster church.[2]

The first Norman prior, Guimond, was a scholar and it is thought that a school where learned men assembled was attached to St Frideswide's, which may have been the cradle of the university. Certainly St Frideswide's held the earliest university chest and acted as timekeeper for Oxford disputations. The 'canons of Oxford', mentioned in the Domesday Survey, however, belonged to the previous foundation, thought to consist of nuns and priests, who were the heirs of St Frideswide's original monastery. Although evidence for the existence of the Saxon monastery has now been found by the archaeologists, faith rather than radiocarbon dating is still required to authenticate the legend of St Frideswide herself. Oxford is quite prepared to take her on trust as a local saint (even Chaucer's carpenter invokes the name of Frideswide when he finds his undergraduate lodger up to no good) and she is honoured every year on her patronal festival, 19 October, when town, gown and diocese assemble at her shrine and the Dean of Christ Church delivers the Feast of St Frideswide sermon.

Sceptics, however, say that although St Frideswide's relics were venerated in the priory church, nothing whatever is known about her and that the Augustinian canons had thought up the story that she was an Oxford saint as a fund-raising effort to rebuild their church. They point to the canons' fabrication of a deed entitling them to hold a fair on spare ground by the conventual buildings and, undeniably, there is such a deed with a false Chancellor's seal in the university archives.[3] There is, however, a list of English saints with the places of their burial, which states that 'St Frideswide rests at Oxford', and this was written a century before the canons in question had arrived on the scene. Furthermore, it was William of Malmesbury, a careful historian, who visited St Frideswide's priory shortly after the Augustinian canons had been installed in 1122, who set down what was known about the saint in his *Gesta Pontificium Anglorum*. A recent discovery[4] suggests that there already was a written life of St Frideswide even before William of Malmesbury's text. The story, which was embroidered on by local sentiment, culminating in the flamboyant scenes depicted in the Burne-Jones window in the cathedral, was quite simple. St Frideswide was the daughter of a king and was sought in marriage by another king, but having taken a vow of chastity she escaped from him, first into a forest and then to Oxford, where her suitor was struck blind. His sight was restored by her prayers and he departed, leaving St Frideswide to found the Oxford monastery, where she spent the rest of her life.

The traditional dating of St Frideswide's life is about 680 to 735. St Frideswide's priory church was burned down by the Danes in 1002 but the tomb of the saint appears to have been unharmed, for when King Ethelred established a new convent in 1004, he is said to have placed the shrine in the centre of the church instead of on the south side as previously. A shrine, then, was mentioned before the Augustinian canons took over and translated the relics to another place with great pomp and ceremony in 1180. Then, in 1289, the relics were translated to a more splendid shrine, to which Henry III and Edward I made pilgrimages.[5] The shrine was desecrated in the Reformation of 1538 and pieces of it subsequently used in steps and walls of the college. In Victorian times the shrine was rebuilt with these reclaimed fragments, the missing mouldings of the jigsaw puzzle being filled in with wood. During the 1985 excavations, which preceded the making of the cloister garden, an arched stone moulding and several other fragments were found, which exactly fit the substitute wooden pieces. The garden-maker felt this was a sign of approval for the garden by St Frideswide herself, and returned to the project with renewed enthusiasm.

The proposed garden was not to be limited to the time of St Frideswide herself, when so little was known about gardening, but would reflect the whole history of the site from Saxon times until the Reformation and its subsequent incorporation into the college. No evidence for a planted garden was found during the archaeological investigation which would give an indication for a basic plan. The best-known representation of an early cloister garth, which could be used as a precedent, was that of an ideal monastery drawn up by the Benedictine monastery of St Gall in Switzerland in 830.[6] A monastery had to be self sufficient so that there were a number of peripheral service buildings employing laymen, and also guest houses. The cloister was at the centre of the monastery, the inner sanctuary kept for the monks themselves, and the main arteries of their communal life between refectory, dormitory, library, warming room and church. The cloister walks were quiet places for study, meditation and exercise looking out on to a green space. St Frideswide's conventual buildings followed this traditional pattern, with its cloister, as customary, on the south side of the church. In the St Gall plan the cloister garth was intersected by paths and there was a cistern in the centre; similarly the basic plan of the St Frideswide's garden is of cloistered walks around a green enclosure.

Although the early cloister gardens were of the simplest kind there were many other monastic gardens, including orchards, herbaria and vineyards shown in the St Gall plan. The monks were highly skilled gardeners and the common Latin of all monastic orders allowed their knowledge to circulate throughout Europe; herbals were copied and plants and plant lore exchanged. There would certainly have been a physic garden with medicinal herbs near the infirmary of the Augustinian priory of St Frideswide, vegetable gardens, an orchard and, perhaps, as the Grey Friars had in Oxford, a paradise garden where the sacristan could grow flowers for the altar and for St Frideswide's shrine. Monastic paradises were usually situated adjacent to the monks' cemetery on the northern side of the church. The word paradise comes from the Persian *pairidaeza*, meaning an enclosure, and occurs in the Old Testament as 'pardes' to indicate a garden, whence it came to be seen as the Garden of Eden. Paradises with pools and shady trees had been taken by the Muslims to Sicily and thence to Europe by the Normans. The European garden became part of mediaeval symbolism showing man's attempt to come to terms with the bewildering complexity of the external world in a way he could understand. Because of their organic nature plants were seen as actual prototypes of the divine.

The intensity of the feeling and symbolic unity of plants with the living world is seen depicted on St Frideswide's shrine. The little face of the Saxon saint looks out from garlands of leaves sheltering her from the world as they did when she hid as a fugitive in the forest outside Oxford. When Dean Liddell preached the St Frideswide's sermon in 1889 he drew attention to the leaves and fruits carved on the shrine as identified by Dr Druce, the author of *The Flora of Oxfordshire*: on the south side, the greater celandine, the maple, buttercup and columbine; on the east the vine and hogweed; on the north the ivy, oak and sycamore;[7] and on the west side the whitehorn and bryony.

St Frideswide's shrine; the face of the saint

The garden itself was a complete allegory, not only in Guillame de Lorris's thirteenth-century secular *Romance of the Rose* depicting the allegory of earthly love, but in the religious *hortus conclusus*. This was a special enclosed Mary garden with mystic symbols based on the Song of Solomon. 'A garden enclosed (*hortus conclusus*) is my sister, my spouse; a spring shut up, a fountain sealed.......a well of living waters.'

The Virgin herself was the *fons signatus*, sealed against all but God. Madonna and child in the garden themes appear in numerous poems and paintings in the fourteenth and fifteenth centuries[8] and the Mary garden is still being depicted much later in emblematic literature, such as in the frontispiece of Henry Hawkins's *Partheneia Sacra* of 1633. In mediaeval illuminations allegory and personification go hand in hand; the lily is a symbol of purity and so the Virgin becomes a lily, and in the Song of Songs, 'I am the rose of Sharon, and the lily of the valleys.' The Madonna lily, *Lilium candidum*, is the best known of symbolic Mary flowers and was often grown in monastic paradises for lady chapel decorations; the rose is also attributed to her as the Queen of Heaven, the violet is associated with her humility. In St Bernard's words, 'Mary is the violet of humility, the lily of chastity, the rose of charity, and the glory and splendour of the heavens.' The tapestries of Mary sitting in her *hortus conclusus* have a stylized millefleurs background, a carpet of flowers beneath her feet, the flowery mead of Chaucer's poetry with its daisies, sweet violets, wild strawberries, periwinkle, daffodils, speedwell and trefoil. The St Frideswide's garden is set in a flowery mead, a turf lawn 'with flowers sweet embroidered all' and incorporates the symbols of the *hortus conclusus*, the small railed enclosure, Mary's 'well of living waters' and the Mary flowers, the Madonna lily, roses, violets, Rose of Sharon, lilies of the valley and marigolds, which appear in mediaeval records as St Mary's gold, as it was thought that such a glorious and shining flower must be an emblem of the Virgin.

The medicinal Doctrine of Signatures was an ancient belief[9] which was still given credence in the seventeenth century. As all material objects were manifestations of God it was thought that plants bore the signatures of their virtues 'as it were in hieroglyphick'. Consequently, plants with red juices staunched wounds, those with yellow sap cured jaundice, and liverwort, *Anemone hepatica*, with its liver-shaped flowers, would cure diseases of that organ. The womb-shaped birthwort, *Aristolochia durior*, meaning 'best for childbirth', was introduced from European monasteries and seems to have been grown by nuns in early physic gardens. It is said to have been grown by the nuns of Carrow Abbey since the twelfth century and was recorded still growing there in 1793,[10] and much more recently it was found growing at Godstow nunnery outside Oxford. It still grows in the fellows' garden at Jesus College, Cambridge, which was formerly the garden of the nuns of St Radegund. Seed from the Cambridge nunnery birthwort has been given to the new St Frideswide's garden.

According to Pliny,[11] a mother who wanted a son should use birthwort with the flesh of an ox. Signature remedies were apparently of no avail to poor Catherine of Aragon, nor could St Frideswide herself help when Henry VIII's first wife came to pray at the shrine. The Court had retired to Abingdon in 1518 because of plague in London and word was sent to Wolsey that 'the Queen is with child and prays God heartily it may be a prince, to the surety and universal comfort of the realm'.[12] It was Cardinal Wolsey himself who brought the Queen to St Frideswide's shrine in the priory church in April 1518 to pray for a son. Seven years later he obtained permission to dissolve the monastery and founded, in its place, a Renaissance college greater than any other in Oxford or Cambridge. The Queen was told that in Wolsey's college 'literature would be so encouraged that men would resort to England from all parts of Christendom' and that she would be made 'a participant of the prayers of the college, for which she gave Wolsey great thanks and was marvellously glad'.[13] The Queen's emblem, the pomegranate, was carved on one of the doors of Cardinal College, and as the fates of Wolsey and Catherine of Aragon are so interwoven, a pomegranate tree has been commemoratively planted in the new cloister garden. Wolsey fell from power in 1529 and his unfinished college with him, when he was unsuccessful in his negotiations with the Pope to obtain Henry VIII's divorce from Queen Catherine. Wolsey's school at Ipswich, his birthplace, which was to have supplied scholars for his Oxford college, (planned in the same relationship as Winchester and New College and Eton and King's), did not get off the ground: its foundation stone can be now seen in the chapter house at Christ Church. Shakespeare's epitaph on Wolsey in *Henry VIII* is spoken to the dying Catherine of Aragon.

> Ever witness for him
> Those twins of learning that he rais'd in you,
> Ipswich and Oxford! one of which fell with him,
> Unwilling to outlive the good that did it;
> The other, though unfinish'd, yet so famous,
> So excellent in art and still so rising,
> That Christendom shall ever speak his virtue[14]

It was not until 1546, sixteen years after Cardinal Wolsey's death, that Henry VIII refounded his college as Christ Church, a joint foundation of college and cathedral for the new see of Oxford. No attempt was made to complete the part of Wolsey's college that remained unfinished until the seventeenth century. What the Cardinal had intended to do with St Frideswide's priory church and claustral buildings is a matter for speculation. He had demolished the outlying buildings and three bays in the western part of the church and cloister in the making of the college Great Quadrangle and had planned a great chapel on the north of the quadrangle which would have outshone even the glories of King's College chapel in Cambridge. The cloisters and Priory House had been restored in 1499 by Bishop Sherborne of Chichester, a great friend and ally of Wolsey[15] and it is unlikely that he intended to demolish more than the western claustral range containing the cellarer's offices, already removed. The east side of the cloister with the chapter house and Priory House still remains today, but the buildings on the south were converted first into a library and then into undergraduates' rooms. When Sherborne's cloisters were restored in 1638 they were, of necessity, left three-sided.

A trellis railing copied from a mediaeval illustration of an *hortus conclusus* now gives the essential mediaeval sense of enclosure to St Frideswide's garden. Also taken from mediaeval illustrations are the raised beds and earthenware pots with their wicker supports. The garden is seen at its best from the stone seats beneath the traceried windows of the cloister arcade. Along the trellis railing grow flowers identified in the borders of the illuminated Epistle Book which Wolsey gave to his college in 1528: roses, lilies, carnations, borage, flax, irises, narcissi, everlasting sweet peas, heartsease and violets.

It is in Wolsey's Epistle Book in the college library that the illumination of St Frideswide and the ox with her priory in the background is to be found. Clearly there was no wish on Cardinal Wolsey's part to question her right to be called Oxford's patron saint and in all his actions he sought to perpetuate the name of the saint, to whose shrine he had brought Catherine of Aragon on pilgrimage. His college was dedicated to the Holy Trinity, the Virgin Mary and St Frideswide and in his statutes provision was made for masses in her honour. Wolsey may in fact have intended that her shrine should remain in the priory church so that pilgrimages could continue there away from the intended college chapel. By the Cardinal's special wish, the first service in his new college was deferred until her feast day, 19 October, 1526.[16] It was after Evensong on the Feast of St Frideswide, 1985 that the Bishop of Oxford blessed the new garden in the presence of the Lord Lieutenant, the Dean and Chapter, Vice-Chancellor and the Lord Mayor with these words. 'We render thanks to Thee O Father, Who hast given us this precinct to be a place of beauty and refreshment, linking the centuries together in a common faith. We render thanks for the love and skill of those who lived long ago, for the inheritance that we have received from them, and for the ability to enjoy and maintain our tradition in peace. We pray that thy blessing will rest upon this garden and upon the going out and coming in of all who visit it, and that it may serve to the wholesomeness of thy people in body, mind and spirit.'

4 Profit and Pleasure in the College Gardens

The colleges which were founded on the sites of dissolved monastic houses actually inherited their means of self-sufficiency. When Sidney Sussex took over the Grey Friars site, it included the 'inclosure, circuit, ambit and precinct of the late House, and all messuages, houses, buildings, stables, dovehouses, pools, waters, orchards, gardens, land and soil thereto pertaining and all the walls, ditches and enclosures'. They may also have inherited lay gardeners with monastic gardening skills. Before the days of printed books instruction was passed down by word of mouth and a good gardener accumulated knowledge as he worked the earth. A treatise on gardening, written about 1440, records reasoned instructions for growing fruit, herbs and flowers, which probably came from a monk:

> Thre ynchys depe they most sette be
> And this seyde mayster John Gardener to me.[1]

One tradition the colleges did not take over from the monasteries was vegetarianism. Not for the fellows were there unrelieved messes of bean and leek pottage; roasts of every kind were the order of the day in their kitchens. Colleges bordering the rivers in Oxford and Cambridge kept swanneries, which would have delighted Chaucer's worldy monk, who found, away from the cloister, that a fat swan made a very good roast. Grazing cattle could not be kept over the winter and carcasses had to be salted down and preserved. Culinary herbs and spices, such as parsley, sage, tansy, fennel, coriander, cumin and mint, for sauces and stuffing to disguise the saltiness of the winter meat, were in great demand. Crab apples were cultivated for verjuice which was used extensively in preserving and pickling. King's College had a large kitchen garden and orchard and hops were grown in the launderers' yard, where the poles could do duty for hops as well as washing. Vines were extensively cultivated; Corpus Christi guild already had a vineyard in 1348, King's

The coat of arms of Lady Margaret Beaufort, the foundress of Christ's College, on the oriel window in First Court

The Nunn's Garden at Queen's, the mediaeval atmosphere persists today

Hall was buying new poles and rails for theirs in 1418 and Trinity Hall had a vineyard within a few years of its foundation in 1350. In Oxford, New College was able to grow vines on its section of the town walls most successfully.

Each college appointed its own garden master or equivalent from among its fellows, who was responsible for labour in the gardens. In the smaller halls and hostels all the inmates had to lend a hand. The gardens were specifically mentioned in the Aularian Statutes[2] drawn up by the University of Oxford at the end of the fifteenth century to give internal regulations to the seventy or more unendowed halls still existing. Fines were instituted for disordering rushes and straw with which the floors were strewn, spilling liquor on the table cloths and defacing walls, doors or windows. All these offences were punishable by a fine of a farthing, but the worst offence which carried a halfpenny fine was for running over grass or breaking down plants. Costs had to kept down and on the day or days appointed by the Principal, all members of the hall were to be ready to help 'put the garden in order and to work usefully in it for the benefit and honour of the Hall'. Failure to do so was punishable by a twopenny fine. The statutes of Balliol College allot a small plot of ground to each chamber for the growing of herbs and vegetables. This is reminiscent of the arrangement of a Carthusian monastery where every monk had his own garden plot attached to his cell, but at Balliol the individual gardens were the result of the numbers of small plots attached to the various tenements that were incorporated into the college.

The Queen's College, Oxford, founded in 1341, even produced a surplus of herbs, beans, onions and garlic which was sold to the town. In addition to their ' 'ortulanus', who in 1358 was called John Godspede, the Queen's College employed casual labour, mostly female. Although it was within the town walls and unable to expand, it also had in its confined space a vineyard and as well as the cauliflowers, hyssop, savory, thyme and borage mentioned in the bursar's rolls, it grew hemp and flax for its own table linen. In Cambridge a fragment of the old Peterhouse kitchen garden wall can be seen near the hall. In 1374 it was recorded that parsley, cress, garlic, leeks and other vegetables were being grown in this garden with a considerable area laid down to vetch and clover. The garden (*virgultum*) to the west of the college was set apart for crocus. This was the *Crocus sativus*, which was very important in mediaeval times for drugs, flavouring and its yellow dye. It was probably introduced into Britain by the Romans, but as with many other of their introductions it died out and was reintroduced sometime in the fourteenth century, grown chiefly in East Anglia, particularly at Saffron Walden. It needed large grounds as it is calculated that it takes 4,300 blossoms to produce a single ounce of the finished product.[3] Peterhouse evidently had a large crocus ground and dried the stigma in the usual way in a specially prepared *caminus croci*.[4] Saffron was also grown at King's Hall in 1383 and at Oxford it was recorded as growing at the Queen's College in 1415. It is not clear whether the dried saffron stigma were used only for culinary and medicinal purposes or if it was a herbal colouring for illumination. When planted at Pembroke, Cambridge in the 1450s it was seen to be 'to the public advantage of the college',[5] so that although milder in appearance, it seems to have been an horticultural asset as other crocus displays are in modern Cambridge.

Although a seventeenth-century Warden[6] maintained that the garden at New College had been 'ancyently not for pleasure and walking, but for Profitt', there must still have been pleasure in the profit gardens, growing their herbs, fruit, vegetables and crocuses. The vines which were often made into arbours would always have been attractive visually and for their shade. Lincoln College, Oxford records a payment 'for mendying the seat under the bay-tree' and elsewhere, references to the early gardens being 'for cooks and bachelors' suggest that some part of the ground was set aside for the relaxation of the fellows, if only as sitting places in herb gardens and orchards.

Real pleasure gardens or pleasances, the 'bowers of bliss' of mediaeval romances, belonged essentially to the ladies. It is tempting to believe that the Queen's College figures so much in Oxford's mediaeval garden history, not because it alone had efficient bursars who kept separate gardeners' accounts from 1341, the year the college was founded, until 1469, but because it had Oxford's only woman founder. The statutes make it clear that Queen Philippa, the wife of Edward III, was a 'foundress rather than a patroness', although her chaplain, Robert Eglesfield, is honoured as co-founder. Queen Philippa was a keen gardener as the two Queen Eleanors of Castile and Provence had been before her. It was Eleanor of Castile, the wife of Edward I, who probably brought the hollyhock, then called the Spanish rose, to England. Queen Philippa introduced rosemary, which was to become such a favourite plant in Tudor gardens.[7] It was in 1338 that she received from her mother, the Countess of Hainault, a copy of a treatise on rosemary and some cuttings from her garden at Antwerp. According to the English version of the treatise on the virtues of rosemary, the plant had never been known in England before that time. Friar Daniel's herbal refers to Queen Philippa's herber (the word commonly used for a garden), and particularly praises a perfumed single pink he had been given from it, which was 'wonder sweet and it spiceth every liquor that it be laid in, and principally red'.[8] Perhaps she also gave it to John Godspede to grow for spicing the fellows' wine in the loving cup which on gaudy days accompanied the traditional 'boryes hede' stuffed with rosemary. Queen's had a number of separate herbers entered through doors in the walls in addition to the productive herb and kitchen gardens. One of these was a chapel garden in which flowers may have been grown for the altar and fumitories for incense. There is still today a little garden entered through a passage and a gateway, called the Nunn's garden, which is very reminiscent of the type of enclosure that would have been in the garden of Queen's in mediaeval days. By 1407 Queen's had built a fountain in the main garden and continued to derive both pleasure and profit from all its gardens.

Cambridge had no less than six colleges founded by noble ladies. Their Queens' College was founded by two queens, hence the position of the apostrophe. It is the most domestic looking of all the colleges. The first was Queen Margaret of Anjou, the eighteen-year-old wife of Henry VI, the founder of next door King's College, who thought it desirable that a Cambridge college should be founded by a Queen of England to 'laud and honneure of sexe feminine'. Queen Margaret was the daughter of King Rene, Duke of Anjou and Count of Provence, who was the most famous horticulturist of his time. He created a number of gardens at his many French castles and is credited with the first introduction of the carnation into northern France.[9] Any gardening that his daughter might have encouraged at Queens' would have been confined to the strip behind the range of buildings on the north side of Old Court, which included the library, since the Carmelite friary still occupied the site between Queens' and King's College. Queen Margaret's feminist college building project unfortunately withered during the Wars of the Roses, however, and after her husband was defeated she returned to her native country and her college nearly expired. It did not have to wait as long as King's College to be completed, however, for it was taken under the wing of Queen Elizabeth Woodville, the wife of Margaret's husband's enemy, Edward IV. She gave the college its statutes and built a cloister court in 1461, nearer the river which, when the sixteenth-century President's Lodge was added, was to give Cambridge its prettiest postcard.

The Lady Margaret Beaufort, mother of Henry VII, certainly gave a great deal to Cambridge and her coat of arms with supporting yales (strange mythical beasts with rotating horns) can be seen over the gatehouse of St John's College and at Christ's College. She did not live to see the building of St John's College but had been much in evidence when Christ's College was founded in 1505. The founder's coat of arms can be seen, not only in the usual place on the college gateway, but also on an oriel window in the present Master's Lodge across the First Court. This was part of the set of upper chambers 'built for our use', the Master having his accommodation on the floor below. The Lady Margaret did in fact make frequent use of these rooms when she descended on the college to see that her wishes were being carried out. She wanted to know everything that was going on right down to the laundry arrangements and how the fellows entertained themselves. She doubtless also gave specific instructions about the garden beneath her windows which she could enter by an external staircase. Noble ladies were used to opening their windows on to flower gardens, pools and orchards. The days of fortified houses with internal looking windows were over. Even in the fourteenth century, before the Wars of the Roses, Queen Philippa had windows looking on to her herber and when she visited the Prior of Ely a long chamber with windows opening on to the garden was built specially for her.[10]

The Lady Elizabeth de Burgh, the Lady of Clare, who founded Clare Hall in 1338 with the idea of a community of teachers and students living together, was also a great lover of gardens. She was the granddaughter of Edward I and lived at Clare Castle in Suffolk, where she had a great herber and a maydengarden under the maidenstower of the castle, with a pool and a lady walk.[11] Although Clare College has beautiful gardens today, nothing remains of the buildings and gardens of the Lady Clare's foundation but there would certainly have been windows looking out on to the riverside gardens. Another of the early colleges was founded by her friend the Countess of Pembroke, who at the same time founded a nunnery at Denny Abbey and enjoined the fellows to visit the nuns for 'ghostly counsel'. The last of the foundresses' colleges was Sidney Sussex, built on the site of the suppressed friary in 1589 by the Countess of Sussex, who bequeathed two-fifths of her estate to found her college.

The noble ladies may have been the first to tip the scales in favour of pleasure rather than profit in gardens, but the study of classical literature by the humanists soon made pleasances masculine, as well as feminine, retreats. Erasmus, the prophet of the English Renaissance, maintained that gardens were indeed 'design'd for Pleasure; but for honest Pleasure, the Entertainment of the Sight, the Smell and the Refreshment of the very Mind'.[12] Had Epicurus not taught in a garden? A college, where there were neither monastic restrictions nor family encumberances, was an ideal place to cultivate the open air life and scholarly habits of the ancient philosophers. As in Thomas More's *Utopia*, the fellows entertained one another in discourse in garden retreats and enjoyed the company of visiting humanists. Of these the most important was Desiderius Erasmus himself who stayed both in Oxford and Cambridge, where he said he found more piety and temperance in the colleges than in any house of religion. At Oxford in 1499 he met Grocyn, Linacre, More and Colet, and in Cambridge, John Fisher, who persuaded him to return and live at Queens', where he was President.

Erasmus stayed in Cambridge from 1511 until 1514 and was Lady Margaret's Reader in Greek and Professor of Divinity in the university. He particularly enjoyed working in the upstairs library at Queens' looking out into the garden. His own apartments were adjacent to what has now become known as Erasmus's Tower and from them Fuller said he had 'the best prospect about the colledge, namely, upon the river into the cornefields and country adjoining'.[13] He particularly delighted in the walk on the other side of the Cam, which became known as Erasmus's Walk. There must still have been plenty to watch in the way of river activity since Fuller said it compensated for the loss of Erasmus's native Rotterdam. The land on the west of the river had been bought from the town in 1475, possibly through the support of the Queen. It was at first called the pondyard which was surrounded by a mud wall. In 1504 it was laid out as part garden and part orchard and was hedged in 1511. In 1547 the ditch on the south side was deepened to form an island. This island with its riverside groves and acre and a half of inner garden must have been one of the most delightful spots in Cambridge. Willows were mentioned at an early stage and thousands of honeysuckles and privet bushes were planted in the 1570s on the island garden, now, sadly, occupied by the modern Cripps Court.

King's College had already begun the severance of the town from the river bank by acquiring town fields to extend their gardens across the Cam soon after its foundation. By 1450 a new large garden on the west side of the river, comprising nearly three acres including a lake with an island surrounded by embattled walls and towers, had appeared on the scene. Walking and other forms of exercise were in keeping with the humanist philosophy on the training of young men. A sphaeristerium or ball court is mentioned in colleges in the late fifteenth century while tennis, bowls and archery were played in most colleges. One of the 1443 statutes expressly forbids fellows or scholars 'to throw or shoot stones, balls, wood, earth or arrows or anything else, or to play any games' within King's College or its close or garden for fear of damaging their precious window glass. The tennis courts with their penthouse roofs were all pulled down but can be seen on the early maps of Oxford and Cambridge. Trinity College, Cambridge made a bowling green in the garden it had inherited from King's Hall, which still exists in the fellows' garden. Fuller was to recommend bowling as a recreation which (besides refreshing) 'teaches men's hands and eyes mathematics and the rules of proportion' and undoubtedly Trinity excelled in her mathematicians.

In Oxford, members of Magdalen College also had the privilege of pleasant walking. Not only had they their cloister walk for wet weather but orchards and riverside walks more extensive than those of any other college. The sixteenth-century college gardens and Cherwell walks are well illustrated on the Agas map. Magdalen had been built outside the city wall on the site of the St John's hospital from which it inherited a

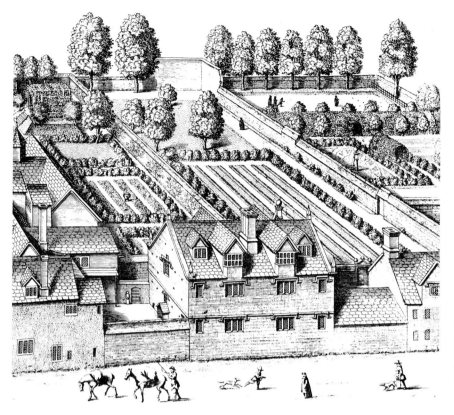

Bowling at Pembroke College, Oxford, from Loggan's illustration which also shows the old-fashioned tunnelled arbors

flourishing physic garden, orchards and fishponds. The college had to build its own walls round its extensive grounds in 1466. These embattled stone walls along Longwall Street are often mistakenly thought to be part of the town walls. The rural walks, which were later referred to as the 'green natural cloister of our Academe', have always been one of the delights of residence at Magdalen. Henry VII presented the college with a she-bear, probably from Woodstock, in 1509, so it appears that they kept some kind of menagerie. The founder had not chosen the site because of these rural delights, however, but with a view to the possibility of building extensions. Waynflete was aware that it might be thought that his college offered the possibility of real country pursuits and in his statutes sought to curb any hunting or hawking aspirations of the fellows by forbidding any member of the college to keep 'a Harrier, or other Hound of any kind or Ferrets, or a Sparrow Hawk, or any other Fowling Bird, or a Mavis or any other Song Bird'. In spite of these regulations, however, a visitation report by the Bishop of Winchester's commissary records in 1507 that 'Smyth keeps a ferret in College, Lenard a sparrowhawk, Parkyns a weasel.' Dogs kept for pets, rather than for field sports, became an increasing nuisance and were forbidden in most colleges. Dr Routh, President of Magdalen from 1791 to 1854, called his dog a cat in order to comply with the founder's statutes. No such deception was apparently necessary at Magdalene, Cambridge, for in the north-west corner of the fellows' garden can still be seen the Victorian pets' cemetery, with miniature tombstones both of dogs and cats from the Master's Lodge.

5 Elizabethan Oxford and Cambridge

The Renaissance and the Reformation had made great changes in sixteenth-century Oxford and Cambridge. The new nobility and gentry sent their sons in increasing numbers to benefit from the broad humanist education as a training for public life. The new colleges were there to receive them and the old ones enlarged their premises, and, according to Paul Hentzner, the Elizabethan traveller, all had fine gardens. Visiting Oxford in 1598, long after the dissolution of the monasteries, he was quick to note the advantages of reformed monastic retreats. 'The students lead a life almost monastic; for as the monks had nothing in the world to do, but when they had said their prayers at stated hours, to employ themselves in instructive studies, no more have these...as soon as grace is said after every meal, every one is at liberty either to retire to his own chambers or to walk in the college garden, there being none that had not a delightful one.'

In the reign of Queen Elizabeth, gardening was transformed by new ideas in design and by the availability of the new plants, recorded in Gerard's *Herball* of 1597, which had been brought back by those who sailed in the Queen's name to discover new lands. The cult of the Virgin Queen replaced the religious imagery of the mediaeval Mary gardens. Queen Elizabeth is depicted in her portraits in association with the Virgin eglantine and the Tudor rose symbolizing the peace of the nation through the unity of the white rose of York and the red rose of Lancaster. In the emblematic imagery of Spenser's *fayre Elisa* she is likened to garden flowers;

> See, where she sits upon the grassie greene,
> (O seemly sight!)
> Yclad in Scarlot, like a mayden Queene,
> And ermine white,
> Upon her head a Cremosin coronet,
> With Damaske roses and Daffadillies set:
> Bay leaves betweene,
> And primroses greene,
> Embellish the sweete Violet..

Christ Church, the garden and royal apartments first used by Queen Elizabeth I in 1566

43

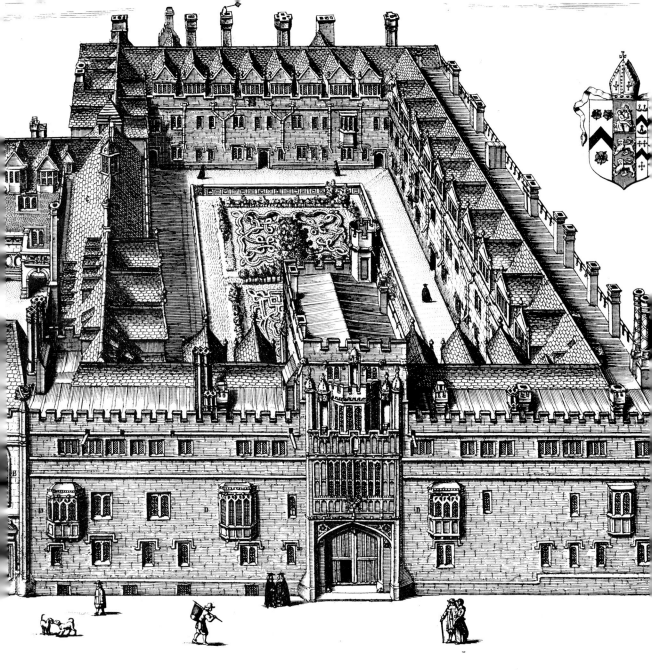

The Brasenose quadrangle with knot gardens, from Loggan

Queen Elizabeth did not build royal palaces as her father did, she encouraged her courtiers to vie with each other in building prodigy houses and gardens in which to entertain her. By means of her progresses she showed herself with great pomp and pageantry to her subjects all over her realm, and strengthened the image of the crown as the unifying force in the nation. She indicated that she would like to pay state visits to Cambridge and Oxford to demonstrate the importance she attached to the universities and her 'dear, dear scholars'. Cambridge, where Sir William Cecil, Secretary of State, was Chancellor of the University, was to be visited first in 1564. Cecil worked out a detailed programme which was the blueprint for future royal visitations. All scholars had to be present and cry out '*Vivat Regina!*', lowly kneeling' as she passed by, and if, as in the case of the August visit to Cambridge, they were on vacation they must be recalled. An orator was to tell the Queen how happy they were to see her, 'being adorned with all kind of good literature, which is rare and marvellous in a woman'.[1] Disputations and plays should be arranged for her and boxes of conceits and gloves presented to her, and the church bells should ring out. The Queen seems to have been inundated with gloves, one pair being presented to her in memory of her great-grandmother, the Lady Margaret Beaufort, foundress of Christ's and St John's, and also with sweetmeat conceits of which she was very fond. The Oxford proctors went across to the briefing so that they would be ready when their turn came. Oxford was honoured two years later and Cecil's instructions were carried out down to the last comfit.

The records suggest that most of the Cambridge boxes of conceits were bought at the grocers, but the colleges that had good orchards and confectioners may have produced their own sweetmeats. The art of comfit-making was that of covering with sugar 'all kinds of seedes, fruits and spices'. It included such mouth-watering conceits as candied violets, marigolds, roses, borage, almonds and all kinds of fruits, musk, ginger and cinnamon comfits.[2] On the Queen's progresses to country houses the sweetmeats were part of the banquet, usually served in a special garden house during the outdoor evening entertainment. The idea of banquets was a development from the mediaeval 'voyde', which was a dainty repast taken in an antechamber while the main feast was being cleared from the hall where the furniture was being rearranged for post-prandial entertainment. Late fifteenth-century Household Orders read 'The King never taketh a voyd of comfittes and other spices, but standing.' Dessert, which has the same derivation as voiding, is still taken in another room in Oxford and Cambridge colleges for the same purpose of clearing the hall. In Cambridge there is a record of the preparation of a 'travelling banquet' being presented to King Charles I on a visit. He ate very little of it but gave the twelve-year-old Prince Charles a good store to put in his pockets.[3] In 1626 when the Duke of Buckingham dined at Trinity, he took his 'bankett' at Clare Hall.

It is true to say that the same things happened on royal visits with little variations in both universities. If Cambridge can claim that Queen Elizabeth slept there first, Oxford was favoured first with visits by King James in 1605 and in 1614. Then Cambridge heard that the King would grace them with their presence the following year and forty shillings was 'expended in going to Oxford' to see how to entertain a Stuart. As it turned out the King visited Cambridge twice in 1615 so that they could taunt triumphantly.

...... you cannot say
The King did go from you in March
And come again in May.

The Stuarts were lodged at Trinity College, King Henry VIII's royal foundation, but when Queen Elizabeth visited Cambridge in 1564 their chapel was still being built and she chose to stay in the Provost's Lodgings at King's College. A window in the north east of King's chapel was removed so that she could have direct access to the Provost's Lodgings through a covered walkway in his garden.[4] After Evensong, on her way back to her apartments, she received her first consignment of four pairs of gloves and the obligatory, 'six boxes of fine comfits and other conceits..which she thankfully took'.

When in 1566 the Queen visited Oxford, she stayed at Christ Church in the apartments Wolsey had planned for the reception of royal visitors. In the east range of the quadrangle there were a series of separate chambers with folding doors which could be thrown open for the Court.[5] Here too the Queen was able to attend church services by a direct route through the garden under her apartments, but there was no necessity to knock holes in the cathedral as there was already a side door for the purpose. Christ Church's problems were concerned with how to get the Queen into the upstairs hall to see the play, as Wolsey had unfortunately fallen from power before the staircase was properly finished, and no adequate arrangements had been made since that time. The only finished staircase into the hall, but unthinkable for the Queen, was up the stone steps leading from the kitchen. A door was, therefore, made upstairs in the south end wall of the east range and a wooden gallery, like those used in garden walks, erected on supports to lead directly into the ante-hall. Shakespeare's comments that Christ Church was

...... though unfinish'd, yet so famous,
So excellent in art and still so rising[6]

would have struck home to the Queen who saw the aerial stairway being built around her.

One item in the expenses 'against the Queen's coming' is £3.7.10 for 'divers women making garlands and gathering ivy' to decorate the wooden posts and fifteen lights were hung along the gallery.[7] Doubtless the Queen received her usual offering of comfits for the evening entertainment as she walked along her carpenters' gallery. The crowd surged up the kitchen stairs to see the Queen and the Court in the hall and, unfortunately, a side wall gave way in the press crushing three people to death.[8] The Queen sent her surgeon and the Vice-Chancellor to cope with the crisis and the play went on. The effects were spectacular and in one scene of a hunting party the fox and hounds were brought into the quadrangle with the actors standing at the windows crying 'Nowe! Nowe!'. The Queen was delighted and said 'O excellent, those boyes are readie to leape out at windows and follow ye houndes'.[9]

The Hamond map of Cambridge and Agas for Oxford show the college gardens much as Queen Elizabeth would have seen them on her visits. There would have been much work for the gardeners in getting ready for the Queen, who was particularly fond of fragrant perfume. Quantities of herbs and flowers were needed for nosegays and strewing; sweet fennel, lavender, roses, pennyroyal, basil, hyssop and tansy, which was used as a disinfectant against the plague. The Queen brought her own strewing woman for sweetening her apartments and repelling vermin on her progress visits, and after her attack of small pox in 1562 she required for her toilet a constant supply of white rose petal water which would 'take away the pocke-holes'.

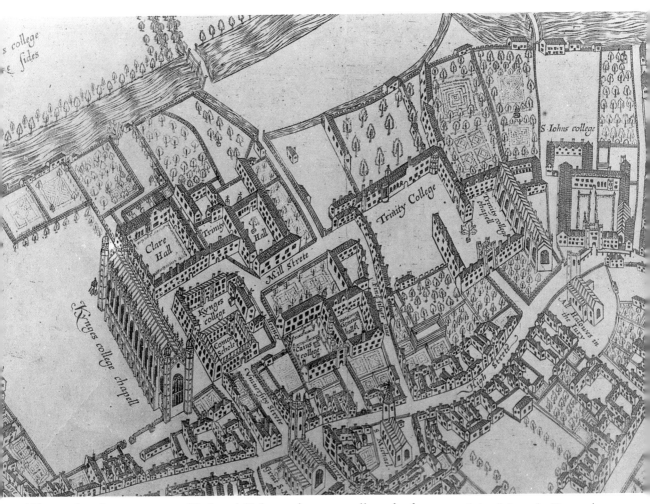

The orchard was a great Tudor delight and every college had one. Bowling alleys were sometimes set up in the orchards. William Harrison in his *The Description of England*, 1577, wrote that the improvement in the skills of orchard gardening was as great as that of horticulture and that the country was 'never furnished with such variety as at this present...we have most delicate apples, plums, pears, walnuts, filberts..in comparison of which most of the old trees are nothing worth'. Apricots, almonds, peaches and figs in the orchards provided what Sir Hugh Platt delightfully describes in *The Garden of Eden* as a 'growing banquet', which greatly increased the pleasure of eating fruit and comfits in the garden arbours. 'What can your eye desire to see, your eares to heare, your mouth to taste, or your nose to smell that is not to be had in an orchard with abundance and variety?', wrote William Lawson.[10] The ill-fated Nicholas Ridley learned St Paul's Epistles in the orchard of Pembroke at Cambridge, 'the sweet smell thereof I trust I shall carry with me into Heaven'.[11]

Undergraduates, although excluded from the delights of the orchard, clearly made frequent raids into forbidden territory as one Elizabethan diary of a Cambridge undergraduate (later to become Master of Sidney Sussex) records.

A detail from the Hamond map of Cambridge showing the gardens and orchards as Queen Elizabeth I would have seen them on her visit in 1564

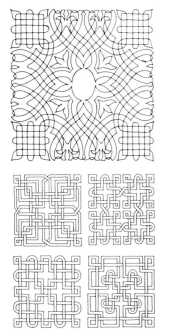

Knot patterns from Thomas Hill's The Gardener's Labyrinth. *Bottom: the top right pattern closely resembles the All Souls High Street garden*

Sept 15 My crapula in eating peares in a morning...
July 22...my grief for being excluded out of the orchard....
July 23...for eating so many plums, although thou heard many died of surfeits.
July 28 My over bold spech to Mr Montagu of Mr Bainbridge saying he was in his coler when he put us out of the orchard.
August 8...my longing after damsons when I made a vow not to eat in the orchard.[12]

At St John's College, Oxford the best garden and orchard were kept locked and reserved exclusively for the most senior members, 'the upper ten' who went to considerable lengths to see that the regulations were observed. A decree of 1584 ruled that:

it was condescended....to binde all the students of the College, not excepted, that no person whatsoever, Master, Bacheler, schollar, chaplayne, commoner, servant, or poor scholler, shall from this day forwarde come or entre into the garden (or being a stranger) here called the tenn Seniors garden in the Grove, except he be one of the simpliciter tenne seniors, under the payne of every man that shall make default for every tyme to forfeyte tenne shillings. The like penaltie is agreed to fall uppon those that shall eyther make any keye to the said garden dore, or use any other man's keye, or use any keye that he shall finde except he be the scholler or servant of one of the tenn simpliciter seniors, sent by his Master to do some service there.[13]

The head of the college usually had his own lodgings with sometimes a small garden plot or orchard attached, but in some, such as Lincoln College, the statutes said that he should have no greater privilege than the first choice of rooms. The clergy had found themselves free to marry in 1533 and heads of houses in Oxford and Cambridge took advantage of this provision, which often meant considerable rearrangement of the college layout and the building of walls to provide separate gardens. Cambridge, always in the lead in Reformation zeal, had got off to an early start. At Queens' Dr Heynes, who became President in 1529, married as soon as arrangements could be made with the college. He seems to have acted by advance knowledge to get himself a private family garden by testifying in 1532 that 'whereas the president of this College hath before this tyme no garden appointed severalli for hymself nether for frute, nor to walk in...now...the said President shall have, enjoy, and take from hensforth the Garden or Orchard over against the College brode gates with all the frutes growing within the same to his own propir use' and 'hensforth shall have no parte nor dividert of suche frutes as growth within the Colleges grett orchard'.[14] Mrs Heynes was so delighted with her lodge, garden and fruit that when her husband died in 1537 she was loathe to leave it all and married the incoming incumbent, Dr Mey. He was able to make further improvements as he was then able to acquire the neighbouring site of the Carmelite friary and the stone from their buildings. The President's Lodge was turned gradually into a virtual country house with its gallery and own pleasure grounds.

Fellows, although in holy orders, were not allowed to marry and were often forced to give up their combination rooms in order to extend the Master's accommodation. It seems that Henry VIII had not intended anyone in the colleges to take advantage of the relaxation of clerical celibacy as the statutes for Trinity College specifically state that nobody, not even the Master, was allowed to marry. However, as the Trinity lodge was to be used for royal reception, the custom grew up of obtaining leave from the monarch to take a wife to preside over the hospitality of the lodge.[15] The game was up for protestant matrimony when Mary became Queen in 1553 and married heads had to withdraw until 1559 when her sister Queen Elizabeth could reinstate them. Not that it was then all plain sailing, for the Virgin Queen was irritated by too obvious a presence of married bliss, and in 1561 issued an edict that 'no Manner of Person, being either the Head or member of any College...within this Realm, shall have or be permitted to have within the Precinct of any such College, his Wife or other Woman to abide and dwell in the same'. Her Majesty felt that wives, children, and nurses were an offence 'to the Intent of the Founders, and to the quiet and orderly Profession of Study and Learning'. Fortunately, although the previous President of King's had been married, Philip Baker, who entertained the Queen in 1564, was a Romanist at heart and had not succumbed to matrimony. He had nothing to conceal and the accounts merely reveal that he was a glutton and inordinately fond of sweetbreads.[16] His successor in 1569, Dr Goade, was married, however, but testified that his 'wyf is not kept within the quadrant of the college, wher as yet I think she never came twice'. His lodgings between the chapel and the High Street were conveniently separate from the rest of the college, but Dr Whitaker of St John's said that his wife was 'kept in town', his lodgings being embedded within the college.[17]

The first official ladies did not appear in Oxford until 1550 (nearly twenty years after their Cambridge counterparts) when Richard Cox, Dean of Christ Church, a former Cambridge man, installed his wife in his lodgings. Christ Church as cathedral college was in a peculiar position as canons were permitted to marry after the Reformation. Peter Martyr, invited by Cranmer to England from Florence, was made a canon of Christ Church in 1550 and with him came his ex-nun wife Catherine Dampmartin. It was their example that opened the matrimonial floodgates in Oxford colleges and, according to Anthony Wood, it was 'looked upon as such a damnable matter by the Roman Catholicks and others too, that they usually styled them Concubines, and the Lodgings that entertained them and their children Stews and Cony-buries'.[18] At first Mrs Cox and Mrs Martyr lived in adjacent lodgings on the St Aldates front, but the Martyrs, who were next to the Great Gate, soon had to move over to old Priory House in the cloister to avoid the jeers and bricks thrown by those opposed to clerical matrimony. In the garden Canon Martyr erected a two-storeyed stone building (still visible in Loggan's map of 1675) so that he could get on with his commentaries on the Epistles in peace. Poor Catherine died after only two years and was buried in the cathedral near the desecrated shrine of St Frideswide. The next year when Mary came to the throne, the Coxes were forced to leave and Peter Martyr fled the country. The Roman Catholic commissioners

More knot patterns. Top: one of the All Souls knots

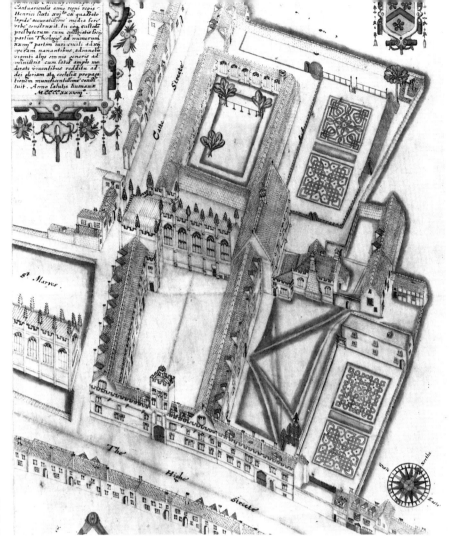

The Hovenden map of All Souls clearly showing the knot gardens

dug up Catherine's body and threw it on a dung heap in the new Dean's stableyard. Six years later under Queen Elizabeth her bones together with those of St Frideswide were buried *permixta et confusa* in one common grave with due ceremony. The Queen invited Peter Martyr to come back but having acquired another wife he preferred to stay where he was 'fearing another mutation'.[19]

Two of the married canons deprived under Mary did feel secure enough to return under Queen Elizabeth, but they were rehoused well away from the main part of the college in buildings in Peckwater and Canterbury quadrangles with some ground around them and their own exit to side streets. Other married canons appeared on the scene and in the general shake up there were acrimonious disputes about seniority and location of lodgings.[20] Wolsey of course had never intended a cathedral attached to his college and there were no precincts. His idea had been for quite modest chambers for his college canons and many problems were created by the new phenomenon of family canons. Being on Fish Street or by the noisy south gate was not very popular and space for gardens and orchards was at a premium. It was easy enough to carve out one new garden within the precincts of the college as the first married Rector of Lincoln did, but there was a limit to the number of canons' gardens that could be made before the canonries were built on the north side of the Great Quadrangle in the seventeenth century. One married canon with lodgings on the landless entrance front was allowed to rent the garden by the cathedral, formerly the monastic cemetery, which had been converted into the garden of the royal apartments. The family would have had due notice to remove themselves if a royal visitor was expected. The largest garden, which included the old infirmary garden, belonged to the Priory House, and before the Dean moved into the Deanery at the end of the east range its orchard was reserved for his use. Waste land to the south of the college had to be used to make other family gardens. Fortunately, there were the meadow walks for what Wood called the 'bawling Children' from the canons' 'cony-buries'.

The Oxford and Cambridge college layouts, depicted on the Hamond and Agas maps, show knot gardens set near the buildings and in the groves and orchards. Knots had begun to be popular in Henry VIII's reign and were very fashionable during the Elizabethan age. One of the features which delighted the owner of a knot garden was that it was green all the winter, the plants being low-growing thyme, hyssop, cotton lavender or box. The last was not so popular as it had a sour smell and the clippings of the sweet-smelling herbs could be used for strewing floors. In 1575 Lincoln College recorded a payment of 6d 'for herbs to sett our knotts'. If these were interlaced over and under they were known as closed knots, and the more intricate and enknotted the more stylish they were. The open knots with wider spaces allowing for walking were more suitable for growing flowers in. The pattern chosen by Brasenose College, as seen in the Loggan engraving, was the double-noosed knot invented by the Duke of Buckingham for hanging two men simultaneously.

An open knot garden of geometrical wedge shapes has been made at Emmanuel College by John Codrington. It is very appropriate that it should be Emmanuel that has an evocative Elizabethan garden since it is one of the only three colleges founded in Elizabeth's reign, the other two being Sidney Sussex in Cambridge and Jesus in Oxford. The knot garden is in New Court and was made in 1960 after the lawn had been destroyed by the renovation of the kitchen. The triangular form of the box-edged beds allows paths to cross fan-wise from two corners of the court. Sometimes the interstices of the Elizabethan knot shapes were filled with gravel, crushed bricks, powdered tiles or mineral substances and in his design for Emmanuel, John Codrington has used coal. As the garden is situated outside the old kitchen culinary herbs are used in the beds; the winter savory, recommended by Izaac Walton for cooking pike, elecampane, which could be made into a paste like marzipan, applemint for salads, tansy used for tansy cake and as a fly-repellent in the kitchen, angelica, eaten like celery or candied for confections, lovage for soups and stews, marjoram, rosemary, and thyme which college cooks would have used to flavour the meat destined for the sixteenth-century high table. A Cambridge man, Thomas Tusser of Trinity Hall, had published his highly praised final version of *Five Hundred Points of Good Husbandry*, four years before Emmanuel was founded, explaining when to plant the 'seedes and herbs for the kitchen' and what herbs and roots

*The modern knot at
Emmanuel*

to plant for using in salads and sauces and 'to boile or to butter'. Most of
the herbs are familiar to today's cooks, but many of the vegetables listed
would be considered weeds, and flowers such as marigolds, 'pot
marigold' (*Calendula officinalis*), are no longer considered to have
culinary uses. If Thomas Coghan's *The Haven of Health*, 1596 was
heeded, balm, *Melissa officinalis*, would certainly have been extensively
used in college cooking for he said it was 'greatly to be esteemed of
students for by a special property it driveth away heaviness of mind,
sharpeneth the understanding and encreaseth memory'.[21]

The knots were originally patterned shapes to contain herbs and
flowers but the design became an end in itself, particularly after the
influence of strapwork devices brought from Flanders in the 1560s.
Garden knot patterns were adapted from the linear designs used for
carving, embroidery, book bindings and frets and a greater emphasis
placed on the strap effects. *A Book of Sundry Draughts*, published by W.
Gedde in 1615, commends his designs as 'principally serving glaziers and
not impertinent for plasterers and gardeners'. When recreations of knot
gardens are made today, such as at the Tudor House museum in
Southampton, it is particularly effective if the pattern is copied from
wood or plaster work in order to give historical unity between the house
and garden.

One of the most influential books on Renaissance garden design was *Les Plus Excellents Bastiments de France* by Jacques Androuet du Cerceau, published in 1576, in which he gives illustrations of the great gardens of Gaillon, Blois, and Verneuil, showing elaborate knots and *deambulationes* or carpenters' work galleries. These covered walkways, often planted with vines, were very popular in college gardens. In 1575 Jesus College, Cambridge called in a 'frenche man' to help with the vine-covered carpenter's gallery in their fellows' garden.[22] Thomas Hill wrote the first English gardening books and in his *The Gardeners Labyrinth*, 1577, he gives instructions for making the covered walkways and knot gardens seen in du Cerceau's book. Fortunately, there is a most detailed plan of a Renaissance college garden, complete with covered galleries, arbours, cut hedges and marvellously intricate knot gardens. This *Typus Collegii* of the 1590s was made for the humanist Robert Hovenden who became Warden of All Souls in 1571. He was the first married Warden to take office and built new lodgings on the High Street to the east of the original ones. As the Rose Inn next door was derelict this was bought for a new garden, which the Warden began to lay out in 1574, and no doubt his wife Catherine Powys from Abingdon took a keen interest in its design. All Souls clearly had copies of Thomas Hill's books so that no 'frenche man' would have been needed to erect the vine-covered galleries seen in *Les Plus Excellent Bastiments de France* if Hill's instructions in his *Most Briefe and Pleasant Treatyse* of 1563 were carried out. He explains how these 'herbars' should be framed with ash or willow poles and covered with branches of vine or melon.

The design for the All Souls knots must certainly have come from Hill's *Labyrinth* of 1577, where he gave detailed instructions for 'Proper Knottes to be sette with Hysope or Tyme'. The Hovenden cartographer shows them in aerial perspective much more clearly than those shown by du Cerceau in the French castle gardens. The 40ft square intricate knot patterns[23] in the Warden's garden extracted from Hill's fantasy knot were repeated in the fellows' garden. It is unlikely that the gardener could have set out the patterns on his own and it is intriguing to think that he might have been assisted by some mathematically minded fellows. Another interesting thought is that the knots might have taken final shape for Queen Elizabeth's second progress to Oxford in 1592.

The Elizabethan feel for linear design and the love of matching conceits and symmetry in frets and knots extended to courtyards, garden terraces and forthrights or paths. The haphazard mediaeval arrangement of college buildings gave way to a design conceived as a whole with symmetrical courts and quadrangles, axially aligned gateways and through vistas into gardens. Trinity College achieved its symmetrical Great Court with its central fountain under Thomas Nevile, who was appointed Master by Queen Elizabeth in 1593. Three wings of the old buildings had to be pulled down to achieve the space and the clock tower moved stone by stone to line up with the chapel. The new fine gateway was ornamented with a statue of Queen Elizabeth who could look down on the largest college court in Cambridge, even grander than Christ Church's completed Great Quadrangle was destined to become.

6 Botanical Gardening

The sixteenth century saw the birth of botanical science, which was at first primarily related to medicine, but, when plant husbandry passed from the monasteries to the great Elizabethan country houses, became increasingly used in the service of gardening. In mediaeval Oxford and Cambridge physic was part of scholastic studies, but the Renaissance had brought new ideas of acquiring knowledge through direct observation and unlocked old stores of classical wisdom, which had been obscured in the mysticism and superstition of scholasticism.

For Chaucer's doctor, who would have been licensed at either Oxford or Cambridge, medicine was typically part of the comprehensive natural philosophy of Aristotle whose authority in the universities was supreme.

> With us ther was a Doctour of Phisyk,
> In al this world ne was ther noon him lyk
> To speke of phisik and of surgerye;
> For he was grounded in astronomye.
> He kepte his pacient a ful greet del
> In houres, by his magik naturel.
> Wel coude he fortunen the ascendent
> Of his images for his pacient.
> He knew the cause of everich maladye,
> Were it of hoot or cold, or moiste, or drye,
> And where engendered, and of what humour;
> He was a verrey parfit practisour.[1]

The books the doctor in the Canterbury Tales had read included Gaddesden's *Rosa Medicinae*, written in 1309. John Gaddesden belonged to a group of medical men who flourished at Merton, in spite of the fact that the college statutes, designed to promote the secular priesthood, specifically forbade the study of medicine. Chaucer's learned doctor had also read 'Esculapius and Deiscorides, and eek Rufus, Old Ypocras, Haly, and Galien', but he would not have studied these in the

*The Botanic Garden,
showing the founder's gate
and the Magdalen tower*

55

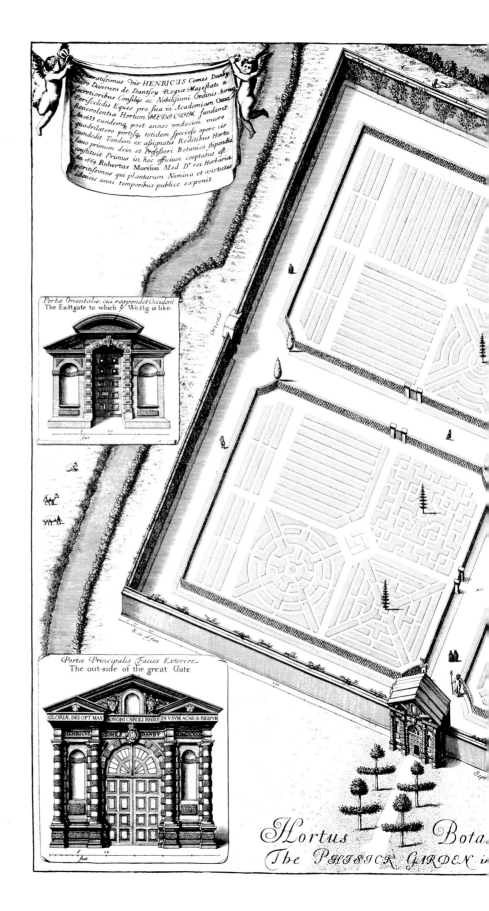

Illuratissimus Vir HENRICUS Comes Danby
Baro Dauvers de Dantsey Regiæ Majestati a
Secretioribus Consilijs ac Nobilissimi Ordinis Aureæ
Periscelidis Eques pro sua in Academiam Oxon
Benevolentia Hortum MEDICUM fundavit
An 1633 eundemg, post annos undecim muro
quadrilatero portisg, totidem specioso opere cir
cundedit Tandem ex assignatis Reditibus Hortu
lano primum dein et Professori Botanico stipendia
constituit Primus in hoc officium cooptatus est
An 1669 Robertus Morison Med Dr rei Herbariæ
peritissimus qui plantarum Nomina et virtutes
Suneis anni temporibus publice exponit

Portæ Orientalis, cui respondet Occident
The Eastgate to which ye Westg. is like.

Portæ Principalis Facies Exterior
The out-side of the great Gate

GLORIÆ. DEI OPT MAX   HONORI CAROLI REGIS   IN VSVM ACAD & REIPVB

HENRICVS COMES   DANBY FVNDATOR

Hortus   Bota.
The PHISICK GARDEN i

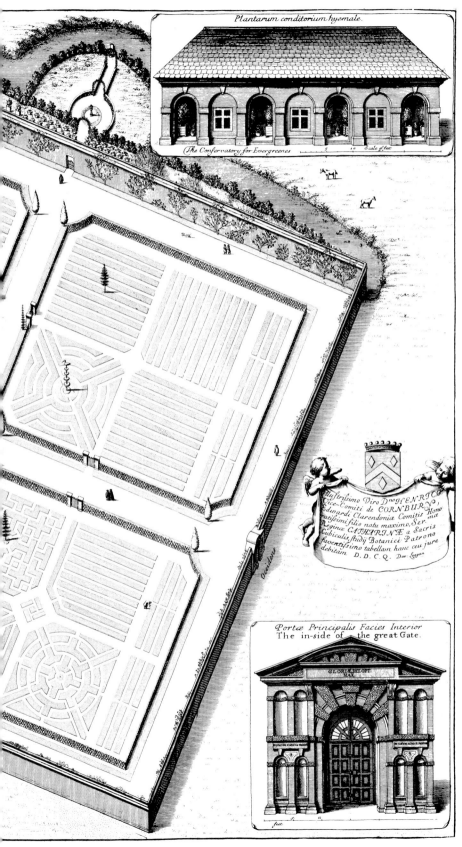

The Hortus Botanicus, *as shown by Loggan in 1675. 'The Conservatory for Evergreens' was probably the first greenhouse in the country*

John Tradescant the elder
(c. 1570–1638)

original. It was the outstanding Oxford humanist Thomas Linacre of All Souls who was said to have been the first Englishman to read Galen in Greek and when he translated his *Methodus Medendii* in 1519, Erasmus rejoiced that scholars read now 'Galen by the help of Linacre, speaking better Latin than they ever before spoke Greek'. Linacre also studied the *Materia medica* of Dioscorides, the great compendium of the medicinal uses of plants which was rediscovered in the Renaissance.

It was Thomas Linacre who first promoted the new ideas for the study of medicine and medical botany in England. He accompanied an embassy sent by Henry VII to the court of Rome and went on to take a degree of doctor of medicine with great distinction at Padua. On his return to Oxford he formed one of the brilliant circle of Oxford scholars, which included John Colet, William Grocyn, and William Lilye. On the accession of Henry VIII Linacre was appointed the King's physician. Cardinal Wolsey was also one of his patients. Linacre saw the need to supplement the academic studies which the universities could provide by a more professional body. In 1518 he founded the Royal College of Physicians which extended the privilege of licensing medical practitioners from Oxford and Cambridge to London. Later he also founded two readerships, one in Merton College, Oxford and one in St John's College, Cambridge. Anatomical studies as such had to wait until the next century in Oxford and Cambridge, when Padua, Bologna, Rome, Paris and Montpellier were already flourishing centres.

Botany as well as anatomy had first taken root in European universities. There were many in Oxford and Cambridge who found it hard to turn from the precepts of Christian scholasticism to pagan classical Renaissance studies, but Erasmus pointed to John Claymond of Magdalen College, Oxford, whose character he said would do much to 'win over those who are apt to assert that the new studies corrupt men, and are unfavourable to Christian piety'. In 1483 Claymond had written his *Notes and Observations on the Natural History of Pliny* and the rural walks and environs of Magdalen College must have helped him to appreciate Pliny's love of Nature. The tower in the garden, mentioned as being repaired in Magdalen's records in 1513, may have been a Pliny type pavilion for looking abroad into the Cherwell meadows.

William Turner, a learned commentator on Dioscorides and a field naturalist is often called the father of English botany. His *Libellus de re Herbaria Novus*, published in Cambridge in 1538, was one of the earliest botanical books. William Turner had studied medicine at Pembroke Hall, Cambridge, and was appointed to a junior fellowship and to various college offices. He was deeply involved in the teachings of Latimer and Ridley and when he visited Oxford in 1540 he was put in gaol for preaching without a licence. On his release he was proposed as Provost of Oriel or President of Magdalen but the fellows would not elect him. He spent some time abroad furthering his studies in France, Italy and Switzerland, where he met the great naturalist, Gesner. Turner was a true child of the Reformation, with an unprejudiced mind and ability for objective study. At that time there was no authoritative work on the English names of plants which would relate to the continental herbals and in 1548 he published *The names of Herbs in Greek, Latin, English, Dutch and French, with the common names that herbaries and apothecaries use.* By then he had become physician to the Lord Protector, the Duke of Somerset, who was greatly interested in plants and laid out fine gardens at Syon. In 1551 he became Dean of Wells but had to retreat once more to the Continent on the accession of Queen Mary. The two-way flow of scholars across the Channel in times of religious persecution greatly fertilized botanical ideas.

William Turner's *New Herball* was published in complete form in 1568, the first volume having appeared in 1551. It was dedicated to Queen Elizabeth with whom he said, he was proud to have conversed in Latin when she was a young princess. Its illustrations were taken from the *De Historia Stirpium* of Leonhart Fuchs (in whose honour the genus Fuchsia was named) but its English text included original descriptions of native plants. Turner often draws attention to the difference in nomenclature in the north and south of the country. It was still difficult to identify plants, however, before the advent of systematic botany.

Jacob Bobart the elder (1599–1680)

The herbal was a most important contribution to botany, medicine, and gardening in the sixteenth century.[2] The most famous and influential herbal was that published by John Gerard in 1597, which was able to update Turner's work with the plants that had been brought back to England by Elizabethan travellers for new country house gardens. John Gerard, who was in charge of the plants that came to Lord Burghley's gardens at Theobalds in Hertfordshire and in the Strand, was one of the first to realize the implications of this floricultural revolution. At first there had been exchanges between amateurs but, as more and more new gardens were established, the need for propagating and selling plants became apparent. Gerard set up one of the first nursery gardens at Holborn, and in 1596 he published his catalogue, a list of what he grew there, 'all manner of strange trees, herbes, rootes, plants, flowers, and other such rare things'. The next year he published his *Herball or General Historie of Plants*, dedicated to Lord Burghley, who had done so much to promote gardening. Gerard, who was a barber-surgeon, was also curator of the garden at the College of Physicians, and was primarily concerned with the medicinal properties of the new plants, which, as Harrison described, were 'dailie brought unto us from the Indies, Americans, Taprobane, Canarie Iles, and all parts of the world'.

Although there were now commercial nurserymen, Gerard recognized that there was no permanent place in England where the plants could be nurtured and studied and he recommended to his employer Lord Burghley, who was still Chancellor of Cambridge, that a physic garden should be set up within the university,[3] similar to those attached to the universities of Montpellier, Pisa and Padua for teaching medical students. Whatever beneficial side effects this might have had for decorative gardening, its primary aim would be to make absolute 'that noble science of phsicke' as 'having recovered the facultie of Simpling a principall and materiall part thereof'. The whole world of plants was made for the use and benefit of man 'for medicine to recover health', according to Gerard, and even the 'very brute beasts' had found out their hidden virtues. The

The garden today showing the Professor's House

wealth of material from the New World was in urgent need of investigating to promote hitherto unknown cures. Gerard's proposal that Cambridge should set up an establishment for this purpose with himself as head was never acted upon as Lord Burghley died in 1598 soon after receiving Gerard's request.

It was, however, at Oxford that such a garden was to be founded some twenty years later, where botany, medicine and practical gardening were to become linked for the first time in systematic study. As was intended at Cambridge it was primarily founded for 'a Nursery of Simples and that a Professor of Botanicey should read there, and shew the use and virtue of them to his Auditors', according to Anthony Wood. It was Henry Danvers, Earl of Danby, from Christ Church who being 'minded to become a benefactor to the University, determined to begin and finish a place where learning, especially the faculty of medicine might be improved'. Lord Danby leased from Magdalen College five acres of meadow land outside the city walls, which until 1290 had been the cemetery of the Jews in Oxford. It was low lying and four thousand loads of 'mucke and dunge' had to be used to raise the land above the Cherwell flood plain and prepare the ground to receive the plants. The foundation ceremony for the Physic Garden (which in 1840 was renamed the Oxford Botanic Garden) took place on 25 July 1621 with Dr Clayton, the new Regius Professor of Physic giving the oration. James I linked his chair with the Wardenship of the Ewelme almshouses, a retreat near Oxford which remains one of the delights of the Regius Professor of Medicine today. The walls of the Physic Garden which were to be as 'well fair and sufficient as All Soules Colledge walls, Magdalen Colledge Tower, or any of the fairest buildings in Oxford both for truth and beauty' were not finished until 1633. The gateways were as fine as those in the finest country house in England. They were built by Inigo Jones's master mason, Nicholas Stone, in 1632 in the mannerist style of his later St Mary's porch, reminiscent of Serlio's portals. The pedimented archways terminating the walks are similar to those built by Nicholas Stone at Kirby Hall in Northamptonshire.

Thomas Clayton, who signed himself 'His Majesty's professor of Physicke, Oxon', wrote in commending Parkinson's *Theatrum Botanicum* that 'Oxford and England are happy in the foundation of a spacious illustrious physicke garden, completely beautifully walled and gated, now levelling and planting with the charges and expences of thousands by the many wayes Honourable earle of Danby, the furnishing and enriching whereof and of many a glorious Tempe, with all usefull and delightful plants, will be expedited by your painefull happy satisfying Worke.' A new note was to be found in John Parkinson's book, for he was as concerned with the ornamental delights of the plants as with their medicinal value. The word 'curious' was often used in connection with plants, especially for those introductions brought in by the explorers. There is little doubt that Henry Danvers intended his Oxford Physic Garden to be a repository for curious plants as well as to provide the drugs necessary for the medical faculty. His brother, Sir John Danvers, had a garden at Chelsea which was highly praised by Aubrey who said of him: 'He had well travelled France and Italy, and made good observations. He had in a fair body an harmonicall mind. He had a very fine fancy, which lay chiefly for gardens and architecture.' John Tradescant, gardener to Charles I, whose famous Lambeth garden across the Thames which displayed 'all nature's varieties' would have been well known to the Danvers, was invited to be the first Keeper of Oxford's Physic Garden.

John Tradescant,[4] described by Parkinson as 'a painful industrious searcher and lover of all nature's varieties', was the first true plant explorer. Like Gerard, he was in charge of the gardens of a great country house and also had his own London nursery garden for propagating and selling his curious plants. His employer was Lord Salisbury, Lord Burghley's son, who exchanged Theobalds, where Gerard had been employed, for Hatfield at the King's request in 1607. He travelled in North Africa and the Mediterranean countries and in 1618 he became the first botanist to visit Russia, whence he brought back cones for the first raising of the larch tree in England. A journal of his travels is preserved in the Bodleian library, which also holds a book known as 'Tradescant's Orchard',[5] containing drawings of fruit possibly cultivated at Hatfield.

Probably through ill health, as he died the following year in 1638, John Tradescant was unable to take up the Oxford post, but it is possible that some of his rare plants may already have been sent to Oxford. In 1617 Tradescant had become a member of the Virginia Company, which was to become a channel for his introduction of many North American plants including the spiderwort, *Tradescantia virginiana*, which was grown at the botanic garden, where it was to become one of the most valuable plants for cytological research. John Tradescant the younger made three visits to Virginia and brought back many more new plants, including the tulip tree and the swamp cypress. During their plant hunting expeditions the Tradescants acquired all manner of curiosities, including shells, fauna and precious stones, which were inherited by Ashmole and presented to Oxford. The Tradescant rarities, which had been in the nature of baubles for Londoners in their Lambeth museum-cum-garden-centre, became the basis of scientific study in the Ashmolean Museum in Broad Street.[6]

Having been unable to get John Tradescant as his *Horti Praefectus*, Danby finally discovered, in 1642 when he was staying at the Greyhound Inn opposite Magdalen College, that the tenant, Jacob Bobart, a retired soldier from Brunswick, would be ideal as Keeper of his Physic Garden. What was needed in those troublesome times was clearly a good practical gardener to take care of the exotic plants that had been arriving, and, as no more building could be undertaken, Bobart could continue to live in his premises just across the road. It proved to be an excellent solution as Jacob Bobart assiduously carried out his contract with the founder for 'dressing, manuring and planting' the Physic Garden until his death in 1679. Bobart was always remembered in Oxford as a remarkable eccentric. He is shown in all his portraits with an enormous beard which on rejoicing days he used to have tagged with silver. Anthony Wood adds to the beard legend with his anecdote of 'Mark Colman, a melancholy distracted man, sometime a singing man at Christ Church, walking in the

The East Gate, by Nicholas Stone, as fine as any country house

62

Physic garden, catch fast hold of his beard crying "Help! Help!"; upon which people coming and enquiring of the outcrie, Colman made reply that, "Bobart hath eaten his horse and his tayle hung out of his mouth".'

To add to Bobart's strange appearance visitors usually found him accompanied by a goat. This did not detract from the old soldier's undoubted skill in his profession. Dr Plot described him as 'an excellent gardener and botanist' and the Revd John Ward,[7] who in later years became a botanist of some standing himself, wrote with enthusiasm of what he had learned from Bobart in the days before a professor of botany was appointed. He noted how he spread white sand under his plants so that he could see where the seeds needed for propagation and distribution fell. In 1648 Bobart produced a catalogue of plants growing in the Physic Garden, listing about 1,600 different species and varieties. He was clearly a very versatile and practical man and to eke out a living during the Civil War, when he received no stipend, he set up a stall in Carfax and sold there the fruit from the trees and vines he had trained along the garden's stone walls to the greatly increased population in the royalist capital.

In Commonwealth Oxford there was an increased interest in his garden as some Puritan academics believed that by making the earth bear fruit a new Eden would be called forth. Ralph Austen's *The Spirituall Use of an Orchard*, published in Oxford in 1653, not only gave instructions for planting but aimed at promoting puritan ideas. Austen had his own nursery in Oxford and so great was his trade that he estimated that he could sell 20,000 plants a year from his seedlings and grafts.[8] The college orchard planting was not entirely spiritual in the sense intended by Austen according to Anthony Wood, who maintained that home-brewing became popular when the fellows were no longer able to frequent taverns and tippled in their own rooms. Certainly the Parliamentary Visitors reported in 1651 'some Fellows of Newe Colledge abusing themselves by excessive drinking', but the fellows professed innocence. Although the colleges largely preferred ale and had their own brewhouses, there was a new interest in cider following Austen's experiments on apple fermentation. Experiments with grafting vines in the Physic Garden produced a 'white Frontiac grafted upon a Parsley Vine'[9] which also proved popular, give or take the Parliamentary Visitors. Bobart was always available to give advice on grafting but there is nothing to indicate that Bobart himself believed in scientific utopias or the Millenium. He did find, however, that dung from New College's 'house of office' when rotten was 'excellent soil to fill up deep holes to plant young vines'.

William Coles of New College published in 1657 his *Adam in Eden*, in which he tried to bring together all that was known in the art of physic gardening and at the same time revive the Doctrine of Signatures in the search for scriptural bounty. He called on academics to garden wholeheartedly so that those 'wearied with over-much study' should find refreshment. He pointed to his Warden, Dr Pinck, who had been sentenced to imprisonment by Parliament but allowed to return to Oxford on bail, and as a 'very learned Man, and well versed in Physick, and truly he would rise very betimes in the morning even in his later dayes, when he was almost fourscore years old, and going into his Garden, he would take a Mattock or Spade, digging there an houre or two, which he found very advantageous to his health'. In his obituary notice he was referred to as the 'pride of Wykeham's garden, cropt to be made a flower in paradise'. Cambridge fellows also engaged in down to earth gardening. Joseph Mede of Christ's College was often to be found in the fellows' garden 'very busy (at due hours) and sometimes knuckle-deep, when he would say smiling, 'Why? this was Adam's work in his Innocency'.[10]

On all sides scientists were taking an interest in practical aspects of their experiments whether in grafting or testing for good fertilizers. Many books based on the real observation of plants in the Physic Garden were published in Oxford. *The History of the Propagation and Improvement of Vegetables by the Concurrence of Art and Nature* by Robert Sharrock of New College in 1659 was dedicated to the great master of 'vegetative philosophy', Robert Boyle. Bobart was undoubtedly lucky in having Boyle as a near neighbour until 1668 and from him he learned rudimentary methods for over-wintering plants. Both Boyle and Evelyn were interested in the conservation of plants and it is not surprising that Oxford probably had the first house for conserving 'greens' in the country. This early greenhouse, illustrated by Loggan, was 60ft long and had an arcaded front and solid roof in the manner of an orangery. In severe weather it was heated by a gardener hauling around the pathways a grated iron wagon filled with burning charcoal. It was not until 1691 that Evelyn, after discussion with Wren and Hooke, published a design for an internally heated greenhouse, and this means of housing tender greens became a real Royal Society interest. Bobart also gained tips on mulching from Boyle and one year counted 500 balusters on his double pomegranate tree and took pride in presenting his large figs to the Vice-Chancellor. The Physic Garden undoubtedly played a major part in the promotion of vegetative philosphy and there were reciprocal benefits between the garden and gardening fellows of colleges. Many wondered how Cambridge could manage without one.

A plan for a Cambridge botanic garden had been made in 1696[11] and it was still being discussed in 1724 when Richard Bradley, a fellow of the Royal Society, was elected the first Professor of Botany. In the preface to his *Survey of the Ancient Husbandry and Gardening*, published the following year, Bradley wrote:

'For this new Foundation of a Physick-Garden at Cambridge is yet an Affair of much great Concern, as it will conduce to the general Health of Mankind, by instructing those who are any ways related to the Practice of Physic, in those Plants and Druggs which they are to use ... as the young Gentlemen who study Physick at the University, will then have opportunities of knowing the Plants and even the Druggs they are to use, which hitherto has not fallen directly in the way of such students.'

The Professor appealed for donations and mentioned the benefits already found in European universities with botanic gardens, but completely ignored Oxford, whose students had been studying drug plants in the garden for a hundred years. It is clear from the preface, however, that Bradley intended the Cambridge garden to have a much wider scope than that of the Oxford Physic Garden by including experimental agricultural improvement.

'This I hope to compass, as soon as a Physic Garden is completed at Cambridge, where, besides collecting such plants as are used in physic, and choice vegetables from foreign countries, a little room may be spared for experiments tending to the improvement of the land, which may be the means of increasing the estate of every man in England; for in such an undertaking every kind of soil must be used, and every situation imitated.'

Professor Bradley was in touch with all the successful horticulturists of his day and was clearly interested in the hybridization of plants. He gave no lectures in the university and received no money from them but devoted his time to pioneering garden journalism. This did not further the cause of the planned botanic garden and it was not until 1763 that Cambridge finally acquired one.

Long before Bradley's appointment, however, botany had been studied as an important part of seventeenth-century natural philosophy. Pre-eminent in this field was the naturalist John Ray,[12] who entered Trinity College in 1646 and was a fellow and tutor until 1662. He botanized in the countryside around Cambridge and in 1660 published a catalogue of the area.[13] He began to make a series of journeys covering the greater part of Britain and together with his pupil, Francis Willughby, he attempted a systematic description of the whole organic world, Willughby the animals and Ray the plants. Bobart's list of plants growing in his Physic Garden was drawn up in alphabetical order without any attempt at classification. Ray was a pioneer of systematic classification, which even included a rudimentary exploration of the sexuality of plants.

Ray started a herborizing tradition which helped to shape the future course of botany in Cambridge. By his rooms at Trinity College he had a small botanic garden which he shared with Newton's tutor, Isaac Barrow, and in his *Historia Plantarum* he refers to the plants growing there, which included the tobacco plant of which he says 'it sometimes endures the winter as I proved in Cambridge'.[14] Dr Richard Walker carried on his gardening example and in 1748 Salmon pointed out that although Cambridge had no botanic garden, many exotic plants, including pineapples, bananas and the coffee shrub, were to be found in his garden.[15] In 1761 Dr Walker presented the university with land for their own botanic garden in the centre of the town on the site of an Augustinian friary which had an ancient watercourse. He expressly stated that he wanted the work that Ray had begun carried on in the garden.[16] It was laid out by Dr Martyn who had followed in Ray's footsteps by perambulating the county with his students showing them the plants described by Ray and making additions to his catalogue. John Ray had taken part in the Cambridge Commonwealth physico-theological discourses and at the Restoration was one of the first generation of the Royal Society, which consolidated the pioneer work in the 'interrogation of nature' in Oxford and Cambridge during the 'twenty troublous years'.

7   The Restoration

The Civil War brought great changes to the universities. New building stopped and gardens were turned into parade grounds. The majority of the dons and undergraduates were for the King, but Cambridge could give little support with Cromwell's troops quartered in the town. Cromwell was MP for Cambridge and virtually its dictator. Although it was the military headquarters of the Eastern Association supporting Parliament, Cambridge, unlike Oxford, saw nothing of the actual fighting. Treasuries were ransacked however, fellows were turned out of their beds when their chambers were converted into prisons, and the cherished orchards and walks in the colleges were despoiled.

'For besides the cutting down of our Walks and Orchards ...they have cut down the Woods and Groves belonging to our Colleges, and sold them before our eyes to a great value...they have pulled down, demolished and defaced five or six faire Bridges of Stone and Timber belonging to severall Colleges, and have spoyled a goodly Walk with a new Gate.'[1]

Oxford became a garrison town when, from 1642 until 1646, it was the centre of the Royalist cause and Charles I took up residence at Christ Church in whose hall parliaments met and ambassadors were received. Queen Henrietta Maria and her entourage were accommodated at Merton and a door was made in the Corpus wall to give her access to Christ Church. This door in the cathedral garden is now planted with roses and lilies as a record that it was made for the 'Rose and Lily Queen'. The courtiers moved into college rooms and the colleges had to lay in stores of food for a siege. Lincoln College seems to have found time to put its knot and rose garden in order, even when Cromwell's troops surrounded the city and a cannon ball hit Christ Church hall. In their account for 1645 is recorded; '5s.0d for cutting the box-knot, the rose trees and hedges'.[2] Some of the Oxford college gardens still have traces of

The fortifications shown on de Gomme's map (next page) were later made into a garden feature at Magdalen College

67

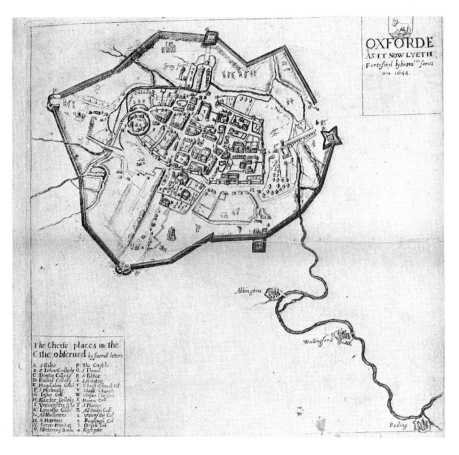

OXFORDE
AS IT NOW LYETH
Fortified by theſe forces
an .1644.

The Cheiſe places in the
Citie obſerued *by ſeuerall letters*

A	s Giles	P	The Caſtle
B	s Iohns Colledg	Q	S Thomas
C	Trinitie Colledg	R	S Ebbe
D	Balliol Colledg	S	S Aldates
E	Magdalen Colled	T	Chriſt Church Col
F	S Michaell	V	Chriſt Church
G	Iesus Coll	W	Corpus Chr Coll
H	Exeter Colledg	X	Merton Coll
I	Vniuerſitie ſtr	Y	S Maries
K	Lyncolne Coll	Z	All Soules Coll
L	All Hallowes	1	Vniuerſitie Col
M	S Marting	2	Braſenoſe Col
N	Corpus Market	3	Oriell Coll
O	S Petters Baily	4	Eaſtgate

Abbington

Wallingford

Reding

Sir Bernard de Gomme's
Defences of Oxford, 1644

Civil War fortifications reused as garden features, such as the terrace embankment on the east side of the private fellows' garden at Wadham. The Cherwell and Thames water meadows were flooded, and the Magdalen walks were extended to a bastion commanding the Cherwell, called Dover Pier after its commander, the Earl of Dover.[3] Addison's Walk, banked above the water ditches, is the best example of a war earthwork being used to advantage as a garden feature. The gardens were much frequented by the courtiers and their ladies and an entry in the *Brief Lives* of John Aubrey, who was at Trinity College, suggests that their behaviour shocked some of the clerical dons. 'Our grove was the Daphne for the ladies and their gallants to walke in, and many times my lady Isabella Thynne would make her entry with a theorbo or lute played before her.' The ladies used to come to morning chapel 'halfe dressed, like angels' and the President was heard to say to one of them, 'Madam, your husband and father I bred up here, and I knew your grandfather; I know you to be a gentlewoman, I will not say you are a whore; but gett you gonne for a very woman'.

When Charles I was defeated and the gay ladies, portrait painters and pastry cooks who had followed the Court to Oxford had left, university life picked up again. Cromwell was made Oxford's Chancellor in 1650 and Puritans were intruded as heads of colleges in both universities. Oxford and Cambridge rejoiced greatly at the end of the Commonwealth and Puritanism, however, and bonfires were lit in the towns and colleges.

Charles II was duly proclaimed at King's College on 12 May 1660 with all the soldiers unsuitably placed on the top of the chapel to give a volley of shot. Altars that had been pushed out into the middle of college chapels to make tables were returned to their original liturgical positions, and all tokens of monarchy that had been plastered over were restored. There was a clamour for maypoles to be set up in the streets of Oxford on Restoration Day, the jollity continued all night and, according to Wood, the Puritans 'tack'd about to participate of the universal joy'. The King's Head was able to display its sign again and the dons could drink openly. The Carfax Conduit flowed with claret for the citizens. New College added the King's arms to its parterre and Magdalen pointlessly chopped down the trees that had been planted in 'fanatick times'.[4]

Nevertheless, the Interregnum had 'yielded a harvest of extraordinary good and sound knowledge in all parts of learning' as Clarendon pointed out in his *History of the Rebellion*, and a remarkable sanity had prevailed in the universities in extraordinarily difficult circumstances. Dr Wilkins, the Warden of Wadham, fostered that freer air which saw the brilliant dawn of natural science in the universities. There were divided loyalties in college common rooms (he himself being married to Cromwell's sister while the uncle of his most distinguished pupil, Christopher Wren, was imprisoned in the Tower) and politics and religion were shunned wherever possible in favour of the neutrality of natural philosophy. Wilkins's lodgings provided a centre for a group of illustrious scientists including Wren and Sprat, Seth Ward and Willis from Cambridge, and others such as Robert Boyle, who came to Oxford to escape 'the madness of that dismal age'.[5] They began to reason freely on the works of Nature and, one by one, the preconceived notions that had been handed down uncritically were brought out into the light and examined. To the great natural scientists in Oxford and Cambridge, Nature was a conceptual whole, the law by which the universe proceeded, and their enquiries ranged over ever widening fields. Wren, that 'miracle of a youth', set up an observatory in the Bodleian tower, and Boyle, the most diligent of all the 'enquirers into the works of Nature', established a laboratory in the High Street, opposite the Queen's College. His demonstrations there included work on an air pump which led to the discovery of his law relating the pressure and volume of gases, and his assistant Robert Hooke of Christ Church made, through a microscope, the first identification of the cell on which life is based.

The Wadham garden, first laid out in 1651, was a remarkable reflection of the enquiring minds of Dr Wilkins and his colleagues. John Evelyn, who saw it shortly after it had been made, took great delight in the experimental nature of the garden with its transparent beehives, speaking statue and artificial rainbows. Joke fountains and automata of all kinds filled the seventeenth-century mannerist gardens in great houses, but the Wadham speaking statue on top of the mount was not just to trick and amuse; it was a serious experiment by the Warden, who was preoccupied with language and voice projection, and hoped to find a way of teaching deaf mutes. The speaking statue with pipes into his study was set up for this purpose but clearly startled unscientific visitors to the garden. Dr

Plot, who was conducting other empirical enquiries which led to the publication of his *Natural History of Oxfordshire* in 1677, was full of admiration for another of the Warden's contrivances 'whereby of but few galons of water forced through a narrow Fissure, he could raise Mist in his Garden, wherein a person placed at a due distance between the Sun and the Mist might see an exquisite Rainbow in all its proper Colours'.[6] It was the future builder of St Paul's and of the All Souls sundial who had made the dials and vanes on top of the transparent ornamental beehives.[7] Evelyn describes many more of the ingenious devices that the Warden and his protégé had set up in the Wadham garden, 'a variety of shadows, dyals, perspectives, and many other artificial, mathematical and magical curiosities, a way-wiser, a thermometer, a monstrous magnet, conic and other sections, a ballance of a demi-circle, most of them of his owne and that prodigious young scholar, Mr Chr. Wren, who presented me with a piece of white marble, which he had stain'd with a lively red very deepe, as beautiful as if had been natural'.[8] Evelyn, who was in spirit one of the Wadham set, was the greatest influence on the science of gardening, which he saw as a fundamental part of natural philosophy. He had been at Balliol in 1637 but left at the outbreak of the Civil War. His great classic on gardens, the *Elysium Britannicum*,[9] which is still in manuscript, contains all his ideas on garden design and plants and the workings of the kind of 'hortulan elaboratory' he had so much admired in the garden of his 'most obliging and universally curious' friend, Dr Wilkins.

Dr Wilkins moved to Cambridge in 1659 to become Master of Trinity College and, in the words of Bishop Burnet, 'joined those who studied to propagate better thoughts, to take men off from being in parties, or from narrow notions, from superstitious conceits, and a fierceness about opinions'.[10] The promotion of reconciliation and latitudinarianism had come from the Cambridge Platonists, a movement which outlasted its Commonwealth beginnings to have far-reaching effects. Ralph Cudworth, who was Commonwealth Master of Clare Hall and later of Christ's College, published in 1678 *The True Intellectual System of the Universe* which prepared the way for eighteenth-century deism. Joseph Worthington, the Master of Jesus College, was also a Cambridge Platonist, and his letter to Dr Sterne, whom he had replaced at the Commonwealth and who was now to replace him, is a model of latitudinarian consideration, especially in the matter of the transfer of the orchard fruit. 'I must not omit the giving you an account of your orchard fruit. A little after your going hence, I caused the summer fruit to be gathered, which were layed up, and lookt to every day, that none might hurt the other. Glad should I have been that you enjoyed them in their perfection, which you might, if you had returned, as we expected: but now summer apples have lost both the fair look and tast. As for winter fruits...I employed some to gather these, as the uncertain weather would permit. I think the last will be gathered today...The apple loft over the founder's chamber will be filled with them. I mean with those that are gathered from the trees. As for those that fell in the gathering, or fell by the winds, they are layd up in another place. It is one of the dayly employments of my wife, to look that none of them hurt their fellows.'[11]

The Wadham experimental garden laid out in 1651

70

D. Loggan delin. et Sculp. cum Privil. S.R.M.

71

Dr Sterne returned thanks for such kind efforts but gave instructions for the apples to 'be beaten for cyder', which it is to be hoped that the Worthingtons were also invited to drink at his Restoration party.

Trinity College was the stronghold of Cambridge Platonism, and it was into this humane and intellectual society that Isaac Newton, at the age of eighteen, matriculated in 1661. John Ray was still mathematics lecturer at the time but resigned in 1662 because he felt unable to accept the precise wording of the Anglican Act of Uniformity, although he remained in communion with the Established Church. Newton's tutor, Isaac Barrow, equally great as a mathematician and a divine, was one of the fellows, who, although a royalist, was not dislodged in the Commonwealth and could accept the new oath required and so bridge the change from Roundhead to Royalist rule in the college. In 1660 he was appointed Regius Professor of Greek and in 1664 first Lucasian Professor of Mathematics, which he resigned in 1669 in favour of his pupil, who had been made a fellow two years before. In 1672 Barrow became Master. Barrow's amazingly unselfish action in acknowledging the intellectual supremacy of Newton was typical of the enlightened atmosphere of Trinity, which became to Cambridge in the 1660s what Wadham had been to Oxford in the 1650s. The seeds of the decline in natural science can be seen in Oxford at the Restoration and the return to orthodoxy. There was no equivalent of the Cambridge Platonists to perpetuate the toleration and new empirical attitudes to natural philosophy fostered in Commonwealth Oxford. Mathematics, which had been fundamental to the thinking of Wilkins, Ward, Wallis, Boyle and Wren declined, whereas in Cambridge the institution of the tripos examination firmly established its reputation as an outstanding school of mathematical science.

Newton's contribution to the Enlightenment is best expressed in the well-known couplet of Alexander Pope;

> Nature, and Nature's laws lay hid in night:,
> God said. Let Newton be! and all was light.[12]

His formidable intellect in the fields of mathematics, astronomy, optics, and natural philosophy is embodied in the marble statue of him by Roubiliac in the Trinity ante-chapel, which so impressed Wordsworth;

> Of Newton with his prism and silent face,
> The marble index of a mind for ever
> Voyaging through strange seas of Thought, alone.[13]

The great Oxford empiricist natural scientists had consciously banded together in the Commonwealth to support each other and exchange ideas in common rooms. Newton was supremely self-sufficient and it was in his garden he often walked in lonely and concentrated thought. His rooms were on the first floor in the Great Court between the Great Gate and the east end of the chapel and there was a wooden structure leading down from his elaboratory into the garden. Humphrey Newton describes this little world of natural science enshrined in the elaboratory and garden that is clearly seen in Loggan's *Cantabrigia Illustrata*.

'About 6 weeks at spring, and 6 at the fall, the fire in the elaboratory scarcely went out, which was well furnished with chymical materials as bodyes, receivers, heads, crucibles, & ......Near his elaboratory was his garden, which was kept in order by a gardiner... When he has sometimes taken a turn or two has made a sudden stand, turn's himself about, run up the stairs like another Archimedes, with an Eureka, fall to write on his desk standing without giving himself the leisure to draw a chair to sit down on.'[14]

It is sad that the Loggan chess board garden of neat mathematical squares which had seen Newton deep in thought on his immortal *Principia* has now disappeared. In its place is a grass plot, often piled up with bicycles, on which an apple tree, taken from the stock of the proverbial one at his home near Grantham, has been planted by his college; it first bore fruit in 1954. It was Newton's friend William Stukeley who was responsible for the apple story. Newton had retired to his home, Woolsthorpe Manor, near Grantham, when Cambridge was ravaged by plague in 1666 and it was in the garden there that the notion of gravitation came into his mind, according to Stukeley, 'occasioned by the fall of an apple, as he sat in a contemplative mood. Why should that apple always descend perpendicularly to the ground, thought he to himself. Why should it not go sideways or upwards, but constantly to the earth's centre?'[15] Whether or not the story is apocryphal, Newton was, like many other academics, very interested in apple growing. In 1676 he sent to Oxford for some of Ralph Austen's best mind-soothing cider apple grafts to grow in Cambridge, but the order came too late because Austen had died.[16]

David Loggan's depictions of Oxford and Cambridge colleges at the Restoration enable us almost to walk into their gardens and to become acquainted with their historical features. The Wadham mount can be seen, but with the departure of Wilkins to Cambridge the speaking statue was replaced by the figure of Atlas, and all the other ingenious contrivances were removed. Loggan shows the gardens in detail, exactly as they were, down to the last gravel path, shrub, kitchen bed, or woodpile, rather than the more schematic representations shown by Hamond and Agas of the Elizabethan gardens. Donnish games can be seen in progress on fives courts and bowling alleys. Loggan, who lived in Holywell in Oxford, was appointed engraver to the university in 1669. He took many years over *Oxonia Illustrata*, which he probably began in 1663. In the preface to *Cantabrigia Illustrata*, which he undertook after his completion of the Oxford survey, he explains his technique of accurate delineation by examining 'from some distant point the roofs of all the buildings which came within my field of vision, all the objects which the subtle and varied art of architecture brought under my notice in the different materials which it employs; to draw them first on paper, then to engrave them on copper, and lastly, to print them properly'. There is little doubt that Isaac Newton took a great interest in the Oxford engraver who professed to be delineating his garden so accurately by submitting 'everything to the closest examination of the mind, as well as of the eye; to observe the limitations imposed by optics as well as by Geometry'.

Loggan's print of Trinity College shows besides the now vanished gardens in the front of the college the Great Court with its fountain, completed at the beginning of the century, six grass courts, cobbles and pathways, much as it is today, but the grass plots are surrounded by railings which were removed in the early eighteenth century. Emmanuel is also seen with railed courts and the fellows' garden divided into two parts by a tunnel arbour, possibly covered with vines, a bath and summerhouse. A brewhouse or *cerevisiarium* is much in evidence at the end of the old monastic fishpond. Christ's has an avenue terminated by a classical summerhouse and a large Master's garden containing drying ground, a pigeon house, beehives and a pool, which is now the setting for the busts of two famous sons, the Cambridge Platonist Ralph Cudworth and John Milton. Nearby is an ancient tree now known as Milton's mulberry, which is shown on Loggan and is probably one of the 300 planted in 1608 at King James's injunction. Jesus and Emmanuel also planted mulberry trees at this time. The Pembroke print shows the fellows' garden divided by a thick embattled hedge, one part of which is a bowling green. The Master's garden has espaliered fruit trees and elaborate beds, one of which is a floral sundial with a large wooden gnomon in the centre. Queens' also has a sundial in the fellows' garden, beyond which is the bowling green with seats and a summerhouse and a door leading to a bridge providing access to the garden and grove across the river. In the front court of Caius can be seen a miniature mount with a spiral path edged by stone balls and a column on top. There are terraces along the river bank at Trinity Hall and St John's which has an extensive kitchen garden, a bowling green and a wilderness across the river. Sidney Sussex also has a large kitchen garden across 'the ditch'.

All these college garden features can also be seen in Loggan's *Oxonia Illustrata*, which was intended to some extent to be a companion volume to Wood's *History and Antiquities of the University*, published the year before, in 1674. The table of contents gives, opposite each plate, a reference to the page of Anthony Wood's work where a description of the college represented is to be found. It is amusing to fit Wood's gossip in his diaries into Loggan's engravings. At Merton in *Oxonia Illustrata* the open knot garden and carpenter's work arbour can be seen and above it a stylish summerhouse with sixteen steps leading up to it. As a viewing point for Christ Church meadow it appears unnecessary as there is a good lookout from the terrace formed in the city wall. All is made clear by Wood's description of this feature and the rest of the alterations made by Lady Clayton, the Warden's wife:

'New trees planted, arbours made, rootes of choice flowers bought etc; All which tho unnecessary, yet the poore college must pay for them and all this to please a woman. Not content with these matters, there must be a new summerhouse built at the south end of the warden's garden, wherein her ladyship and her gossips may take their pleasure, and any

Emmanuel College, Cambridge, where the monastic fish pond, clearly defined in Loggan's print, still survives.

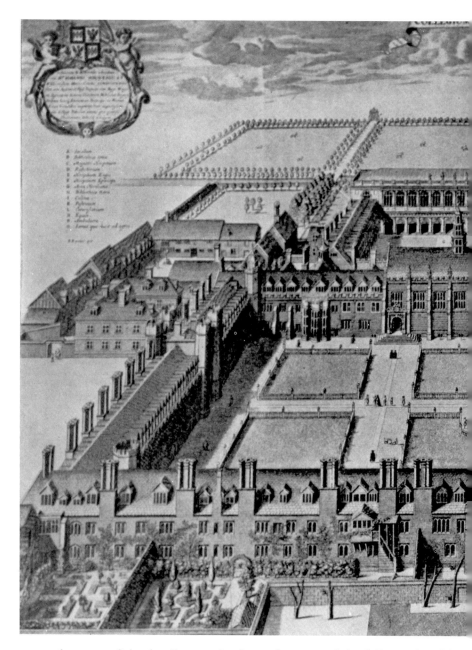

eaves-dropper of the family may harken what any of the fellows should accidentally talk of in the passage to their owne garden.'

Anthony Wood lived opposite Merton and would himself be in a good position to observe from his upstairs windows Lady Clayton's spying tactics. Many of the college gardens would have changed little since the beginning of the seventeenth century; even above Pembroke's new floral sundial the old herber persists. Balliol, with its small pleasaunce entered through a herber, its narrow beds and trained fruit trees, could scarcely have changed since the time when Evelyn was there in pre-Civil War days.

One of the most revealing of the Loggan prints is of the Great Quadrangle of Christ Church. All the canons had to be reappointed at the Restoration, their half-finished canonries on the north side of the

Trinity College, Cambridge, from Loggan's Cantabrigia Illustrata *showing in the bottom right-hand corner Newton's elaboratory and garden*

quadrangle finished and new gardens made on the foundations of Wolsey's intended chapel. Some of the canons were very interested in gardening and set about the planting enthusiastically. One of them, Henry Compton, who was a friend of John Ray, was a sponsor of plant collectors, and when he became Bishop of London in 1675 he made the gardens of Fulham Palace famous for exotic trees and shrubs. Another eminent collector was Dr Pococke, made a canon at the Restoration, and given the lodgings behind the south-west tower seen on Loggan. The distinguished orientalist had already been at Christ Church before the Civil War, after his return from being chaplain to the Levant Company at Aleppo. He is credited with obtaining the first plants of the cedar of Lebanon and raising them in his Berkshire rectory. One of Oxford's most

famous trees is Pococke's plane in the Priory garden at Christ Church, probably the largest oriental plane in the country, the girth of which was recorded by Gunther as 19ft 3in in 1911. It was planted in 1636 from seeds brought back by Pococke. He also had a flourishing fig tree growing on his canonry wall. Loggan clearly shows the new planting of Broad Walk by Dean Fell. In 1670 Wood noted that seventy-two elms had been planted each side and that an ancient water course on the north side had been stopped up. The wartime earthwork was not removed immediately. As in Wolsey's days it was débris from the building enterprises that had formed the base of the walk, which was at first given the name of White Walk, later corrupted to Wide Walk and then finally to Broad Walk.

Only Loggan's New College shows the real fashionable embroidered look in the garden, although Exeter has also sported a coat of arms in box. The box scrolls and heraldic parterre could be admired from the mount at New College, so well illustrated by Loggan with its column and sundial on top. The sixteenth-century Agas map shows the garden divided into strips either side of a central path with a single tree in each plot as the only ornamental feature, but by the end of the century the mount had appeared. In 1648, according to Warden Woodward, it had

The Restoration garden at New College

been 'perfected with stepps of stone and setts of ye hedges about the walks'. There is no actual date for the making of the parterre to the west of the mount, first described by Anthony Wood in 1658, but as the fellows wish to ascend, it would suggest there was a formal garden beneath, which could best be seen from above. Parterre was a new word brought from France and although, like the knot garden, was designed to be seen from above ground level, it was meant to be seen as a whole and not to be walked in. It was often arabesque and curved within the rectangle, rather than the simple geometrical patterns or the strap shapes of the Elizabethan All Souls knot. It was usually laid out in box, this being more manageable than the hyssop and lavender used for knot edging. There was a centre gravelled walk with compartments on either side balancing one another. It was the Mollets, the French royal gardeners brought over by Henrietta Maria, who had introduced *parterres de broderie* to England. New College was in the lead in introducing parterre gardening in balanced quarters, all to be viewed from an elegant mount. Their records show that they were assisted by 'Mr Bobart' in their schemes but it is not clear which of old Bobart's sons was involved, Jacob, or Tilleman, a professional landscape gardener.

The oriental plane at Christ Church planted in 1636 by Pococke from seeds he collected in Aleppo

One garden in *Oxonia Illustrata* is shown as particularly formal and that is the *Hortus Botanicus*. Bobart had presumably laid out his Physic Garden of the 1640s based on some rough system of classification for medicinal purposes and had decided which part of the garden was best suited to the exotic plants he collected. But it is unlikely that the old soldier had any hand in the formal design of the garden illustrated by Loggan. This was the work of an eminent botanist, physician and gardener who was, in every sense, a true man of the Restoration. Robert Morison, who was appointed by Charles II as first Professor of Botany in Oxford in 1669, had served the Stuart cause with passionate devotion. He had graduated at Aberdeen University in Latin, Greek and philosophy and turned his attention to natural philosophy with the idea of studying medicine. He was badly wounded fighting on the Royalist side in the Civil War and fled to France, where he resumed his medical studies. He took his degree in medicine and devoted himself to the study of botany under Vespasian Robin, the King's botanist. Robin recommended him to Gaston, Duke of Orleans, the brother of Louis XIII, who appointed him physician to his household and superintendent of his famous garden at Blois. Morison searched for rare plants for the garden and began a treatise on the classification of plants. Queen Henrietta Maria was the sister of the Duke of Orleans and visited Blois with her son, the future Charles II, during their exile and there they met Morison. All the royal parks had to be remade when Charles II returned triumphantly to England and Morison was invited to be superintendent of his royal gardens while acting as the King's personal physician. Morison dedicated his *Blois Hortus* to Charles II.

The appointment of a professor who had studied the ornamental uses of plants in royal gardens as well as their medicinal properties was to add a new dimension to the work of the Oxford Physic Garden. Not only had Morison grown accustomed to the formal gardens of the great Renaissance château of Blois,[17] but he had spent some time at Fontainebleau, the royal garden laid out by Claude Mollet for Henrietta Maria's parents, Henry IV and Marie de Medici. Morison set about designing the sophisticated partitioned plots with 30-ft wide walks for the Oxford garden such as he had been used to for setting off his rare plants at Blois. While superintendent there, according to Dr Plot, he noticed a 'white striped Dulcamara...creeping through lime and other Rubbish of Buildings' and cultivated it. Later in Magdalen grove the Professor found a striped sycamore seedling growing and brought it across to the Physic Garden for Bobart to cultivate. Morison's striped plants are still preserved in the present collection of variegated chimaeras in the Botanic Garden, which developed a specialized study of the nature of variegation.[18] The example of the striped sycamore shows well the combination of scientific and gardening interests initiated by the Oxford Physic Garden. In today's Genetic Garden, valuable research is undertaken in the beds arranged to demonstrate variegation and genetically-controlled breeding systems, and gardeners and flower arrangers are also indebted to this interest in chimeral variegation, particularly in grasses and hostas striped or outlined with white tissue.

Bobart, a key figure in Oxford's garden history, died, aged eighty-one, in 1679 and was buried in the churchyard of St Peter's-in-the-East. His memorial is inscribed: 'to the pious memory of Jacob Bobart, a native German. A man of great integrity, chosen by the founder to be the keeper of the Physic Garden'. Professor Morison who had been greatly assisted by having such a down-to-earth physic gardener, was killed in a coach accident in 1683 and Bobart's son, Jacob, took over both posts. After Morison's death he completed Part 3 of his unfinished *Plantarum historiae universalis Oxoniensis* in which Hearne said he was greatly assisted by Mr Dale of the Queen's College who 'put it into proper Latin for him'. He also circulated a seed list for exchange among botanic gardens, which proved to be the beginning of a world-wide service. One of the plants he introduced to the Physic Garden was the *Senecio squalidus*, a native plant of Sicily, which was to give Oxford its own weed, the Oxford Ragwort. It escaped over the walls and when the railway cuttings were made it spread all over the country, thriving on the volcanic conditions. Bobart died in 1719 and his plant collections were taken over by his great friend William Sherard of St John's, who had travelled extensively and had contributed many plants to the garden. At his death, Sherard bequeathed his books and herbarium to the university and endowed a chair of botany, stipulating that it should never be held by a cleric. He asked his friend Dillenius from Darmstadt to be the first professor and directed that thereafter the appointment should rest with the Royal College of Physicians and not with the university.

8 The Grand Manner

Restoration benefactions were to give Oxford and Cambridge many new buildings in the height of architectural fashion, and in future the colleges would think in terms of layouts, rather than unconnected gardens to offset them. New ranges were gradually put up in most colleges with the increased demands for accommodation. The poor scholars sharing sleeping quarters had largely been replaced by the gentlemen commoners who wanted their own rooms. Although the new ideas were for alignment and unity, this could not always be achieved in the older colleges that had grown organically as needs arose. The only two old foundations which removed all their important buildings that existed prior to the seventeenth century and could achieve unified schemes were Clare in Cambridge, which had had the materials intended for new buildings commandeered by Cromwell, and the Queen's College in Oxford.

It was Christopher Wren's architectural ideas that inspired post-Restoration building. It was fortunate that in 1661 he had returned to Oxford after four years at Gresham College to become the new Savilian Professor of Astronomy to succeed Seth Ward. He was then twenty-eight years old, one of the 'race of young men provided against the next age' under Dr Wilkins at Wadham. The ability for making models of the moon and of the brain, the ingenuity Wren had shown in all his experimentation and, above all, the mathematics which had been fundamental to the clarity of thought of the Wadham set, almost imperceptibly coalesced into an inclination for architecture. The lessons of the Civil War had given the country a new national unity and sense of purpose, which through Wren's creative genius was to be expressed in architecture. At the height of his career in which he was much consulted by both universities Wren said, 'nothing is more acceptable to me than to promote what in me lies any public ornament and more especially in the universities where I find something of a public spirit to be yet alive'.[1] It was fitting that his earliest works had been university buildings.

The Robinson screen giving a Versailles touch to the garden court at New College

Archbishop Sheldon, a former Warden of All Souls, where Wren was a fellow, felt that Oxford required a building which would provide an appropriate setting for its ceremonies, and provided the money for it.[2] Wren decided that a Roman theatre was best adapted for the performance of university ceremonies and produced a model of the trussed roof it needed for the Royal Society in 1663. His Sheldonian theatre was inaugurated on 9 July 1669 and Evelyn records that it had been resolved to celebrate its dedication 'with the greatest splendour and formalitie that might be' and to draw 'a world of strangers and other Companie to the University from all parts of the Nation'; there were panegyric speeches, triumphal organ music and an oration 'in praise of Academic Learning'; all this lasted from 11 a.m. until 7 p.m. and concluded with 'bells ringing, and universal joy and feasting'. Wren's theatre had provided the baroque setting for a triumphal Restoration ceremony. Evelyn stayed on for a few days after receiving one of the first honorary degrees in the theatre, and was disgusted to find that people had already begun to scratch their names on the Arundel marbles which he had persuaded Lord Howard to give the university and which Wren had built into the niches on the walls beside the theatre. Evelyn, always the practical gardener, advised the Vice-Chancellor to plant holly in front of them. The bearded heads set on plinths in the iron railings outside the Sheldonian, known as 'the Emperors', were renewed in 1867 and some of Wren's decayed originals found their way into Oxford gardens and are now almost unrecognizable. A third set was made by Michael Black in 1972 and they now look out philosophically at the new 'world of strangers' that tourism brings to Oxford. The Arundel marbles have long since been taken indoors.

In Cambridge, Wren began work on the Pembroke College chapel in 1663 at the same time as he drew up his plans for the Sheldonian. This was a benefaction from his uncle, Matthew Wren, Bishop of Ely, who had been imprisoned in the Tower for eighteen years. Matthew Wren had been a fellow of Pembroke before becoming Master of Peterhouse and then Bishop of Ely. He was arrested by the East Anglican Puritans at the outbreak of the Civil War and made a vow during his lengthy imprisonment that if ever he was returned to his see he would express his thanks to Almighty God by erecting a chapel at Pembroke 'for the Ornament of the University, which he always affected with a fervent and passionate Love; and in grateful Remembrance of his first Education, which was in that Place received'.[3] It was with complete confidence that he entrusted the fulfilment of his vow to his young nephew. It was the first college chapel without any Gothic features, being based on a Roman temple by Serlio. The chapel at Emmanuel College with its classical cloister and cupola followed in 1667. Eight years later, in the year he began to build St Paul's Cathedral, Wren designed Trinity College library for the Master, his friend Isaac Barrow, to whom he gave his services free.[4] This closed Nevile's Court and as it backed on to the river bank, woodpiles had to be driven in to the soggy foundation to support each of the pillars. At the opposite end of Nevile's Court, Wren built the balustraded terrace with two flights of steps leading from the hall screens passage into the court. The rostrum has three semi-circular niches built into the west side of the Gothic hall to harmonize with the classical appearance of the arcades and library.

In Oxford, when engaged in his astronomical studies as a fellow of All Souls from 1653–7, Wren discovered a graphic method of computing solar and lunar eclipses and also designed a huge sundial for the college. This was originally in the front quadrangle but was later removed to the wall of the Codrington Library, where it still adds distinction to Hawksmoor's baroque quadrangle. His influence was never far away on his own university and when he returned to Oxford he was consulted by the Queen's College and Trinity College about their new buildings. New College developed a most successful garden quadrangle in two stages. It was originally envisaged as a conventional closed quadrangle in alignment with the Front Quad but there were obvious advantages in leaving one side open to look on to their greatly admired garden. Wren had already in 1668 advocated the abandonment of the closed quadrangle in his Trinity College scheme and, knowing the conservatism of Oxford, added that if benefactors insisted on having one, then 'let them have a quadrangle, though a lame one, somewhat like a three-legged table'.[5] The second stage of the New College development was largely the work of William Townesend, and his buildings, stepped back from those already built by William Bird in 1682, gave the appearance of a perspective stage set from an Italian engraving. The entrance front of Versailles had clearly influenced Wren and others in designing garden courts. At New College the stepping back of the later buildings was almost inevitable to the design when fellows already installed did not wish their views of the garden to be obstructed. In 1714 John Ayliffe described the completed quadrangle with 'its several projections and fallings back in a uniform and elegant manner' as like Versailles. The finishing touch to the palace and park appearance was the linking of the north and south ranges by a handsome, wrought-iron screen with gates to the garden. The screen was erected in 1711 by Thomas Robinson, who had worked for the *émigré* Tijou, famous for his work at Hampton Court, and the money had been provided by the Duke of Chandos. The Michael Burghers engraving of *The Ichonography of New College* of 1708 shows two gardeners measuring the ground where the screen was to be laid.

The completion of the Great Quadrangle at Christ Church had been frustrated by the Civil War. Plans to complete the north range, to build Wolsey's cloisters and the missing hall staircase had begun in 1636, but all work ceased when the college was made Charles I's headquarters. Even the timber from the roofs of the unfinished canonries in the north range was removed during the Interregnum, the Cromwellians having no use for canons. In the first attempted restoration of the Great Quadrangle in 1636 it had been intended to follow Wolsey's plan which included Gothic cloisters. In the 1660s, ideas had changed and it was decided to cover up the low walls which would have supported the cloisters and to smooth back the shafts to form the blind arcade as seen today and on the Loggan engraving. The rhythm of the arcades was continued on the walls of the new canonries on the north side and the east tower was levelled to make the east side of the quadrangle regular and a classical balustrade on the roof substituted for Wolsey's battling.

The Great Quadrangle now assumed a uniform Renaissance appearance which makes an interesting comparison with Cambridge's Great Court at Trinity College, which was completed in the late sixteenth century and, although symmetrical in concept, has variety in its façades and retains its battlements. The central space in the Great Quadrangle at Christ Church was used to enhance the uniformity of the buildings and, in order to increase the impressive effect, the quadrangle was lowered leaving a broad gravel terrace in front of the arcaded walls. Stately steps were built down to the sunken quadrangle and a basin and *jet d'eau* erected in the middle, which served, like Trinity's fountain, as a reservoir. The basin and fountain had been the gift of Dr Gardiner and a Chapter order of 22 July, 1670 records the act:[6]

'Whereas Richard Gardiner, Doctor in Divinity, and Senior Prebend of this Church, hath at his own cost and charges in the Great Quadrangle belonging to this Church made one large bason 40ft in the diameter of stone work and lead well soldered, and in the midst thereof a rock of stone with a large globe covered with lead and gilt, and a fountain of water conveyed through the centre of the said rock and globe by a pipe running through the mouth of the serpent into the said bason, expending in the same work the sum of £250 and upwards, to the great beautifying and adorning of the said Quadrangle; in consideration whereof it is this day ordered by the said Dean and Chapter and they do for themselves and their successors promise and grant that the said bason, rock, globe and fountain shall from time to time be ever hereafter repaired, maintained and kept by the said Dean and Chapter and their successors.'

In spite of such strong words, twenty-five years later Canon Anthony Radcliffe, himself a member of the said Chapter, presented the college with a statue of the god Mercury, the body of lead, the head and neck of bronze to replace Dr Gardiner's globe and serpent; a not unfamiliar occurence in Oxford and Cambridge colleges. Mercury was removed in a student rag by a future prime minister in 1817 and it was a hundred years before it was replaced, although the basin continued to be called Mercury by generations of Christ Church men.

Loggan shows the new Christ Church of the 1670s with the grand uniform quadrangle, the baroque steps, globe and serpent fountain, smooth green lawns and the formal gravel walks. There was nothing to compare with such grandeur in other college quads. The sunken quadrangle gave additional height and consequence to the buildings, but this arrangement would not have been possible if Wolsey's college had been completed, as had been intended in the 1630s, with cloisters. The dominating feature of the Great Quadrangle, Tom Tower, which houses the great bell Tom from Osney Abbey, is missing in Loggan where the gatehouse is shown uncompleted. Only one man was fitted for the

Wren's chapel at Trinity College, Oxford, where he first advocated the design of a garden quadrangle

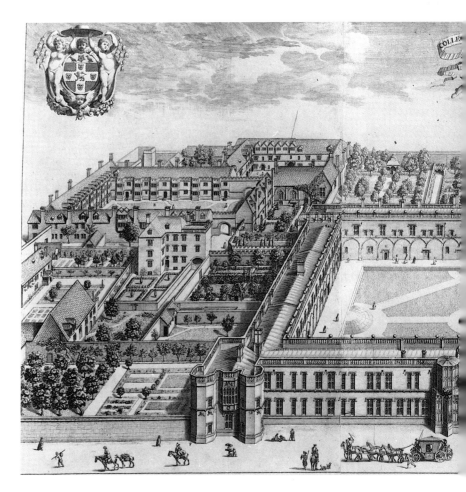

Christy Church by Loggan. The grandest quadrangle in Oxford, before Wren added his Tom Tower in 1682. The canons' gardens and newly planted Broad Walk can be seen

challenging task of building on to the work of Redman, Wolsey's master-mason, and that was Christopher Wren. Whatever his brief from Dean Fell had been, when sending his plan for the tower, Wren informed the Dean in a letter dated 26 May, 1681;

'I am resolved it ought to be Gothick to agree with the Founder's worke, yet I have not continued soe busy as he began. It is not a picture I send you or an imperfect Essay but a design well studied as to all its bearing.'[7]

Not only had Wren to complete the Tudor gateway as seen from the street with all its Gothic business, but also, on the inner side, to complete Fell's elegant Italianate quadrangle with the emphasized rhythm of the blind arcades and classical uniformity. Tom Tower was a wonderful solution uniting the mediaeval and the new enlightenment of thought in which Wren had played so great a part. It is an architectural expression of the idea of continuity between the 'glories of a New World' and respect for the 'remnants of the Old', commended by Dryden in the *Epilogue* to the play performed before the King in Wren's theatre in Oxford. The tower was designed in the year Wren became President of the Royal Society. The two events are eulogized in the Oxford Almanack for 1683, in which the illustration by Michael Burghers shows a group of mathematicians in the foreground paying tribute to Wren and the Royal

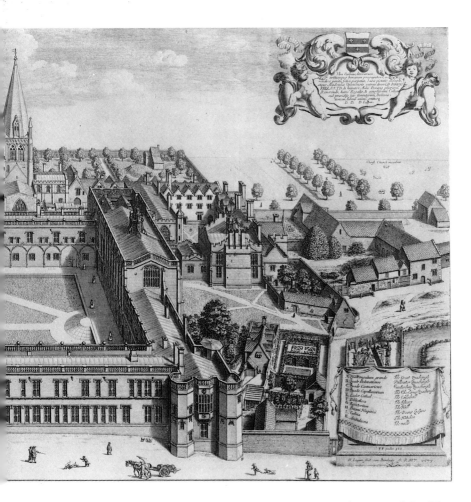

Society with a backdrop of the Oxford skyline newly graced by Tom Tower.

While the various elements of the Great Quadrangle, usually thereafter known as Tom Quad, were brought together in classical uniformity, Peckwater Quadrangle was a complete innovation, not only in Oxford but in the whole country. Many of the young men who occupied its staircases would in later years live in the Palladian country houses which were to spring up all over Georgian England but in 1705 such a building was new indeed. Peckwater was being lived in before Coke of Holkham or Lord Burlington set out on their Grand Tours and fourteen years before William Kent returned from Italy to play his part in Burlington's Palladianism. It had been designed by Christ Church's Henry Aldrich, who was appointed Dean in 1689. Like Wren, he was a man of wide interests – a mathematician, chemist and gifted musician. His mathematical mind and sense of harmony equipped him for his career as a gifted Oxford amateur architect. His Palladianism was the result of academic study rather than dilettante travel. Although Aldrich had travelled as a young man, his enthusiasm for architecture was aroused by contact with Wren and the study of books on architecture in Oxford libraries, and his large collection of Italian engravings. Aldrich's own

The reconstruction of the Peckwater layout in 1978

book on architecture, *Elementa Architecturae Civilis*, published after his death in 1710, contained many quotations from Vitruvius and Palladio. His place as Oxford's virtuoso and arbiter of taste was taken by his friend Dr Clarke, fellow of All Souls, the patron of Wren's pupil, Hawksmoor. Aldrich died before the library planned for the south side of Peckwater was built and the designs for it were made by George Clarke and executed by the talented college mason William Townesend.

Oxford, in close proximity with Blenheim, found itself surrounded with all the baroque ideas and artists. The Christ Church library matches up to the Blenheim concept of grandeur, and with its giant Corinthian columns and broad bays is in startling contrast to the restraint of the rest of Aldrich's quadrangle. Elsewhere in England the Palladian was to oust the Baroque but at Christ Church, because Aldrich had anticipated the Palladian movement, his Peckwater buildings were up before the library was begun in 1717 by Clarke and Townesend in the mood of Blenheim. The interrelationship of the buildings and spaces between them in Peckwater allow an exciting baroque progress. The build-up of sensation to the great baroque palace built for the victor of Blenheim was achieved by changes of level in a mile-long avenue to give the impression of an approach to a distant monumental citadel. Landscape could not be pressed into service in the limited space of a quadrangle and the baroque impression of grandeur had to be achieved through a space and movement progress.

The Peckwater progress is now suitably begun through a triumphal arch at Canterbury Gate, added by Wyatt in 1773. The first sight is of the impressive end of Clarke's massive library, towering over the quadrangle. The central space has baroque grass shapes which serve to unite the Palladian symmetry of the three sides of the quadrangle with the sculptural effects of the giant columns of the two-coloured stone library building. The sweeping curves of the contrasting gravel coloured paths lead the eye through the gap between the library and the west side of Peckwater to the supreme visual satisfaction of Wren's tower. The walk continues round the western end of the library when suddenly, in a more confined space, the cathedral spire bursts on the eye. An additional visual surprise is provided by the reflecting panes of the windows on the main façade of the library: these are alternating convex and concave in the bays so that there is an intriguing reflection of the Peckwater buildings with the spire of Aldrich-designed All Saints above, followed by the view with spire, chimney pots and pediments upside down. Dr Clarke had intended the library, Renaissance fashion, to be on the first floor with an open piazza underneath, but a later benefaction of pictures necessitated the conversion of the arcade into a room to house the bequest and these windows with reflecting panes were inserted.

The central layout of the new Peckwater Quadrangle is shown clearly in *Oxonia Depicta* of 1733 by William Williams. The baroque grass shapes were probably never executed but in 1978 when the quadrangle had to be levelled and resurfaced it was decided to carry out what the eighteenth-century eye saw as the appropriate complement to the buildings of the Oxford amateurs, Aldrich and Clarke. It was only when the shapes had been laid down using the small diagram in *Oxonia Depicta* that it was realised how effective the eighteenth-century eye was in space design. What Williams drew was probably only intended, since, whereas Loggan accurately illustrated what he saw from his chosen vantage point, Williams included in his depictions unexecuted designs he learned of in the course of his survey work and discussions.

The small college quadrangles and courts in Oxford and Cambridge were originally usually laid out as gardens with wooden railings, bordered with rosemary and sweetbriars, and often had seats and arbours. By the time of Loggan most of them had been replaced by grass plots with a single tree. Ideas of grandeur were sometimes taken amiss by conservative Oxonians. Dr Clarke was instrumental in giving a new look to the Brasenose Old Quad which in Loggan is still seen planted with its old-fashioned railed garden with its double-noosed knot. In 1727 he presented his old college with a statue group of Cain and Abel, a leaden replica after Giovanni de Bologna's Samson killing the Philistine which had been presented to Charles I on his visit to Spain and given to the Duke of Buckingham. Thomas Hearne, the Oxford antiquary, commented sourly:

'Last week they cut down the fine pleasant garden in Brasenose College Quadrangle, which was not only a great Ornament to it, and was agreeable to the quadrangles of our old monasteries, but was a delightful pleasant Shade in Summer Time, and made the rooms, in hot seasons, much cooler than otherwise they would have been. This is done, by the direction of the Principal and some others purely to turn it into a grass Plot and erect some silly statue there.'[8]

The Victorians sold the 'silly statue' for scrap in 1881. Dr Clarke gave Worcester College, the former Gloucester Hall, more than a statue, when it was refounded in 1714. He was, as the inscription on their loving cup says, 'almost our Founder'. As well as giving it most of his money and manuscripts, he designed the central block of hall, library, arcade and chapel. The money ran out before the south side of the quadrangle was completed, so that the old monastic camerae have fortunately been preserved to give the college historic continuity.

The most radical changes of layout that Oxford and Cambridge might have had were, as most people now agree, mercifully abandoned in both places.[9] These were the baroque town-planning schemes put forward in 1712 by Nicholas Hawksmoor. The academic scene was to be dramatized by a great complex uniting the towns and universities visually with the lining up of objects as in the Rome of Sixtus V. The Sistine plan was, however, for a sixteenth-century Rome much shrunken within its ancient layout where vistas could be opened to distant classical buildings. There was little scope in Oxford and Cambridge for intersecting vistas on an heroic scale, which was perhaps just as well as today pleasure is derived from unexpected views of spires and domes from mediaeval lanes, and the contrast of small town houses and grandiose college buildings. Hawksmoor's baroque town schemes were produced on his own initiative.

It was Dr George Clarke who brought Hawksmoor to Oxford, when he was working at Blenheim. His first commission was for the Clarendon Press building, next door to Wren's Sheldonian, and he was also consulted at Queen's College. Hawksmoor then produced his grand Oxford design which included a *forum civitatis* at Carfax with colonnaded buildings and a central Trajan's column to replace the Conduit. A much altered Brasenose College would have had a new quadrangle opening on to the High, a new university church would have been built where Hertford College now stands and New College Lane would have been widened and straightened on the axis of the Bodleian with an underground road, a *Pausilyp*, planned under the New College mount. A circular, domed library was to be attached to the Bodleian. Although his scheme was rejected, the baroque concept of Radcliffe Square as seen today was master-minded by Hawksmoor.[10] The Radcliffe Camera, built later by James Gibbs, the Bodleian complex, St Mary's and All Souls give a unique sequence of architectural experiences in space and movement. Hawksmoor's true monument in Oxford is the North Quadrangle at All Souls with the Codrington Library and the twin-towered range of buildings. The design for the great south front was not carried out and the Warden, who had been a generous benefactor, complained that 'he Designs Grandly for a college', and after Hawksmoor and his patron, Dr Clarke, had died and the indefatigable mason, William Townesend, who had had a hand in most of the new buildings, was in his seventies, the Warden wrote with much relief 'I reckon now, Hawksmooring and Townsending, is all Out for this century'. Enough was enough, he felt, in a venerable university where the buildings 'were so strangely altered and encreased that if our old Founders and Benefactors were to rise from the Dead they would not know Oxford even in Oxford'.[11]

Hawksmoor's ideas of unification by axial planning extended to vistas into the landscape. The baroque concept of such spatial design had come from Rome and from Le Nôtre. The Renaissance ideas of symmetrical gardens within boundary limits had been replaced by central axes as at Versailles, and the extension of vistas by the use of claires-voies, perspective and optical illusion. Hawksmoor was disgusted that Oxford and Cambridge, being ideal for overall spatial planning, covering buildings and landscape, still favoured haphazard layouts. At St John's College, Hawksmoor advised that to achieve this unity of building and environment a bridge should be built over the Cam on the main axis of the college through the gateways of its three courts which would give a pleasant vista 'thro the body of ye whole fabrick'. The existing arrangement 'being without any regard of ye fronts or sides of the Colledge, so very ungracefull and inconvenient that seems rather by chance to belong to the Coll: than by any intention: tis true it leads to a walk of trees which is an Avenue leading to nothing and would be no worse if the Bridge was elsewhere than in the present scituation which sufficiently condemns it selfe without any farther evidence as being irregular unseemly and barbarous unfitt to be contiguous to so noble a house in a place where so many strangers come'. He then asked for a plan of the river front of the college adding that 'I need not put you in minde how exact the Italian and French are in everything of this sort and what great benefit they obtain from it'. When the bridge to replace the old wooden one destroyed by Cromwell's men was built on its old off-centre site, in spite of such strong words, Hawksmoor finally vented his frustrations with governing bodies. 'Sir, I can say no more but that my thoughts are still the same as at first, but however I must confess your owne affairs are best known to yourselves, and must therefore submitt the execution of them to your own wisdomes.'[12]

Hawksmoor's master, Christopher Wren, had also been consulted about the alignment of the new St John's bridge and had also had his advice rejected. He too had recommended that it should be placed where the Bridge of Sighs now stands so as to make it 'directly in the middle visto of your quadrangles, and to rayse a new but shorter walke as farr as your ground goes, which may terminate in a seat, statue, summerhouse or some agreeable object'.[13] In order that the bridge might stand at right angles to the opposite banks, he suggested the diversion of the bed of the river westward, by digging 'a new channell of 700ft long 50ft broad and 8ft deep' which he felt would be 'a singular benefit to Trinity College, as well as yours, for it will give them (instead of triangular piece of ground) a regular parterre before their library'.

The regular parterre Wren proposed would have been no more than the elegant lawn that offsets the Trinity College library today. The word lawn did not come into use as mown grass until the 1730s and Miller's dictionary of 1724 defines a parterre in the sense that Wren used it, as 'a level division of ground'. A plain parterre could be merely a bowling green or a grass plot with a statue in it such as many of the colleges had. The intricately patterned parterres used extensively by the French and the Dutch were referred to as parterres of embroidery. 'Plain parterres', according to Miller, 'are most beautiful in England by reason of their turf, and that decency and unaffected simplicity it affords the eye of the spectator.' It was this 'unaffected simplicity' of a regular turf plot, and a canalized river bordered by an elegant arcade of manicured trees that Wren saw as the appropriate landscape to offset his library arcade. His ideas of 'neatnesse and naturall simplicity' should always be seen in mathematical terms. Isaac Barrow, Newton's former tutor, for whom Wren built the Trinity College library, believed that 'God always acts geometrically' and for Wren geometrical figures were 'naturally more beautiful than other irregular; in this all consent as to a law of Nature'.[14] The true test for the 'causes of beauty', he maintained in his *First Tract on Architecture*, was 'natural or geometrical Beauty' and for Wren natural and geometrical were synonymous. Wren only gave the broad outline of the natural geometry he saw appropriate to accompany his buildings. At Hampton Court his plan shows the radiating avenues and semi-circular arcade of trees. The foreground embroidery parterres were designed for William III in the Dutch taste for horticulture that the Glorious Revolution brought to England.

9 The Glorious Revolution and Dutch Gardening

The universities played an important part in the Glorious Revolution. There had been installations of papists and time-serving royal favourites under James II. Two great figures of the Enlightenment opposed these demonstrations of royal authority. In Cambridge in 1687 when the King tried to admit a Benedictine monk without taking the oath of allegiance, Newton led the resistance and appeared before Judge Jeffreys to argue the case for the university. In Oxford John Locke, the Whig philosopher, had supported Lord Shaftesbury in seeking to exclude James II from the succession and had been expelled from Christ Church by Charles II and fled to Holland. Tutors were ordered to instruct their pupils in the doctrine of passive obedience and Whig books were burned in the Bodleian quadrangle at what was, in fact, to be the last public burning of books in England. It was not long, however, before the views of Locke and the Whigs on absolutism were vindicated. James II chose Oxford for a demonstration of divine right, but this time the royal hand was overplayed. In 1687 he expelled over twenty fellows of Magdalen, intending to turn the college into a Roman Catholic seminary. Orange colours were flown in the High Street, the doctrine of passive obedience was ended, and the Glorious Revolution soon followed. Cambridge observed 14 February 1688, as Thanksgiving Day 'for the deliverance of the nation from Popery and arbitary power'.

The arrival of William III from Holland as the constitutional monarch brought new gardening fashions to Oxford and Cambridge as well as the rest of his kingdom. Walter Harris of New College was a great promoter of the King's Dutch gardening. He had come up as Founder's Kin in 1666 and had stayed on and practised medicine in the college and later became physician to William III. He visited the King's palace of Het Loo and in 1699 wrote enthusiastically his detailed account of the gardens of Het Loo in the hope that the 'reading might give some Diversions to the

The close walks and open rows of trees along the Backs, much as Celia Fiennes saw them; (detail from a print by Samuel and Nathaniel Buck, 1743)

95

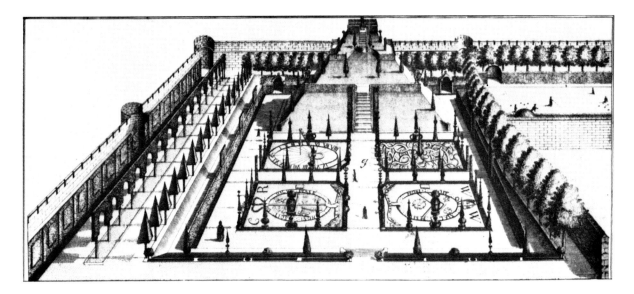

Curious, as the writing was pleasing to me. Also Persons of Quality, and Great Fortunes, may here find many things to Admire, and also to imitate, if they please, when they are taking their Summer Diversions at their Country seats'.

Dutch gardening had taken much from French ideas but the amount of water in the flat part of their country made grand conceptions impossible, so that there was a concentration of garden features in a restricted area. The gardens were divided into compartments with intricate box work, stunted trees and topiary. Daniel Defoe recorded that 'it is since the Revolution that our English gentlemen began so universally to adorn their gardens with those plants we call evergreens'. The King was 'delighted with the decoration of evergreens, as the greatest addition to the beauty of a garden, preserving the figure in the place even in the roughest part of an inclement and tempestuous winter. With the particular judgement of the King all the gentlemen in England began to fall in; and in a few years fine gardens and fine houses began to grow up in every corner; the King began with the gardens of Hampton Court and Kensington, and the gentlemen followed every where, with such a gust that the alteration is indeed wonderful throughout the whole kingdom.'[1]

George London, who with Henry Wise owned the great hundred-acre Brompton Park nursery in South Kensington, which supplied most of the great country houses with their plants, was the King's Master Gardener. London had studied Le Nôtre's garden designs in France and it was because of his combined skills as garden designer and horticulturist that he was asked to plan a physic garden in Cambridge. No such plan has survived and the only reference to the commission is in William Cole's manuscript history of Cambridge,[2] which states that in 1696 the ground for a physic garden had been measured and a plan drawn up by London, the King's gardener, who was paid for his journeys from London. Robert Grumbold assisted in the measuring up of the intended physic garden, but it was not taken any further and Cambridge had to wait another seventy years to achieve one.

The restricted size of many walled college gardens made Dutch gardening, with its attention to horticultural detail, rather than grand concepts, an attractive proposition, but in most courts and quadrangles, however, Wren's natural simplicity of grass plot was retained. Topiary features or 'hortulan architecture' became the rage. The 'tonsile evergreens' mentioned by Pliny were reintroduced into Renaissance gardens. The word 'topiarus' was used for an ornamental gardener in general terms in Ciceronian Latin but in England came to be used specifically for the art of clipping evergreens into various shapes. Fortunately a most lively and percipient young lady toured England, including the Oxford and Cambridge colleges, 'on a side saddle in the time of William and Mary' and her comments on her journeys were later published. She admired the enfilade arrangement of buildings and gardens, the 'through glides and vistos' that she saw, and gives details of the curiosities in cut hedges and trees everywhere to be seen in the new Dutch style gardens. She revels in the fashionable gardens with their gravel and grass walks, alleys of clipped trees, close arbours, topiary work, dwarf trees and 'grates to look through'.

Celia Fiennes took a particular pleasure in visiting Oxford in 1694. The Civil War had virtually been planned at her family's home at Broughton Castle when Oxford was the Royalist capital and it was her grandfather who had occupied Oxford when Charles I withdrew. As Founder's Kin he had been a fellow of New College and his granddaughter inspected his college and said with a patronising air:

'New College which belongs to the Fiennes's, William of Wickham the founder, so I look'd on my self as some way a little interested in that; here I was handsomely entertained by Mr Cross which was one of my Nephew Say and Seale's Tutors when at Oxford.'[3]

She thought the fellows' apartments very well set up that they 'may live very neatly and well if sober, and have all their curiosityes'. The fellows obviously enjoyed curiosities in their gardens and indulged in moveable potted plants which were set out upon the leads above in the summer:

'They take much delight in greens of all sorts Myrtle Orange and Lemons and Lorrestine growing in pots of earth, and so moved about from place to place and into the aire sometymes; ther are severall New Lodgings added and beautifyed here, the Gardens also with gravell and grass walkes, shady, and a great mount in the middle which is ascended by degrees in a round of green paths defended by greens cutt low, and on the top is a Summer house, beyond these Gardens is a bowling-green, and round it a close shady walke, walled round and a cutt hedge to the bowling green.'

Celia Fiennes's description 'walled round and a cutt hedge' only comes to life when read in conjunction with the Williams engraving, where the full extent of the cutwork can be appreciated. The beautiful stone walls, which serve so well as a background for a herbaceous border today, are covered with cut yew panelling, as was the case in most of the colleges. There are cut alcoves and doors in the hedges, evergreen pyramids and pillars and in front of the northern wall is a most complicated line of stilted arched trees, rivalling anything that the New College fellow,

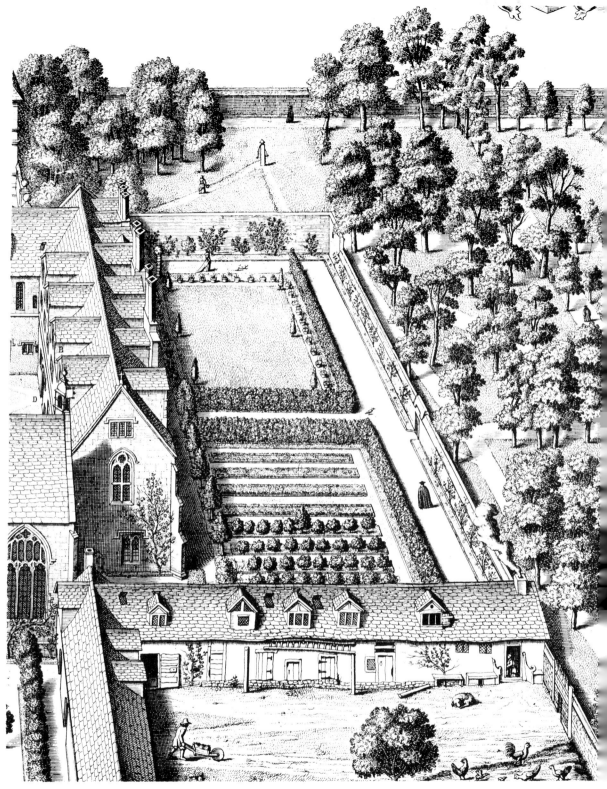

A section from Loggan's plan of Trinity College, Oxford showing the full extent of the Dutch cutwork craze

Walter Harris, had seen and described in the gardens of Het Loo. William Gilpin, the Picturesque traveller-to-be, described the New College garden, as seen from his rooms at Queen's, in 1742 with cut greens still as shown in Williams and topiary additions in the parterre: 'in one compartment you may discover His Majesty's arms cut out in box, in the opposite one they have done as much for the Founder of their College, in the third you have a figure of a sundial cut in the form of a Labyrinth'.[4] At St John's Celia Fiennes had admired the 'fine grove of trees and walks all walled round'. When she saw the garden it was just being laid out in the manner shown in Williams and it was described more fully by Thomas Salmon in 1744. Of the two adjacent gardens, then separated by a stone wall, he says:

'In the first the walks are planted with Dutch elms, and the walls covered with evergreens: the inner garden has everything almost that can render such a place agreeable; as a terrace, a mount, a wilderness, and well-contrived arbours; but, notwithstanding, this is much more admired by strangers than the other, the outer garden is become the general rendezvous of gentlemen and ladies, who seldome fail of making their appearance here at the same time unless the weather prevents them.'[5]

It does seem a little strange, as Mr Salmon comments, that the outer garden with its stunted pollard Dutch elms should have been so popular. These palisades or pole-hedges were popular in Holland and were particularly decried by the next generations as 'green chests on poles'. In *La Théorie et la Pratique du Jardinage* (1709), D'Argenville describes designs of woodwork covering 'tall groves, close walks, quincunces, galleries and halls of verdure, green arbours, labyrinths'. It is difficult to know in which category the St John's outer garden would fit. Perhaps it was a verdant hall with bowling green or palisades with cabinets but, whatever it was, the citizens seemed to enjoy the whimsicalities that the Glorious Revolution had brought to Oxford.

Wadham sported topiary balustrades in its garden and Corpus Christi echoed the sundial in the front quadrangle in topiary. Bobart had yew men guarding the entrance to the Physic Garden, but the formal evergreen craze was taken to an unbelievable extreme at Trinity College. The garden was first planted about 1706 and in the Loggan plan it is shown as quite unambitious and given over to domestic requirements, a vegetable garden, pump and fruit trees trained along the walls. The President's lady walks her dog in a small garden consisting of a grass plot bordered by plants in pots and beyond the walled garden the grove is laid out with gravel walks and unclipped trees. A transformation has taken place in the Williams depiction of the garden. The grove is regimented into pyramids and pillars of evergreens and the usual yew panelling on the stone walls. The most remarkable feature is the labyrinth cut out of block greens called by Thomas Salmon a 'wilderness adorned with fountains, close arbours, round stone tables, and other embellishments'. The wilderness was a formal arrangement of trees in a geometrical pattern, so often seen in the illustrations of Kip and Knyff in the first decade of the eighteenth century. The Trinity wall of yew, cut into regular pilasters and compartments, remained intact for a century and today some of the once tonsile yews can be seen growing naturally through the grille on Parks Road. Celia Fiennes particularly enjoyed the 'grates to look through' in Dutch gardening whereby the passer-by 'discovers the whole to view'.

Celia Fiennes discovered just as much in Cambridge to delight and captivate her.

'St John's College Garden is very pleasant for the fine walks, both close shady walks and open rows of trees and quickset hedges, there is a pretty bowling green with cut arbours in the hedges; Queen's College is old but a stately and lofty building; Clare Hall is very little but most exactly neate; in all parts they have walks with rows of trees and bridges over the river and fine painted gates into the fields.'[6]

Cambridge does not have an equivalent to William Williams's *Oxonia Depicta* covering the height of the Dutch gardening fashions, but there are tentative beginnings to be seen in Loggan's *Cantabrigia Illustrata*, which was dedicated to King William who had 'overthrown the enemies alike of the Church and the Liberties of England'. Peterhouse is seen with evergreen obelisks in its front court and Jesus College is training topiary conceits. College records show examples of greens and gravel gardening with pleached and stilted Dutch limes and elms along the walks. Clare had its pleached lime arcade along the river front as late as 1780. Many gardens had both open and close walks so that the fellows could walk on the open gravel if fine and in the close pleached walks in inclement weather. Improvements were also made in the gardens of the Masters' lodges, particularly at Trinity College by the famous Dr Bentley.

William III, on the advice of a commission of bishops, appointed Dr Bentley as Master of Trinity College in 1700. 'With the help of my God I have leaped over a wall' Bentley boasted in referring to the high wall that divides Trinity bowling green from the lane by St John's, his own college. Then began what a later Master, G.M. Trevelyan, called the forty years' war with the college.[7] Bentley immediately began to transform the Lodge into a mansion, replacing Elizabethan windows with sashes, although the college which was paying for the alterations protested that they spoiled the uniformity of the Great Court (they were later replaced except for the sash windows looking out from the state bedrooms on to the Master's garden). In the Lodge he erected a grand staircase and fine marble fireplaces. He wanted to take over the fellows' Combination Room as he said they hatched plots against him there, and when he made a chemical laboratory in rooms overlooking the bowling green they were suspicious that it was a move to steal their bowling green to add to his garden. The fellows had one of their few victories over the Master on the issue of the bowling green, and the Master confined his activities to the limits of his own garden. The latitudinarian divine, Dr Conyers Middelton, reported in 1720 that 'he is still the same Man he was nearly twenty years ago: the very last year he squandered at least £500 of the college money in the improvement of his Garden, the building of a sort of Banquetting house there, the making of a Terras walk upon the river'.[8] The building was in fact a spacious bath house, a feature popular at Cambridge. At Emmanuel the fellows had their own cold bath and brick changing room and Christ's had theirs set in a little formal wilderness. Peterhouse were even more democratic for the cold bath there was said to be 'much frequented by the students'.

The greens used in the college gardens would have been, besides the ubiquitous yew, Dutch box, juniper, phillyrea, the strawberry tree, bay, myrtle, laurustinus, oleander and pyracantha. A garden, such as that of

Trinity College, would not have been of unrelieved green colour. Variations were made by obelisks and globes of gold and silver hollies which would have stood out against the dark green of the yew panels and columns. Local nurserymen could often supply pots made out of hornbeam in which to grow standard trees. In Oxford the Paradise Nurseries specialized in supplying the colleges with their evergreens and enterprisingly joined forces with the tavern next door to encourage custom. In 1710 Von Uffenbach described the riverside garden which had once 'belonged to the Franciscan friars: 'Next we went on to a garden which they called Paradise Garden. This is hard by an end of the town, near a tavern, which is in connection with it, and at the back of which, on the water, are countless little boxes, partitioned by hedges, where the fellows drink in summer. There are beautiful fruit trees and many yew trees'.[9]

There was a demand for evergreens from local nurseries by the colleges even after the Dutch fashion had been replaced by natural landscaping elsewhere. The colleges were always conservative about their garden improvements even though they were often in the lead in architectural fashions. Dutch designs such as those at Trinity College and St John's in Oxford would have taken years to grow into maturity and would not have been scrapped in their infancy. Trinity still had its Dutch formality when Robert Southey revisited Oxford in 1807.[10] It was Joseph Addison of Magdalen College who first launched the spearhead attack on topiary in his *Spectator* article in 1712.

'Our Trees rise in Cones, Globes, and Pyramids. We see the Marks of the Scissars upon every Plant and Bush. I do not know whether I am singular in my Opinion, but, for my own part, I would rather look upon a tree in all its Luxuriancy and Diffusion of Boughs and Branches, than when it is thus cut trimmed into a Mathematical Figure; and cannot but fancy that an Orchard in Flower looks infinitely more delightful than all the little Labyrinths of the most finished parterre.'[11]

Although Addison's call for a more natural style of gardening went largely unheeded in his own university, it was not long before his cry was taken up by landscape improvers. The garden was seen as an opportunity to reflect the spirit of the age; both Enlightenment and the new national feelings of political liberty were felt to be unworthily represented both by the authoritarian French formality and the fussiness of Dutch taste. The garden, long fettered by French and Dutch ideas, was to develop a more representative native taste, natural and pleasing to the imagination and, as described by William Mason in *The English Garden*, shake off those ideas brought

> Alike, when Charles, the abject tool of France,
> Came back to smile his subjects into slaves;
> Or Belgic William, with his warriour frown,
> Coldly declar'd them free; in fetters still
> The Goddess pin'd, by both alike opprest[12]

10   The Pleasures of the Imagination

As the eighteenth century and the interest in natural scenery progressed, philosophers and poets increasingly challenged the idea that in the realm of garden design natural beauty was from geometry. The triumvirate held to be the philosophical influence behind the dawn of naturalized landscape gardening are Addison, Shaftesbury and Pope. It was largely a reaction from Dutch gardening, rather than from the grand manner, however, which sparked off the changes in taste. It was fitting that the spearhead attack on artificial shows, topiary and all other deviations from nature should have come from a disciple of the Oxford natural scientists and a follower of John Locke. Addison was the first to suggest that the scientific enquiries into the laws by which the universe proceeded would quicken a 'taste for the Creation' and give a new meaning to the 'works of Nature' as demonstrated by Newton, Boyle, Wren, Hooke and Halley. His statement in *The Spectator* that 'a beautiful prospect delights the Soul as much as a demonstration' struck an entirely new note in 1712.[1]

Joseph Addison was, he said, 'ambitious to have it said of me, that I have brought Philosophy out of Closets and Libraries, Schools and Colleges to dwell in Clubs and Assemblies, at Tea-Tables and in Coffee-Houses'.[2] He wrote in the relaxed lucid prose advocated by Dr Wilkins and the Royal Society which did indeed prove so popular that his *Spectator* essays were said to have guided the manners and morals of the eighteenth century, exerting an influence stronger than that of the Bible. Addison was a dedicated scholar and claimed that during his Oxford years he had applied himself 'with so much Diligence to my Studies, that there are very few celebrated Books, either in the Learned or in the Modern Tongues, which I am not acquainted with'.[3] He entered the Queen's College in 1687 and was elected to a post-Revolution demyship at Magdalen two years later on the strength of his skill in Latin versification. He held a fellowship until 1711, although he ceased to teach or reside after 1699. In 1693 he gave an Encaenia oration on the merits

*Rural walks along the
Cherwell gave rise to the
'pleasures of the imagination'*

Joseph Addison
'Great Patron of
Our Isis' groves
Whom Brunswick honours
and Britannia loves'

of the new philosophy, which he claimed had effectively brought an end to metaphysics and scholasticism. He referred to Newton as 'the greatest Ornament of the present age' and also paid tribute to John Locke, whose *Essay Concerning Human Understanding* had been published three years previously.

In his essays on 'The Pleasures of the Imagination', most of which were written in his Oxford days before being published in *The Spectator* in 1712,[4] Addison set out to trace the source of aesthetic enjoyment in the same empirical way that Locke had investigated the understanding. He considered the subject from many aspects, the pleasures to be derived from art, literature, architecture, the new philosophy, and what would today be called the environment. The basis of his aesthetic theory was Locke's insistence that all knowledge was derived from sense perception and experience. He held that beauty was not a quality in the object but the result of form striking an internal sense through the organ of sight. This internal sense which could add the faculty of pleasure to perception he called the Imagination, and he was at pains to emphasize that there was nothing in the Imagination which had not been received by the organ of sight.

Addison applied his theory of the direct psychological effect of form and colour on the beholder to architecture and gardening in a way which now seems oversimplified but was very convincing to the empirical mind. Largeness of scale was the source of great ideas, and for this reason bold classical outlines in buildings and wide prospects in landscape extended the mind and pleased the Imagination more than Gothic detail or fussy gardens. The poet James Thomson took up the theme that 'what is great pleases the Imagination' and called for a 'calm, wide survey' of prospect in landscape. The psychology of grand architectural concepts was then being applied by Hawksmoor, Vanbrugh, Gibbs and the Oxford amateurs. Grand gardens, however, could never be as pleasing to the imagination as wide rural landscape.

'The Beauties of the most stately Garden or Palace lie in a narrow Compass, the Imagination immediately runs them over and requires something else to gratify her; but in the wide Fields of Nature, the Sight wanders up and down without Confinement, and is fed with an infinite variety of Images, without any stint or Number. For this reason we always find the Poet in love with a Country Life, where Nature appears in the greatest Perfection, and furnishes out all those Scenes that are most apt to delight the Imagination.'[5]

Addison's ideas about rural scenes being pleasing to the mind were inseparably linked with classical associations, particularly those aroused by the poetry of Virgil's *Georgics* which he felt were addressed 'wholly to the imagination. It is altogether conversant among the fields and woods, and has the most delightful part of Nature for its provinces. It raises in our minds a pleasing variety of scenes and landscapes'.[6] There was already a strong *beatus ille* tradition in English literature[7] and in the Oxford Interrogation of Nature there had been much discussion about linking the classical philosophy of rural contentment in gardening and husbandry with the new scientific interests. Timothy Nourse, who had been bursar at University College, wrote *Campania Faelix*, which was published posthumously in 1700, in which he extols the beauty of the countryside and the pleasant sight of 'a Field of Corn shooting out of the Earth', and in his *An Essay of a Country House* suggests opening up prospects to enjoy rural scenes.[8]

While pondering his aesthetic philosophy and reading Virgil, Addison at Magdalen College had every opportunity to raise in his mind a 'pleasing variety of scenes and landscapes', which would have been denied to him if he had been a fellow of St John's College, with its topiary gardens. He had rooms in the north-east corner of the cloisters overlooking the Water Walks, which were a constant source of delight to him, and in sight of fields and meadows. At Magdalen Bridge the Cherwell branched into several streams and backwaters giving the

college a large island meadow within its boundaries. The walks round it can clearly be seen on the Agas map of 1578 and extended on the Loggan map of 1675. They have frequently been compared to the classic haunts of the Muses. 'Go into the Water Walks' urged Anthony Wood, 'and at some times of the year you will find them as delectable as the banks of Eurotas which were shaded with bay trees, and where Apollo himself was wont to walk and sing his lays.' William Collins delighted in them, as did Gerard Manley Hopkins and even Gibbon, who otherwise had not a good word to say for his college, fell under their spell when he had rooms in the New Building. The latter had not been erected in Addison's day and he walked out of his rooms over a small bridge into the water walks with gardens, orchards and groves on the western side and the grazed meadow to the east. For a longer walk he could continue on the botanic garden side of the bridge into the Christ Church meadow walks leading to the Thames.

'Philander used every morning to take a walk in a neighbouring wood, that stood on the borders of the Thames. It was cut through by an abundance of beautiful allies, which terminating on the water, looked like so many painted views in perspective. The banks of the river and the thickness of the shades drew unto them all the birds of the country, that at Sun-rising filled the wood with such a variety of notes, as made the prettiest confusion imaginable.'[9]

It was these impressions of walks laid out through natural scenes that Philander recalled in *The Spectator* (article no. 414) when the imagination, he says, delights in a 'prospect which is well laid out and diversified with Fields and Meadows, Woods and Rivers',[10] where a walker could also enjoy the 'rough careless Strokes of Nature', albeit from a gravel path; the 'natural embroidery' of the Magdalen meadow and the willow-covered marsh on the northern side of the raised walk leading on to the Holywell corn mill and its fields were greatly to be preferred to embroidery parterres and other 'artificial shows' as a pleasure of the imagination. In the manuscript essay the sound of bells, so familiar to an Oxonian, is included as one of the delights of the rural walk.

The philosopher and the poet were united in giving high importance to natural rural scenes. What pleasure could the imagination possibly derive from clipped rigid evergreens, abhorrent alike to man and birds, compared to 'Green Shadows of Trees, waving to and fro with the Wind' and sylvan walks where the season's variations could be enjoyed accompanied by shade, movement and the melody of birds? There was already a strong poetic tradition of Albion's glades being the haunt of wood gods, of Orpheus with his lute making 'sweet Music's Power' in the trees and green thoughts in green shades. The time had come for gardeners to listen to the poets and philosophers, particularly as so many landowners in the throes of enclosure and agricultural improvement,

Clare College, Cambridge
had the first stone bridge
over the Cam leading out
into the countryside

107

The entrance to Addison's Walk, from Rowley Lascelles' The University and City of Oxford, *1821*

were replanning their estates. 'But why may not a whole Estate be thrown into a kind of Garden by frequent Plantations, that may turn as much to the Profit, as the Pleasure of the Owner?'[11] wrote Addison. The advice that followed was heeded not only by country house owners but by those Oxford and Cambridge colleges with open rural prospects.

'Fields of Corn make a pleasant Prospect, and if the Walks were a little taken care of that lie between them, if the natural Embroidery of the Meadows were helpt and improved by some small additions of Art, and the several Rows of Hedges set off by Trees and Flowers, that the Soil was capable of receiving, a Man might make a pretty Landskip of his own Possessions.'[12]

Volume III of *The Spectator*, which includes 'The Pleasures of the Imagination' essays, was dedicated to Addison's lifelong friend and patron, Henry Boyle (created Lord Carleton in 1714), who acted on Addison's principles when laying out his estates at Amesbury and Petersham. Addison was undoubtedly the inspiration for the concept of the *ferme ornée* as popularized by Southcote at Wooburn Farm, Bolingbroke at Dawley and in Colonel Dormer's perimeter walks at Rousham near Oxford. Addison visited his friend Lord Bathurst's ornamental farm at Riskins at an early stage and left admiring verses. Ornamental circuit walks round pastoral scenes, the basis of the *ferme ornée*, were in essence what Philander had delighted in when he took his daily walks round Magdalen meadows. In Oxford, Addison was

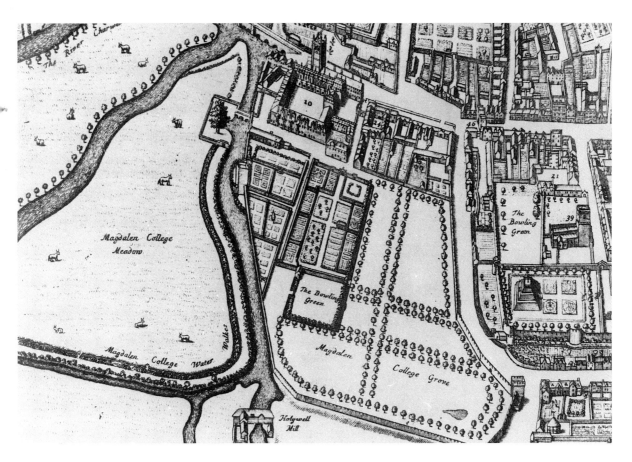

acclaimed in his lifetime as the:

Great Patron of our Isis' groves,
Whom Brunswick honours and Britannia loves.[13]

The Magdalen Walks from Loggan's Oxonia Illustrata, *1675*

The ornamental walks round Christ Church meadow and the Magdalen meadow survive. Since the nineteenth century, part of the Magdalen walks has been called Addison's Walk after the famous alumnus who frequented it. In recent times the wrought iron gates from his house at Bilton, bearing his initials J.A. and those of his wife C.W., have been placed in front of the stone seat on which he loved to sit in the wildest part of the water walks to muse on the pleasures of the imagination.

Cambridge, as seen in Loggan's map, was surrounded by open countryside, and the colleges, particularly those bordering the Cam, were in an excellent position to partake of the newly-found pleasure in the prospect of cornfields. Clare, which was the first college to have a permanent stone bridge over the Cam, variously said to have been erected to give access for building materials or egress from the plague, was the place where all Cambridge could enjoy what today are the communal Backs. Salmon, who reported the Oxonians perversely enjoying the whimsical Dutch gardens of Trinity College, was greatly appreciative of the delights Clare provided for visitors, where 'on the one hand, they are entertained with the View of elegant Buildings, Gardens, Groves and a River and on the other, Fields of Corn, which are equally beautiful at all

'Philander used every morning to take a walk in a neighbouring wood that stood on the borders of the Thames'

seasons of the Year'. Trinity College was also commended for its walks with the same presentation of elegant buildings by the river and avenues of elms leading towards 'cornfields and an open country on the West'. Wren, on the other hand, would not have approved of laying open the adjacent rural scenes to view from the grilles of his library arcade. For him the pleasures of the Imagination were in any case suspect as tending to 'blind the judgement'.[14]

Addison did not write any specific manual on his theories of estate gardening, but his ideas were taken up by Stephen Switzer in *The Nobleman, Gentleman, and Gardener's Recreation*, published in 1715, with proposals for 'Rural and Extensive Gardening', which he also called a 'farm-like way of gardening'. Switzer acknowledged Addison to be 'one of the greatest Genius's of this Age' and quotes freely from 'The Pleasures of the Imagination', while commending other philosopher gardeners, particularly Virgil and Evelyn. The confining walls should be thrown down and the whole estate opened up so that the green fields, meadows and rural scenes could be displayed to delight and enlarge the mind of the beholder. Charles Bridgeman, who was consulted in Cambridge, also gave practical expression to Addison's theories. Both Switzer and Bridgeman agreed with his 'large notions' and decried the 'diminutive beauties' and fussiness of the Dutch taste.

Bridgeman, who was to become Royal Gardener in 1728, was something new in England as a professional landscape designer like Le Nôtre in France.[15] As architects, Wren, Hawskmoor, Vanbrugh and Gibbs were often involved with the broad outlines of the landscape to accompany their buildings, but it was nurserymen contractors, such as London and Wise from the Brompton Nurseries, who usually carried out garden schemes. Bridgeman was an accomplished surveyor and draughtsman and an associate of the best craftsmen and architects of the time. He was a friend of Pope and Prior, and Lord Harley, later the Earl of Oxford, was an early patron. Pope told the Earl in 1724 that Bridgeman was 'of the virtuoso class as well as I and in my notions of the higher class; since Gardening is more Antique and nearer God's own work than Poetry'.[16] Gibbs and Bridgeman worked together at Lord Harley's estate at Wimpole, near Cambridge, in 1720, and in 1724 when Gibbs was consulted by King's College, Bridgeman was asked to lay out the ground across the Cam as an accompaniment to the west side of Gibb's new country-house-like building. The landscape scheme was not carried out but subsequent governing bodies were clearly intending to do so when the front court at King's was finally completed. In 1748 Salmon felt that there was no place in Cambridge 'capable of greater Improvement by cutting Vistos thro' the Grove and laying out the waste ground about it with regular walks and canals, all which is designed to be done (when the remaining Part of the Great Square is finished) according to the plan given by the late ingenious Mr Bridgman', and still in 1763 *Cantabrigia Depicta* repeated Salmon's comments, although by then such a layout would have been unfashionable.

Bridgeman's plan can be seen on the aerial view of King's College drawn by James Essex in 1744. It shows a formal arrangement of a basin off the canalized Cam, a pleached arcade and the vista terminated by a raised circular temple, overlooking the canal, probably designed by Gibbs. It is reminiscent of what Wren had advised for the two other Camside colleges; the canalized river, bridges on a central axis with the buildings, and a summerhouse to terminate the vista. Bridgeman, however, in addition to adding the formal water feature, separated vistas and paths and although the bridge was to cross the Cam opposite the centre of the Gibbs Building, the paths were not continued on the central axis. There is a stylized simplicity in such designs called natural-artificial by Nourse and natura-linear by Switzer, which was not just a transition between formal and naturalized styles but a considered ideal. It accorded with Addison's premise that although 'the works of Nature' were more pleasant to the Imagination than those of art, they were still more pleasant the more they resembled those of art. It was to take several decades before the hand of art was effectively concealed in English naturalized landscape.

New extensions to the pleasures of the Imagination were given by William Shenstone, the poet, and Sanderson Miller, the amateur architect, who were up at Oxford in the 1730s. Miller, who was at St Mary's Hall, did not in fact take a degree but spent six relaxed years in literary and antiquarian pursuits and revelling in the rich associations of

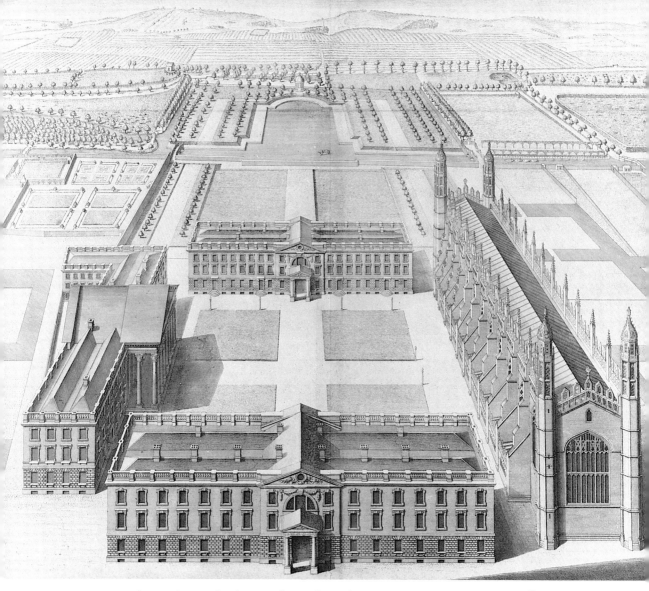

James Essex's aerial view of the Bridgeman garden plan of King's, with the countryside beyond

Oxford's mediaeval architecture. He was essentially a romantic antiquarian and saw turrets, buttresses and battlements with poetic feeling. There was at the time a small circle of antiquarians with a centre at the Bodleian and in 1736 Sir Roger Newdigate, with whom Miller was closely linked, founded the prize in English verse (which still exists) for a subject connected with the history of ancient architecture. Oxford influences can be detected in the buildings that Sanderson Miller designed for his friends; the light domestic Gothic of the Divinity School exterior, the plaster fan-vaulting of Brasenose chapel and the Gothic glazing of windows evoking the traceried windows of St Mary's Hall. Addison had said that the poetic imagination should be fed not only with images of 'great Works of architecture' but also 'in the Ruins of those which flourished in former Ages'.[17] Addison had not thought of artificial ruins as an agreeable sensation but this became a Miller speciality.

Sanderson Miller's particular contribution to the pleasures of the imagination was his linking of local history and landscape. His artificial ruined castles, notably those designed for Hagley and Wimpole, near

Cambridge, were thought by the envious Horace Walpole to bear 'the true rust of the Barons' Wars'. The earliest was built in his own grounds at Radway in 1746 to cap Edgehill at the spot where Charles I had set up his standard before the battle which preceded his winter-quartering in Oxford. Miller collected cannon balls on his estate, and when up at Oxford he had avidly read Civil War pamphlets. The Edgehill tower sought to romanticize the event and to present history in Thomson's words 'unwarped by party zeal'. There was a view of the battlefield from the guardroom tower, where visitors were presented with a sheet locating positions while they were entertained to cold collations. Copses were also planted up in battle formations. 'Surely Edgehill fight was never more fortunate for the nation than it was lucky for Mr Miller', wrote his friend William Shenstone.[18]

William Shenstone, who was a contemporary of Samuel Johnson and Richard Graves at Pembroke, had a liking for good company and old ballads while at Oxford and anything that was considered through history and literature to show native taste. Both Miller and Shenstone introduced into landscape gardening the feel for the picturesque past they had learned in Oxford. Shenstone inherited a small estate in Worcestershire, called the Leasowes, in the 1740s and, on a modest income of £300 a year, he created the most famous of all *fermes ornées*, an Addison 'pretty landskip out of his own possessions' on a pleasure and profit basis. His landscape gardening and pastoral poetry went hand in hand. The inscriptions from the *Georgics* would have delighted Addison, and Robert Dodsley said of his Virgil's grove, where Shenstone gave practical expression to poetic imagery, that 'none ever beheld this grove without a sense of satisfaction; and were one to chuse any one spot of this perfectly Arcadian farm, it would be this'. Even Dr Johnson and Oliver Goldsmith who were critical of landscape gardening approved of the Leasowes.

Shenstone's *Unconnected Thoughts on Gardening* was published posthumously by Dodsley in 1764 and it included the Miller-inspired suggestion that 'wherever a park or garden happens to have been the scene of any event in history, one would surely avail one's self of that circumstance, to make it more interesting to the imagination. Mottoes should allude to it, columns etc record it; verses moralize upon it.'[19] Shenstone developed the ideas of Switzer and Bridgeman in separating paths and vistas by the advice that when an object had been viewed 'the foot should never travel to it by the same path, which the eye has travelled over before. Lose the object, and draw nigh, obliquely.'[20] He went beyond Addison and Switzer's ideas of what could be seen as natural-artificial by advocating that 'apparent art, in its proper province' should 'contrast agreeably' with apparent nature but 'their provinces ever should be kept distinct'.[21] Shenstone's Leasowes was an early example of truly naturalized landscape gardening, where the discovery of art was successfully avoided, and his published thoughts on achieving this were some of the first on the subject. Natural landscape gardening ideas did not make an impact on Oxford and Cambridge college gardens until much later in the century.

11   Landscaping in the Age of Taste

The eighteenth century fostered the growth of a new concept of taste which flourished in the stability of the age. The appreciation of art, architecture and landscape was not merely a pleasurable sensation but a moral sense. Addison's 'polite imagination' developed into a 'fine taste' which was the criterion by which every well-bred gentleman was judged. Taste was aristocratic rather than academic and it was Lord Shaftesbury, the grandson of the 1st Earl, who had given the lead in exploring the principles of discerning taste. In the *Moralists* (1709) he wrote; 'what is beautiful is harmonious and proportionable; what is harmonious and proportionable is true; and what is at once both beautiful and true is of consequence agreeable and good'. Connoisseurship came to replace scholarship in his reflections on manners and taste in the *Characteristics*.

'The mere amusements of gentlemen are found more improving than the profound researches of pedants. I am persuaded that to be a virtuoso is a higher step towards becoming a man of virtue and good sense than the being of what in this age we call a scholar.'[1]

The Dilettanti Society soon had more standing than the Royal Society and the world of fashion spoke louder than the dormant universities. Lord Burlington's Chiswick could do more for culture and the intellect than Oxford and Cambridge.

Shaftesbury emphasized the interrelationship of the arts and sought to provide them with the philosophical backing already allied to scientific thought. John Locke had been his private tutor, but although Shaftesbury was influenced by his powerful intellect and integrity, he could not accept Locke's premise that man came into the world with 'a blank slate' and that all knowledge was derived from sense perception and experience. Shaftesbury saw Addison's Locke-inspired scientific imagination as a barrier to the arts. The neo-classical philosophy of innate ideas, the recognition of beauty through an idea of perfection already existing in the mind, which an artist sought to capture, was more sympathetic to creative imagination. Shaftesbury was a disciple of the Cambridge

The Gibb's building at King's, the 'country house' focus of Capability Brown's controversial proposal to landscape the Backs

The view of Wren's Trinity College library is still much as he would have wished it

Platonists, feeling that their view of reality was more congenial to the arts, which he passionately wished to promote. In particular he supported Ralph Cudworth's *The Intellectual System*, in which he rejected Hobbes's materialism and the mechanistic world of Cartesian thought as 'a dead and wooden world, as it were a carved statue, that hath nothing neither vital nor magical at all in it'. Cudworth and the Cambridge Platonists saw an organic nature animating the natural world, a 'Plastick Life of Nature', which gave Nature back part of its old magic and was much more congenial to poetry and the idea of poetic landscape. Natural objects could have a meaning beyond sense perception and the old ideas of symbolism could be brought into the new realistic studies of the works of nature. The Cambridge latitude men, who sought reconciliation and synthesis in all things, had produced a different kind of idealism, a world beyond the senses more relevant to the arts than classical innate ideas. The aesthetic theories of Addison and Shaftesbury, although seemingly in opposite camps, could be reconciled in this purposely ambiguous concept of nature.

Shaftesbury's dialogue between the two moralists Theocles and the more sceptical Philocles, offered in 1709 a deist kind of Nature worship which would not be out of place a hundred years later.

'O Glorious *Nature*! supremely Fair, and sovereignly Good! All-loving and All-lovely, All-divine!...O mighty *Nature*! Wise Substitute of *Providence*! impower'd *Creatress*! Or Thou impowering DEITY, Supreme Creator! Thee I invoke, and Thee alone adore. To Thee this Solitude, this Place, these Rural Meditations are sacred; whilst thus inspir'd with Harmony of Thought, tho unconfin'd by Words, and in loose Numbers, I sing of Nature's Order in created Beings, and celebrate the Beautys which resolve in Thee, the Source and Principle of all Beauty and Perfection.........The Wildness pleases. We seem to live alone with Nature......... I shall no longer resist the Passion growing in me for Things of a *natural* kind; where neither *Art*, nor the *Conceit* or *Caprice* of Man had spoil'd their *genuine Order*, by breaking in upon that *primitive State*. Even the rude *Rocks*, the mossy *Caverns*, the irregular unwrought *Grotto's* and broken *Falls* of Water, with all the horrid Graces of the *Wilderness* it-self, as representing *Nature* more, will be the more engaging, and appear with a Magnificence beyond the formal Mockery of Princely Gardens.'[2]

Shaftesbury was the philosophical spokesman for the Burlington Palladians, the second generation of Whigs who criticized Wren, baroque architecture and formal gardens. Alexander Pope, who was deeply versed in Shaftesbury's moral philosophy, laid out poetic guidelines for the man of taste and good sense, which included a system of landscape gardening which followed Nature and the 'Genius of the Place' rather than geometry. It was Shaftesbury's neo-classical 'Beautiful Nature' which inspired the mid-century idealized landscaped gardens. This Palladian view of landscape with its abstract ideas of beauty is best described by Isaac Ware in 1750 in *A Complete Body of Architecture*:

'What we propose now in Gardens is to collect the beauties of Nature and to separate them from those rude views in which her blemishes are seen, to bring them nearer to the eye, and to dispose them in the most pleasing order and create an universal harmony.'

Palladio had held that 'Beauty will result from the beautiful form', and in the eighteenth century the decision as to what constituted beautiful forms was taken on empirical lines. Ideas of taste fluctuated and Hogarth wrote *The Analysis of Beauty* in 1753 with a view to establishing what shapes and forms were universally pleasing. He demonstrated in the manner of Addison that beauty was in the eye of the beholder and suggested that what the eye particularly relished was being led 'a wanton kind of chase'.

Waving and serpentine lines were universally acceptable as forms of grace and dominated ideas on landscape gardening as well as on Georgian furniture and decoration. They were already to be found in the rococo fashion of ornament which drew inspiration from natural objects, such as shells, flowers and seaweed, in which the line wandered freely. Some time in the mid-eighteenth century the fellows of Exeter changed the straight garden path, shown in *Oxonia Depicta*, 1733, to make an S curve, clearly to accord with the Line of Beauty. Not only would the eye be led 'a wanton kind of chase' by the serpentine line, according to Hogarth, but from the pleasure it would give to the mind it would make 'what would else be toil and labour, become sport and recreation'. The fellows and visitors are obviously enjoying the walk on the sweeping curve painted by Delamotte. Exeter had always been confined and forbidden to have a bowling green or tennis court because of its proximity to the Bodleian Library, but in the eighteenth century it learned to take advantage of the nearness of buildings of such architectural merit. The south side of the Divinity School gives great distinction to the garden and the terrace walk at the end of the garden affords spectacular views over Radcliffe Square. It is also very pleasant to secure a seat in Duke Humphrey's library overlooking the Exeter garden, for, as Erasmus had said, there is nothing nicer than having a library overlook a garden.

Edmund Burke, in 1757, writing in his *A Philosophical Enquiry into the Origin of our ideas of the Sublime and the Beautiful*, extended Hogarth's artistic analysis of beauty to a philosophical enquiry and further stabilized eighteenth-century attitudes to the psychology and perception of beautiful forms. Burke showed how the beautiful and the sublime acted on emotions and instincts of self-preservation, the one being related to satisfaction, the other to fear. For the theory of mid-eighteenth-century landscape gardening, Burke's definition of satisfying beauty as smoothness and gradual variations was as important as Hogarth's serpentine line. Smoothness, according to Burke, was:

'A quality so essential to beauty that I do not recollect anything beautiful that is not smooth. In trees and flowers small leaves are beautiful: smooth slopes of earth in gardens; smooth streams in the landscape, in fine women smooth skins and in several sorts of ornamental furniture, smooth and polished surfaces.'[3]

Another essential element in a landscaped garden, alongside the beautiful smooth convex and concave landforms and the waving lines, was greenness. Addison had used Newton's ideas to demonstrate that 'the Rays that produce in us the idea of Green fall upon the Eye in such a due proportion, that they give the animal Spirits their proper play'[4] and David Hartley, writing in *The Observations on Man* in 1749, pointed out that 'the middle colour of the seven primary ones and consequently most agreeable to the Organ of Sight is also the general colour of the vegetable kingdom'.

Lancelot Brown, known as Capability Brown, became the professional practitioner of mid-century landscape gardening ideas. His work was the epitome of stabilized beauty and the recognizable harmony of beautiful forms, all in the colour 'most agreeable to the Organ of Sight'. Edmund Burke appears to be describing a Brown park when he describes the satisfying emotions roused by beauty:

'Most people have observed the sort of sense they have had of being swiftly drawn in an easy coach on a smooth turf, with gradual ascents

The landscaping at Exeter was limited by the proximity of other buildings

and declivities. This will give a better idea of the Beautiful than almost anything else.'[5]

If Brown's plan for the Backs had been carried out it would have given Cambridge a landscape setting truly characteristic of the mid-century ideas of beauty. Brown lived nearby at Fenstanton and was first called to advise in Cambridge in 1772 by St John's College, who wished to improve their fellows' garden. Brown, who was a trained gardener, was said by Lord Chatham to have 'sentiments much above his birth' and 'shares the private hours of the King, dines familiarly with his neighbour of Sion and sits down at the tables of all the House of Lords'.[6] He was not, therefore, overawed by Cambridge dons. He was already a friend of one of the fellows, Professor John Mainwaring, the Lady Margaret Professor of Divinity, who was a dedicated landscape improver of his own small estate near Church Stretton.[7] The Professor was also a friend of William Mason who visited him there in 1778.[8] The Master, Dr William Powell, was anxious that Brown's proposals should not be set aside and donated £500 towards the estimated cost of £800. There was some embarrassment about paying the Professor's friend and after some deliberation it was decided to present Brown with a piece of plate to the value of £50 in recognition of his 'services to improving the walks'. Loggan shows the formality of the former walks in the hedged wilderness or fellows' garden, which were said to have been laid out in the form of the nave, transepts and chancel of a cathedral. Today, Brown's moated garden is a delightful retreat of winding walks with aconites, bluebells and daffodils in the spring and a flourishing colony of martagon lilies in the summer.

Brown's work at St John's was for naturalizing a specific area for use as the fellows' garden. In his mind's eye he envisaged a collective landscape scheme involving all the Camside colleges, no doubt encouraged by his friends at St John's, who persuaded the Senate to allow a drawing to be made. The plan 'Presented to the University of Cambridge for some Alterations by Lancelot Brown, 1779' is now in the university library. The Cam was to have been widened into a lake with two long islands and on the western side with college boundaries removed there would have been a leg-of-mutton shaped lawn with clumps of trees stretching from St John's to Queens'. A belt of trees would have hidden a new communal carriageway, where Queen's Road now is, which turned to cross the Cam at the two public bridges. King's College would have had the central position as the great house in the Brown landscaped park. Whatever reaction King's College had to the proposal, as Hawksmoor found, there were many 'wisdomes' to be consulted and the other riverside colleges were unwilling to be relegated to adjuncts in the park. The plan was rejected even though, according to George Dyer, it was hinted that 'the expense would have been scarce worth mentioning; a noble Duke, then residing in one of the colleges, having proposed to set it afoot by a subscription of £1,000'.[9] Following the example set by St John's the university presented Capability Brown with an inscribed silver tray by way of compensation.

George Dyer of Emmanuel College, historian, poet and gardenist, writing thirty-five years later in his *History of the University and Colleges of Cambridge* wondered to what extent Brown's plan was capable of being realized and whether it would have received the gratitude of posterity. Certainly today's thousands of tourists would not have appreciated Brown's beautiful but static landscape as much as the lively Backs scene with its vista of little bridges, beginning with the wooden one at Queens', culminating in the St John's Bridge of Sighs, which they now enjoy from undergraduate-driven punts. A variety of enchanting views can be seen from the stone bridges at Clare and Trinity and it is small wonder that Queen Victoria thought she was in Venice.[10] It is the proximity of the ancient buildings at the Queens' and St John's end of the Cam, with their walled gardens, contrasted with the open lawns of King's and Trinity that gives variety and interest to the scene. Brown would have taken the widened river further from the colleges and the individual bridges and access to riverside walks would have been sacrificed for the

*The Cam and the St John's
Bridge of Sighs today*

effect of the landscaped lake and islands. The barge activity on the river, so admired by Erasmus from the Queens' walks, would have been confined to the western channel and hidden from view of the colleges by the banks of the island. The tree-lined walks which Dyer praised as 'peculiar beauties adapted to the place' would also have been lost. An avenue of limes had been planted beyond Trinity bridge in 1672, terminating in a vista of Coton church, and at Clare in 1690, and when the elegant wrought iron gates were added in the early eighteenth century, the approach to the colleges had the appearance of the country house avenue. Brown's avenues would only have begun across the communal carriageway, the present Queen's Road.

Many felt that what was needed had, in fact, already been done by King's and Trinity before Brown drew up his plan. The ground between the river and the Trinity library had been turfed in 1760, much as Wren would have wished, and in 1771 King's upgraded the riverside area. The ground between Gibbs Buildings and the Cam was freed of bowling green walls and other enclosures, and levelled under the direction of James Essex. The horses were removed to the other side of the river, which was still as in Bridgeman's time, a rough unimproved meadow with ditches and canals. The area, which had been known as Chapel Yard, was then sown with grass seeds and fed from time to time with sheep to get it 'into good and ornamental condition'.[11] The resulting effect of greensward and elegant classical buildings probably gave Brown the idea for a collective Backs landscape. The term the Backs, which is now so evocative of the Cambridge academic landscape, was not used until the nineteenth century. In the seventeenth century they were merely referred to as the 'backsides' of the colleges and their relationship to the river was functional and not scenic, although by the time of Loggan, most of the riverside wharves had gone, leaving stairs on the banks for disembarking goods and passengers. In Henry VI's original plan for King's College there was a kitchen court and offices nearest to the river. The Backs, as we now know them, were made possible when William Wilkins drew up the plans for completing King's College in 1818. The centrally placed old bridge was in a ruinous condition and was rebuilt in its present position in a line with the avenue planted some sixty years previously on the south side of the lawn and now continued on the west bank. The lawn was sloped down to the river, taking away the reinforced river embankment, and giving it its present landscaped appearance.

Lancelot 'Capability' Brown whose ideas on abstract beauty dominated the mid-eighteenth century

George Dyer felt that Cambridge, the ancient seat of learning, had got it right and that 'the Genius of the Place' did not require collective landscape improvement. 'Let us distinguish', he said 'between a nobleman's pleasure ground and a spot to be adapted to the health and exercise of students, to academic retreats which invite meditation.'[12] Dyer, a friend of Wordsworth[13] and disciple of William Mason, author of *The English Garden*, is a valuable commentator on the change of taste in the 1780s and 90s. He pointed to Mason's landscaping precepts:

> But learn to rein
> Thy skill within the limits she allows;
> Great Nature scorns control; she will not bear
> One beauty foreign to the spot or soil.

It was the riverside walks, beloved for centuries, which gave Cambridge its special character, Dyer felt, and wrote of Queens':

'Let no one leave these grounds without going to the end of that walk by the side of the river, and let him thence look to the view on the opposite side, nor let him say, it is the best in Cambridge, or is well enough for Cambridge: though it has not hill or dale, perhaps, of the kind it is the best anywhere for it has grand objects, which amply compensate for the want of other beauties.'[14]

What Dyer felt was needed was more variety and less regularity in the college walks. 'It may be admitted that the public walks of our sister university have some superior claims over these we are now describing; the walks are generally more winding, without so many formal strait lines and acute angles; the trees have greater variety of foliage (and consequently you have bolder lights and shades) and there is more of underwood and shrubbery amidst their fine oaks, beech, birch and elms.'[15] Wadham, Balliol and St John's all had informal groves underplanted with flowering shrubs. Oxford was fortunate in having its Paradise nursery gardens[16] and also Penson's gardens near the Botanic Garden (the sites of their gardens are commemorated by Paradise Square in Westgate and Penson's Gardens near the Botanic Garden) and the

Wadham's informal groves, typical of the small-scale landscaping in colleges

accounts show that the colleges were supplied with hornbeams, white hawthorns, syringas, honeysuckle, Lombardy poplars, viburnum, euonymus, laburnum, bird cherries, lilac, wayfaring trees, hypericum, mountain ash, almonds, sweetbriars, laurustinus, dog's-tooth violets, crocuses and crown imperials for their groves. When George III paid his first visit to Oxford he declared that his dominions did not contain such a specimen of gardening skill as he saw in the four acres at St John's.[17]

In Cambridge, Sidney Sussex, like St John's, Wadham and Balliol, had no riverside landscape to use to its advantage and it too concentrated on gardening skills. Dyer praised its fellows' garden, later sacrificed to make way for the New Court, and its walks 'agreeably winding, with variety of trees and shrubs intertwining, and forming the whole length a fine canopy overhead; with nothing but singing and fragrance and seclusion; a delightful summer retreat, the sweetest lover's or poet's walk, perhaps in the University'.[18] There was a time and place for all kinds of gardening, which enhanced the character of the college, however, and the straight walks of Queens' were also praised because it was 'rather famous for mathematicians and divines than poets; and it has been observed that mathematicians and divines are apt to walk in straight lines and poets in curves, as the former are apt to be more uniform and regular in their literary pursuits than the latter'.[19]

In his writings Dyer sought to promote college feelings and the poets found walks and gardens associated with famous men congenial to the romantic mood. Oxford, of course, had similar feelings. 'Beautiful as are St John's Gardens, who would not exchange them for the very walks and alleys along which Laud, in all the pardonable pride of collegiate lionizing, conducted his illustrious guests, Charles and Henrietta? Who does not grieve that we must now inquire in vain for the bowling green in Christ Church, where Cranmer solaced the weariness of his last confinement', wrote Thomas James in *The Carthusian*. Wordsworth, who was at St John's, Cambridge from 1789 – 1791 could not 'print ground where the grass had yielded to the steps of generations of illustrious men unmoved' and

> All winter long, whenever free to choose
> Did I by night frequent the College groves
> And tributary walks.[20]

In Brown's wilderness he was enraptured by an ash tree with 'boughs exquisitely wreathed':

> Often have I stood
> Foot-bound uplooking at this lovely tree
> Beneath a frosty moon.

Later poets were to remember the college avenues with the pleasure of association as did Tennyson, who was at Trinity in 1831, in his lines written in memory of Arthur Hallam:

> Up that long walk of limes I past
> To see the rooms in which he dwelt..[21]

The psychological theory of association, which came to replace purely visual pleasures of the imagination, had been set out by the Revd Archibald Alison in his *Essays on the Nature and Principles of Taste*, published in 1790. Burke's abstract view of beauty ignored reference to association, but Alison stressed that what made a scene beautiful in the mind of the beholder was its associations and historical connections and 'every analagous idea that has place in the memory'. This encouraged a sense of place and historical sensibility. Dyer wrote that 'it is natural for people to receive gratification from the history of the places where they were educated as from revisiting them',[22] and he would have endorsed Thomas Salmon's view that the gardens and landscapes evoked powerful college memories. 'To whatever Distance the young Gentlemen remove, when they have finished their Studies, they must ever retain an Affection for these charming Seats of the Muses.'[23] Alison's obituary notice praised his presentation of the universe as 'a great mirror to the mind of man... and that in contemplating the fairest scenes, we are ourselves half creating their loveliness'. Such ideas which encouraged subjective reactions were seen in the words of Southey, as 'a matter of feeling, which is a better thing than taste'.[24] Landscape gardening, the very epitome of universal taste and aristocratic standards, had to adapt in the nineteenth century to accommodate the new romantic attitudes.

12   The Picturesque

The concepts of the Beautiful and the Sublime, as defined by Edmund Burke, were major preoccupations of the mid-eighteenth century. By the end of the century, however, a new category had been formulated, that of the Picturesque, which was to have lasting effects on aesthetic judgement, travel and rural planning. In terms of landscaping, the Beautiful, as defined by Burke and practised by Brown, was only used in a limited way in the 'Seats of the Muses', and if any fellow had contemplated the Sublime in college gardening it has not been recorded. Shaftesbury's 'horrid graces' had little to do with Oxford and Cambridge and were kept for the vacations. The ultimate in sublime semi-religious experiences was a visit to Switzerland and the *Alpine Journal* reported that 'if you met a man in the Alps, it was 10 to 1 he was a University man, 8 to 1 (say) that he was a Cambridge man and about even betting that he was a fellow of his college'.[1] Many were cast in the sublime role of the Byronic hero. Childe Harold was himself at Cambridge from 1805 until 1808 and the weir above Grantchester where he swam is still known as Byron's Pool. His rooms at Trinity were in the top attic of the tower at the south-east corner of the Great Court, where he kept a pet bear,[2] there being a statute forbidding the keeping of dogs. His tutor noted that he was a youth of 'tumultuous passions'.

While Napoleon's troops were still in Europe, however, the cult of the Sublime was restricted to the Lake District, which was the focal point of the English romantics. Thomas Gray, who was at Cambridge, first at Peterhouse and then at Pembroke from 1742 until his death in 1771, was one of the earliest of the Lake District enthusiasts. In college he was content with a window box and keeping nature notes, but impressed on his colleagues the sublimity of the mountains which were 'extatic, & ought to be visited in pilgrimage once a year, none but those monstrous creatures of God know how to join so much beauty with so much horror'.[3] His devoted friend and admirer, William Mason, a fellow of Pembroke, who became his literary executor, published his *Journal of a*

The Greek revival at Downing

The Cam in 1840 showing picturesque improvements

visit to the Lakes in 1775 with his *Letters* and this fanned the flame of interest in the Lakeland and picturesque travel. In 1812 George Dyer wrote an ode 'After Making a Tour of the Lakes on a visit to Wordsworth and Southey written at the Spot described by Gray'.

The theory of the Picturesque was set out by Uvedale Price in his *Essay on the Picturesque* in 1794. This was to have an important influence on nineteenth-century picturesque architecture and landscape gardening. The idea of the Picturesque had been in circulation for some time, however, and its real pioneer was the Revd William Gilpin. He entered the Queen's College, Oxford in 1740 and left in 1748, and unlike many of his contemporaries read widely. 'I remember in my time', he wrote, 'half our young fellows used to read scarce any thing besides classic writers, and that only for the sake of their latin and greek. This is a sad way of study'.[4] His own outlook was influenced by Addison, Pope, Locke and particularly Shaftesbury, whom he admired as an aesthetician and moralist, although rejecting his deism. Having been brought up in Cumberland he already had a native preference for the natural scenery unspoilt by man which Shaftesbury extolled.

Gilpin had been taught to draw by a gifted father and kept up his hobby all through his life. He spent part of his youth at Scaleby Castle and at Carlisle where his father was garrisoned.[5] At Queen's he said he lived in the old chambers which had been formerly occupied by the Black Prince with windows looking out on to the Oxford City wall. 'This wall', he wrote, 'to another spectator would afford no pleasure nor indeed to me upon any other account than as it puts me in mind of those at

Carlisle.'⁶ Gilpin's view of venerable objects was not so much romantic as picturesque, by which he meant 'a term expressive of that peculiar kind of beauty, which is agreeable in a picture'. In letters to the family he describes in detail the immediate view from his windows of New College garden with its flower parterres, yew tree pillars, shady walks and arbours, but when he comes to describe Magdalen grove beyond he does it on the picturesque principles which were to become a life's obsession:

'As Objects now begin to lessen, you must expect a fainter Description, agreeable you know to the Rules of Painting. Beyond the Gardens then the next Thing is a most beautiful Grove which at once charms both your Eyes and Ears. The one is charm'd by the Linnet, the Thrush and the hoarse Musick of Crows and Rooks, than which no noise is more agreeable to one; the other by Deer playing among the Openings of the Trees, and a noble new Building which is so shaded and cover'd with oaks and Elms that it appears to me like an old romantick Castle rising out of a Wood, or if you please a Scaleby. My View is bounded in Front by this Grove; for variety upon each side there is an Opening into a most delicious Country, which abounds with Green Fields, Trees, Spires, Villages, and in short wants nothing but a little more Water, and two or three of your Scotch Mountains to make it a most compleat Prospect.'⁷

After taking his degree Gilpin was for many years a schoolmaster at Cheam, where he was at pains to cultivate a 'picture-making faculty' in his pupils when they read the classics. In a notebook he listed for them what he found picturesque in Virgil's Aeneid – a hero resting after battle, glittering armour, a sea nymph pushing a ship, the sea in a storm and rocky and woody scenery.⁸ Many of the picturesque ideas were heroic attitudes suitable for a history painting, which is consistent with the use of the word in the early eighteenth century and his own statement that 'by Picturesque I mean precisely nothing more than such ideas as can be formed into a picture'. Gilpin was himself largely responsible for the change of emphasis in the term picturesque, so that by the end of the century it was used almost exclusively to describe scenic beauty. In 1768 he published an *Essay on Prints* for the instruction of the large new public for whom cheap prints had become available. He showed how to apply the principles of painting to the examination of prints to enable the layman to appreciate such matters as 'design, disposition, keeping and the distribution of light'.

From cultivating a picture imagination when reading and studying the composition of pictures it was a short step for Gilpin to suggest that the traveller should use the same faculty in viewing landscape. In the Cheam school holidays Gilpin travelled to out-of-the-way places 'in search of picturesque beauty' and, for his own amusement, recorded with descriptions and on-the-spot sketches what he found to be 'pencil-provoking' in the Wye Valley, the Highlands, the Lakes and other picturesque regions of Britain. Although these journeys were made in the 1770s, it was not until Gilpin had left Cheam and become Vicar of Boldre in the New Forest⁹ that he was persuaded by his friends to publish his 'Picturesque Tours'. They were immediately popular and Gilpin's association of pictures with the appreciation of scenery became a craze,

St John's today, the ultimate in the Picturesque in Cambridge

131

132

which is best described by Jane Austen who, according to her brother, was at a very early age 'enamoured of Gilpin on the Picturesque'. The fashionable Tilneys in *Northanger Abbey* were seen to be 'viewing the country with the eyes of persons accustomed to painting and deciding on its capabilities of being formed into pictures' and when Henry Tilney delivers his 'lecture on the Picturesque' the young heroine is instructed on 'fore-grounds, distances, and second distances – side-screens and perspective – lights and shades' in true Gilpin style.

Although Gilpin himself never set out to advise on improving landscape according to principles based on picturesque observation, he was, nevertheless, a great influence on the high phase of landscape gardening.[10] After the death of Capability Brown in 1783 many so-called Brownian landscape gardeners took what they saw to be his improvement formula of shaven lawns, pieces of water, clumped trees and perimeter belts, and applied it wherever they were working, regardless of the character of the region. This was frowned upon by the generation that had acquired a new sense of regionalism from Gilpin's *Picturesque Observations* on the Wye (1782), the Lakes (1786), the Highlands (1789) and the New Forest (1791), which had taught them how to analyse the face of a country and to observe how differently Nature works up landscape in different regions. By proving that the homeland was picturesque, or worthy of painting, Gilpin had broken the spell of Italian landscape and opened the way to a whole new British school of landscape painters. Systematized improvement imposed on a region was now seen to be contrary to picturesque taste. A formula of smooth round forms, gradual deviations, clear margins, serpentine lines and the elimination of nature's 'false accidents' was beautiful but not picturesque. It was ruggedness and sudden deviations, catching lights on uneven surfaces and embowered scenes that a painter really liked. Gilpin had shown in *Forest Scenery*, Nature's picturesque planting in the 'skirts of the forest', the brushwood, twisted trees, broken banks and exposed roots of trees as well as the picturesque forms of the trees themselves.

William Mason, whose precepts in *The English Garden* George Dyer extolled, was a friend of Gilpin and was partly responsible for the publication of his *Picturesque Tours*. He translated Du Fresnoy's *De Arte Graphica* and had, according to Gilpin, 'very picturesque ideas'. He was garden adviser to the 2nd Earl Harcourt at Nuneham, five miles south of Oxford, where in 1772 he laid out his influential picturesque flower garden. Gilpin had suggested in his *Remarks on Forest Scenery* that any designer of artificial landscape would do well to study the natural planting of the forest which furnished endless varieties of form and grouping, projection and recess, and islands and peninsulas of wild planting on forest lawns. Mason took this up by suggesting that garden lawns should also be planted in imitation of forest lawns with underwood tufts and mazy spaces. His Nuneham island and promontory

A picturesque shrubbery at St John's College, Oxford, from The Oxford Almanack, *1783*

The formally planted mount allowed to grow picturesque at New College

beds with their hollyhocks, pinks, arbutus, willows, small magnolias and other flowering shrubs grouped together were echoed in St John's College gardens, which were painted in 1781 by M.A. Rooker for the Oxford Almanack. The breaking up of empty lawns by such shrubbery planting was particularly favoured in public walking places.

William Mason also laid out a picturesque garden tour at Nuneham featuring the windings of the Thames, the Berkshire Downs and the distant view of Oxford.[11] In 1787 Lord Harcourt acquired the Carfax Conduit, which had been removed from Oxford in a road-widening scheme, as a picturesque feature in his Capability Brown park. The 1st Earl, the founder President of the Dilettanti Society, had abandoned his ancestral home at Stanton Harcourt and chosen this superb site for his new Palladian villa with its views of Oxford's domes and spires, reminiscent of Rome from the surrounding hills. Before he could make the landscaped garden from which to see such picturesque views the old village of Newnham Courtenay had to be removed to a site outside his park. One old widow was allowed to stay and enjoy the view of Oxford and when her cottage was pulled down after her death, a poem was inscribed on a seat by a tree.

> Tho' Thames before her flowed, his farther shores
> She ne'er explored, contented with her own.
> And distant Oxford, tho she saw its towers
> To her ambition was a world unknown.

Oliver Goldsmith, who had witnessed the removal of the village in 1761, later wrote an indictment of Lord Harcourt's high-handed kind of landscape gardening in *The Deserted Village* and commiserated with the old widow who had been left as 'the sad historian of the pensive plain'.[12]

The 2nd Earl Harcourt, who inherited in 1777, was the patron of William Gilpin whom he failed to persuade to accept the living of Nuneham. He wrote his own guide book giving the picturesque stations in the landscaped garden at which to view the framed vistas in typical Gilpinesque style:

'On the left there is a narrow opening that admits a view over the underwood, and the trees in the foreground, apparently uniting with a clump in the garden below, leading the eye to the other masses of wood till it reaches Oxford, which is framed by trees and shrubs.'[13]

Oxford is more naturally picturesque than Cambridge where the most important buildings are stretched out along the Backs. Oxford lies in a hollow and what Matthew Arnold, Professor of Poetry from 1857 to 1867, was to call its famous skyline of 'dreaming spires' cluster together when viewed from rising ground. Even Wordsworth succumbed to its spell.

> Yet, O ye spires of Oxford! Domes and towers!
> Gardens and groves! Your presence overpowers
> The soberness of reason.....[14]

Sanderson Miller had anticipated picturesque vision by seeing buildings in relation to landscape and noting with relish the pinnacles and towers of Oxford 'embosom'd high in tufted trees'. Humphry Repton, at the beginning of the nineteenth century, observed that 'there is nothing more interesting as a picture than the combination of Trees and Buildings; they assist and relieve each other in forming the picturesque Whole, which Painting endeavours to imitate, and for which Oxford has long been celebrated'. New towers and spires appeared in the nineteenth century which could be used to advantage as picturesque features seen from college gardens and groves. W.A. Delamotte lovingly depicted the picturesque period of Oxford college gardens in his *Original Views of Oxford, its Colleges, Chapels and Gardens*, published in 1843. Worcester College made virtue out of necessity and has the only true landscaped garden in Oxford, having its own designed piece of water overhung with trees. An arch from the old monastic foundation is sited by the lake adding a romantic touch of history in character with the picturesque scene. Although the college buildings had been completed by the 1770s, landscaping of the grounds was not undertaken until the beginning of the nineteenth century and then the decision was taken partly for practical reasons. The college's frontage to the Thames had been cut off by the extension of the Oxford canal in 1790. The canal company was dilatory about draining the bordering land in spite of an undertaking given to the college when the land was given. In 1817 the fellows made the swampy, evil-smelling area into a lake and planted specimen trees on the lawns. The landscaping is cleverly done to give the impression of much larger extent. The *Oxford Guide* of 1821 highly praises the college's efforts in laying out 'three acres of land with great taste, embellished with a large sheet of water, well stocked with fish'. The Provost's Lodgings were virtually a Palladian country house and the nineteenth-century engravings depict the Worcester College scene as a gentleman's seat in a

A nineteenth-century engraving of Worcester College showing the garden front of the Provost's Lodgings looking like a Palladian country house with the cottage orné *on the right*

picturesquely planted landscaped park. Another parklike feature is the curly barge board and Regency trellis added to the gable end of the monastic side of the quadrangle, which has the effect of a *cottage orné* when seen from the hanging garden which is brought up to the level of the upper floor by a banked terrace. This raised terrace under which the visitor walks to the landscaped garden through an arched passage is variously said to be made from the excrement of the monastic long room, the stones and rubble of the dissolved monastery and the spoil from digging out the lake.

The same mode of vision that had become an obsession in viewing scenery was now being applied to architecture with buildings and landscape being seen together as a picture. The most picturesque scheme envisaged for Oxford was, however, rejected. In 1801 the fellows of

Magdalen College invited Repton and Nash individually to submit plans for the completion of a new quadrangle which would link the old part of the college with the early eighteenth-century New Building, which stood, as it still does today, isolated like a country house in its deer park. Several attempts had been made in the past to make the connection, but in inviting Humphry Repton, a landscape gardener committed to the new picturesque attitudes, to produce a scheme, some members of the college were clearly anxious to relate any new building scenically to the landscape. Nash and Repton had acted in partnership on buildings and their settings until 1800, when Repton withdrew and took on his son John Adey, who had worked in Nash's office as his architectural assistant. It was John Adey who made the architectural designs for the Magdalen Red Book.[15]

Repton's Red Book: the proposals for Magdalen. Above: the grounds before improvement. Below: after the proposed improvements.

Repton's method of showing intended landscape improvements was to paint a picture of a place as he found it and by means of hinged flaps show what it would look like after his treatment. The illustrations and recommendations were bound with red morocco into handsome volumes which came to be known as Red Books. Brown presented a plan to Cambridge for the improvement of the Backs which, in his customary manner, shows pure landscaping in its own right, to be seen from the windows of the colleges or the banks of the river. Repton, by painting a picture of the intended improvements, gave his clients a series of compositions of buildings and landscape as seen in a Claude painting, which would unfold as the spectator walked. The frontispiece of the Magdalen Red Book has a vignette of two young men in gowns and mortarboards, seated on some learned treatises, who are unconvincingly accompanied by gardening implements and a theodolite. In the centre is a drawing of a gateway at the far corner of the deer park, made out of an old square tower. Repton observed in his commentary that 'as the College boundary Wall is very massive, the gate should rather partake of the ponderous character of a castle, than of the more elegant species of Gothic architecture'. The Red Book includes a dissertation on Grecian and Gothic architecture as Magdalen had appeared open-minded on the subject, and this was afterwards printed in his *Observations on the Theory and Practice of Landscape Gardening* in 1803. Repton proposed to embellish the classical New Building in keeping with the rest of the college. Both he and Nash urged a Picturesque Gothic approach, rejecting a closed quadrangle, recommending that the extension should be a building in its own right, set in the landscape.

Nuneham House, which was sited to enjoy a distant view of Oxford, painted by Paul Sandby c.1760

Repton made much of the fact that Magdalen alone in Oxford had the materials for landscaping but, in all the schemes for the new quadrangle that had hitherto been considered, the college had never seen itself in a picturesque light, enjoying and contributing to the Cherwell views.

'In the various plans which have been suggested by architects only, there seems to have been a total disregard to these local circumstances and advantages that are possessed by Magdalen, over every other College in either of our Universities.....in every design which I have seen for Magdalen, the Command of Property seems to have been neglected and no advantage taken of the adjacent Meadow, and trees or the River Charwell which flows through the premises; but the view towards the East has always been sacrificed, to form an Architectural Quadrangle, which would exclude all benefit from the adjoining territory...Redundance of water is natural to the situation, it would surely be advisable to display this in one broad than in many narrow channels.'

Repton's Gothic castle reflected in the lake certainly looked most picturesque in his water colour. Repton recognized that the meadow 'sacred to Addison', which had given so much pleasure to his imagination, would have to be sacrificed in his scheme and after the walk on the north side of the Magdalen meadow had been removed, a portico named after him was to be built on rising ground. Addison's temple would look out over the lake towards Repton's new Gothic palace.

Nothing was done about any of Repton's building or landscaping proposals. The meadow remained untouched and the threatened walk was henceforth protectively called Addison's Walk. Repton's Red Book was put away on the library shelves as he feared. These books lying on library tables were his greatest advertisement, and suspecting that an academic society would not do justice to this particularly fine specimen, he had fortunately made his own arrangements for it to be seen:

Sir,

In answer to the honour of your Letter of the 16th Jan, the plans which you are so good to mention in terms of commendation, can nowhere be so properly disposed as in the College library to which they relate [Repton had proposed a new library] – and if my part of the plans proposed, meet the approbation of the Society I shall be happy to assist in carrying them into execution – in the mean while as I should be sorry to have them entirely laid upon the shelf of the Library without making them publickly known – I shall request leave of the College to let me shew them to some few personages and perhaps to the King himself if I can procure an Audience for that purpose – I should also wish to have leave from the College to copy one of the Drawings on a larger scale for the purpose of exhibiting it at the Royal Academy – and when the Society shall have had leisure to inspect them – I will trouble you to cause the book to be carefully packed in a box and directed to me at the Salopian Coffee house, Charing Cross, London.[16]

By 1823 the Magdalen project had become history and J.C. Buckler, who was a pioneer in the field of scholarly architectural history, wrote;

'Mr Repton a landscape gardener and Mr Nash a well-known professional architect, severally produced volumes of designs for the disfigurement of Magdalen College and the disposal of its pleasure grounds, touched it is true, with the artist's magic pencil and secured in cases of red morocco and gold, yet, by their preposterous absurdity not to enlarge on their ruinous splendour, consigned to an oblivion from which I shall not risk their escape, by bestowing on them any further comments.'[17]

A mere 'view' was to Mr Buckler a hateful word, 'Who, save, alas, the Sons of Magdalen' he thundered, 'would consent to remove or mutilate one wing of a large mansion because it impeded some pretty object from the view of the other?'

Oxford missed out on a complete new romantic Gothic building when Repton and Nash's architectural schemes were rejected and had to wait for Ruskinian and ponderous ecclesiogical Gothic revival later in the century. James Wyatt did indeed bring Gothic dress to Oxford at the earlier period by remodelling college halls and chapels, and at Christ Church in 1802 he built a new hall staircase in the mood of Fonthill on which he was working at the same time. In both places he revelled, in his customary way, in opening up vistas. At Christ Church this did not, as at Fonthill, involve mock mediaeval buildings in the landscape, but the internal presentation of genuine mediaeval features in a dramatic way. He removed the room on the landing of the staircase and allowed the stairs to sweep up under the fan vaulting to the impressive hammerbeam roof hall, and as seen from Tom Quad he made a succession of Gothic arches leading down to the darkness of the old kitchen.

Cambridge began the nineteenth century with the uncompromisingly classical Downing College, whose porticoes and spacious lawns give it an air of a Stowe landscape garden. Unlike Oxford, however, Cambridge, really did achieve a large scale romantic Gothic castle in 1825 when Rickman gave St John's a new court across the Cam and his partner, Henry Hutchinson, joined it to the old buildings by the picturesque covered Bridge of Sighs. Thomas Rickman was the first architect since James Essex to have a knowledge of mediaeval detail. He first used the now familiar architectural terms in the typological sequence of 'Early English', 'Decorated English', 'Perpendicular English' and in 1817 published *An Attempt to discriminate the Styles of English Architecture form the Conquest to the Reformation*. His work for St John's was carried out with Henry Hutchinson from 1827 to 1831. The design for this fourth court as chosen by the college was to be in red brick and to follow the plan of the famous Tudor second court. What they got was a massive stucco-fronted stone building in the perpendicular style. Ditches and ponds had to be filled in, large balks of timber laid down and massive cellars built to support the four-storeyed building. It gave a new orientation to the collective landscape of the Camside colleges as, instead of facing the canal-like part of the river, it fronted the bend beyond Wren's library and looked down the river. The engravings show it like a fairy palace set in academic groves, the ultimate in the Picturesque in Oxford or Cambridge.

13   Horticulture in Victorian Oxford and Cambridge

In the eighteenth century plants had been treated by the great designers as elements in a landscape composition, and in the country houses flowers were usually banished to the kitchen gardens. In 1805, in response to a growing feeling that horticulture had been neglected in the cult of the Picturesque, the Horticultural Society of London (later the Royal Horticultural Society) was formed 'for the improvement of horticulture'. *The Gardener's Magazine*, first published by John Claudius Loudon in 1826, became the forum for discussion on horticultural matters. It was the first of many periodicals to be devoted specifically to gardening, which encouraged the competitive shows, satirized by Cruikshank.

When, in 1832, William Sawrey Gilpin, the Revd William's nephew, published his *Practical Hints on Landscape Gardening* without mentioning horticulture, Loudon felt obliged to remonstrate in his *Gardeners' Magazine* that 'mere picturesque improvement is not enough in these enlightened times, it is necessary to understand that there is such a character of art as the gardenesque as well as the picturesque. The very term gardenesque may startle some readers, but we are convinced, nevertheless, that this is a term which will soon find its place in the language of rural art.'[1] Loudon had invented the word 'gardenesque' to mean 'as a gardener would like' in the same way as picturesque had been used to mean 'as a painter would like'. Any building would be improved by a horticultural treatment according to Loudon's assessment and when he visited Oxford in 1833 he even suggested that the green space in the Great Quadrangle at Christ Church, surmounted by Wren's Tom Tower, would be improved by flowerbeds.[2]

Loudon's vast literary output in books, encyclopaedias and magazines was readily available for reference and was enormously influential. It is possible that he himself advised on the gardenesque layout of Christ's College in Cambridge. He certainly designed the cemetery grounds in

The Botanic Garden, Cambridge, largely the result of the enthusiasm of Darwin's tutor Professor Henslow

EXHIBITION EXTRAORDINARY in the HORTICULTURAL ROOM.

Cruikshank's satirical view of early nineteenth-century horticulturalists

Histon Road in 1842. At Christ's, paths wind round promontories of mixed flower and shrub plantations. Loudon had admired William Mason's garden at Nuneham and in his early days as a landscape gardener had also followed Gilpin's ideas on forest planting, advocating that exotic trees, shrubs and flowers should be grouped and scattered over lawns 'in the same way that thorns, oaks, hazels and weeds are in the forest'.[3] As he developed his gardenesque style, however, he insisted that it was not the general massing of plants that should be aimed at but the display of the 'individual beauty of trees, shrubs and plants in a state of nature'.

The new steam-heated greenhouses and the introduction of plants from all over the world gave new dimensions to horticulture, which could be best served by Loudon's precepts. The new Cambridge Botanic Garden, when moved from its town site, certainly set out in the 1840s to display on gardenesque principles the 'individual beauty of trees, shrubs and plants' in a natural setting, while, as in Oxford, using the material for teaching purposes. In size, scope and layout it was vastly different from Dr Walker's original Botanic Garden of five acres, given to the university in 1761, which was situated where the laboratories now stand. It was laid out by the Professor of Botany, Thomas Martyn, with the help of Phillip Miller, the Curator of Chelsea Physic Garden, who was called in by Dr Walker 'for his great experience in such an affair'. The appointment of Charles Miller as the first Curator was clearly a wise move as not only was he able to call on his father's encyclopaedic expertise but could obtain plants from Chelsea, for which he only had to pay carriage.[4] It was clearly the intention of Dr Walker that the garden should develop and provide a focus for scientific studies as the Physic Garden did in Oxford,[5] but the buildings round it made it unsuitable for a botanic garden and by the beginning of the nineteenth century the five acre site was much too small to meet the requirements of the vast increase of new species. It has been calculated that by 1800 the number of introduced plants in Britain had risen to 14,000 compared with the 1,600 collected by Bobart in the Oxford Physic Garden in the mid seventeenth century.

It was due to the enthusiasm of Professor John Stevens Henslow, who popularized botany at Cambridge and largely inspired Darwin's taste for natural history, that in 1831 a larger site for the Botanic Garden was found on the Trumpington Road alongside Hobson's Conduit, a stream dug in 1610 to bring water to Cambridge from the Gog Magog hills, which now feeds the lake. Henslow is commemorated by Henslow Walk which crosses the Main Walk, and some of his original greenhouses remain. Most of the plants listed in the 1796 *Hortus cantabrigensis* were gradually transferred from the old garden. These included not only plants donated from Chelsea but also by royal favour from Kew. Sir Joseph Banks had written to James Donn, who was curator of Dr Walker's Botanic Garden in the 1790s, that he was sure that he could 'also rely on Mr Aiton's goodwill to you and that as he has it in his power to send what plants he pleases to Cambridge having had the King's orders for that purpose he will from time to time give you ample increase',[6] and the records show that Banks, who was virtually director of the royal gardens at Kew from 1778 until his death in 1820, saw that the order was carried out.[7] It was owing to his patronage that 7,000 new species were brought into the country including *Rosa chinensis* and *Chrysanthemum indicum*, the ancestors of all our modern roses and chrysanthemums. Joseph Banks had learned his botany when he was up at Oxford from 1760–3 and appreciated the value of botanic gardens for university studies. The teaching of botany was then at a low ebb under Professor Humphry Sibthorp, who is said to have given only one lecture during the thirty-seven years he held the chair, and as the young Banks could find no tutor, he brought Mr Isaac Lyons over from Cambridge. Lyons only stayed a short time, however, preferring to return when Dr Walker founded his Cambridge Botanic Garden. Banks then made his own studies in the Oxford Physic Garden and botanized in Christ Church meadow, where he first noted that Bobart's *Senecio squalidus*, later to be known as Oxford ragwort, had escaped from the garden.

The new Cambridge Botanic Garden was officially opened to the public in 1846 and later the wrought-iron gates from the earlier garden were set up above the water garden. In its forty-acre landscape setting, it soon became a favourite place for walking in for the citizens of

Cambridge. Like its Oxford counterpart it was a

Delightful scientifick Shade!
For Knowledge, as for Pleasure made [8]

but it arrived on the scene when there was a much greater interest in horticulture by the new middle class, and, although he did not live to see it, it fulfilled all Loudon's educational aspirations for displaying in a gardenesque setting a wide range of plants, many of which the public could themselves obtain in nurseries. Clear labelling of plants Loudon felt was essential in public parks and botanic gardens and he had noted in 1833 how greatly hindered the old Cambridge Botanic Garden in the town had been by the numbers of jackdaws who used to remove the wooden labels from plants and take them up into the towers of the five churches and colleges nearby.[9] Loudon felt that dons were particularly conservative in their choice of plants and when he was in Oxford he checked with the local nurseries what they were buying. He learned that whereas they would buy geraniums, roses, night-scented stock and mignonette to put in and around their rooms, they resisted the new calceolarias and fuchsias. Loudon concluded that 'still the taste of Oxford is more for the sensual, than for the intellectual part of gardening'.[10] He did not make a similar check up in Cambridge and died in 1843, almost certainly through overwork in his public-spirited efforts for horticultural education.

Loudon had in fact designed the first publicly-owned botanical garden for the Birmingham Botanical and Horticultural Society, which opened in 1832. The plan drawn up by E. Lapidge for the Cambridge Botanic Garden in 1839 has a close resemblance to Loudon's Birmingham plan, published in his *The Gardener's Magazine* in August 1832.[11] Both have flowing walks in the style of Nash's London parks but with extra areas for conservatories and special plant displays. The plan finally accepted in 1840 by Cambridge University was by Andrew Murray, the first Curator of the Botanic Garden. This has a much more rococo design, which calls to mind the original ideas of Batty Langley, who violently resisted the stiff Dutch gardening, saying in 1728 in his *New Principles of Gardening* 'nor is there anything more shocking than a stiff regular garden'. His irregularity, however, consisted in laying out unbelievably meandering paths round grass plots with statues and other garden features in the mazy spaces. Murray's Cambridge plan has the same effect but it is the herbaceous beds that are shaped in rococo patterns and the paths are merely determined by the way in which the visitor is lead to inspect the plants. Murray's arrangement took care of Loudon's gardenesque precepts for displaying 'the individual beauty of trees, shrubs and plants in a state of nature', but the passion for wiggles, which later became known as gardenesque, was not Loudon's intention. Soon, this type of planting with 'unmeaning flowerbeds in the shape of kidneys and

The Alice Door. This door in the wall of the Deanery garden at Christ Church features in Alice's Adventures in Wonderland

tadpoles and sausages and leeches and commas'[12] was to be condemned and bolder cohesive schemes called for.

Oxford was clearly not satisfied with a so-called Physic Garden when Cambridge had a new Botanic Garden, even though their objectives were the same, and in 1840 Professor Daubeny petitioned for the name to be changed to the Oxford Botanic Garden.[13] Daubeny had himself been appointed by the Royal College of Physicians according to the original frames of the statutes for the Sherardian chair, but he saw no reason to be confined by the purposes implicit in the title Physic Garden, which required him to grow plants for medicine in the garden. Daubeny had come to botany through chemistry and agriculture and as he wanted part of the Botanic Garden for experiments on 'the effects of soils, or of chemical agents upon vegetation', plots were laid out to test the mineral requirements of crops. Daubeny set up the first experiments with chemical fertilizers in this country and by 1843 one of his pupils, John Bennet Lawes, had gone on to found the agricultural experimental station at Rothamsted. Cambridge also forged ahead in studying plants in the interest of science and industry as well as medicine and students from horticultural colleges received practical experience in the garden. There is much general, scientific and historic interest for the public in the identification of plants and the special beds. At Oxford there is a section of the garden set aside for historical roses showing their origin from the wild and development through hybridization. At Cambridge, the chronological bed shows the introduction of plants into Britain following on from a mediaeval flowery mead, through the Elizabethan plant collecting to nineteenth-century oriental introductions.

Until the mid-nineteenth-century, the Oxford and Cambridge beds were set out according to the Linnaean system. Oxford might even have had the great Swedish botanist himself, for when he visited the Physic Garden in 1736, he met Professor Dillenius who disapproved of the young man who was attempting to upset the whole science of botany as it was then understood. However, Linnaeus gave such a masterly analysis of the controversial structure of the ivy-leaved toad-flax growing on a wall of the garden that Dillenius was exceedingly impressed and offered to share his house and salary with him if he would stay in Oxford as his assistant.[14] Linnaeus did not accept the invitation but he later dedicated his *Critica Botanica* to the Oxford professor and named the genus Dillenia after him, for, he said, 'the genus Dillenia being of all plants the most distinguished for beauty of flower and fruit like Dillenius among botanists'.[15]

Daubeny, in 1834, introduced his own systematic beds classified more scientifically 'according to their natural affinities'.[16] His plan, unlike Murray's for Cambridge, shows narrow rectangular beds, still to be seen, which allowed the Professor to lecture from the top to the students standing along the sides. In the 1860s the systematic beds in both botanic gardens were influenced by Darwin's ideas on evolution. When the young Charles Darwin was up at Christ's College in 1827, he little thought that thirty years later his revolutionary theory would split the colleges in both universities. Darwin had delighted in Henslow's natural history excursions and he later remembered that 'no pursuit at Cambridge was followed with nearly so much eagerness or gave me so much pleasure as collecting beetles...No poet ever felt more delight at seeing his first poem than I did at seeing in Stephen's *Illustrations of British Insects* the magic words "captured by C. Darwin, Esq".'[17] His own great work *On the Origin of Species* was to astonish Oxford and Cambridge when first published in 1859. At Cambridge the Professor of Geology, Adam Sedgwick, referring to himself as 'a son of a monkey and an old friend of yours' told Darwin that it had 'greatly shocked my moral taste'.[18] In Oxford, Professor Daubeny introduced the famous British Association debate when Huxley, in reply to Bishop Wilberforce's sarcastic refutation of *On the Origin of Species*, replied that he would rather be descended from an ape than a bishop. Daubeny was a committed evolutionist and gave a party in the Botanic Garden for the victorious Darwinians. He kept monkeys in cages in the Danby gateway which used to be shown to guests and were occasionally to be seen walking down the Iffley road.

The university botanic gardens were always a link between town and gown, giving a strong incentive for the formation of horticultural societies. The Cambridgeshire Horticultural Society was founded as early as 1824, the Oxfordshire Horticultural Society, with Professor Daubeny as patron, came into being in 1830. Their shows were often held in college gardens. Florists' societies pre-dated horticultural societies and there was great florist activity in Oxford and Cambridge in the mid-eighteenth century with feasts being held at various inns.[19] The term florist is now applied to a seller of cut flowers commercially, but from the seventeenth to the nineteenth centuries it referred to the cultivators of flowers for their beauty rather than for their medicinal properties, which was the province of the herbalist. There was a growing desire to arrive at perfection of form and colouring in such florist flowers as carnations, pinks, tulips and auriculas, even before the intensive cultivation to produce new varieties obsessed nineteenth-century horticulture.[20] Bobart was a keen raiser of auriculas and some of his pressed specimens are preserved in his *Hortus Siccus*. The colleges also produced florists. In April 1775 there was an advertisement for the sale of tulips that belonged to the Revd Dr Tottie of Christ Church where they could be seen in flower forming 'the finest collection of tulips in England, annually enriched by importation of the best flowers from Holland'. Dr Walker in Cambridge was also a keen florist, and, on hearing of a brother florist's shooting of himself, he exclaimed: 'Good God! is it possible. Now, at the beginning of tulip time'.[21] Dons and the humblest tradesmen would have exchanged floral secrets at the Town Hall shows, and college gardeners and servants were often enthusiastic members of the local societies.

The University Parks, virtually a landscaped cricket ground with a picturesque pavilion and lodges, were laid out in Oxford in 1863. This was resented by the citizens who had used the land for public walks even before Charles I exercised his dogs there during the Civil War. By way of compensation, the designer of the Parks, James Bateman of Magdalen, who had considerable experience in laying out his own Staffordshire estate at Biddulph Grange, included in his plan an arcade for flower

The Balliol chapel garden with the 'Devorguilla tomb'

shows attached to the cricket pavilion. There was a general approval for Bateman's overall plan but the Vice-Chancellor opposed the 'costliness and inutility' of the proposed arcade.[22] There was still ample scope for civic activities, however, and for Queen Victoria's Jubilee, 7,000 children were entertained to tea there when the mayor provided two engines to work tanks into which 86lb of tea were shovelled, with seventy taps disgorging from a length of pipe.[23] The North Oxford Victorian suburb was built beyond the University Parks and soon filled up with dons.[24] There was no lack of scientific interest in suburban horticulture with professors exchanging notes about soil analysis, the carbon content of the atmosphere and contrivances for watering and heating their conservatories. There was a proliferation of nurseries, commercial and private, in Oxford and Cambridge in the 1880s, to cater for newly married dons caught up in the new zeal for domestic horticulture.

Like the North Oxford suburb, Keble College at the south end of the University Parks, was built in red brick, an innovation in Oxford college building. Built by William Butterfield in 1870 in memory of John Keble, the inspirer of the Oxford Movement, it was blatantly ecclesiological Gothic. The polychrome patterns of chequers, diapers and zigzags were irreverently referred to by undergraduates as 'streaky bacon'. Evergreen foliage was advocated as an accompaniment to Gothic red brick buildings. In North Oxford, yews, hollies, mahonias, aucubas, laurustinus and berberis interspersed with pampas grass and yuccas gave the suburb a distinctive character. Butterfield also built a new chapel for Balliol in 1856 in his favourite striped buff and red stone and emphasized that dark evergreen planting was a necessary accompaniment in the new enclosed fellows' garden planned round it.[25] The effect of the old picturesque landscaped chapel, so delicately portrayed by Delamotte, was transformed by the Butterfield improvements. The taste of the age approved the demolition of the genuine early sixteenth-century chapel in favour of a 'true style' thirteenth-century chapel which, in the view of the ecclesiologists, ought to have been there on the original foundation. Later, when Waterhouse revived the front of Balliol in would-be thirteenth-century castle collegiate, the fellows' garden received additions from both the Butterfield and Waterhouse demolitions of old Balliol, a doorhead with quatrefoils from the old chapel and stone bosses from the original gateway to the college. The bits and pieces piled together make a centrepiece for the garden, sometimes facetiously called the Devorguilla tomb after the lady Devorguilla, wife of John de Balliol, who bought the original three tenements and land on which the college was built.

Ivy was thought to be an essential enhancement to old buildings in Oxford and Cambridge and in some Victorian photographs the colleges are unidentifiable. Even perpendicular architecture was covered by it. The new Victorian so-called restorations received the same romantic treatment, and Butterfield urged that the gardener should get in the roots of ivy even before his Balliol chapel was finished. Dr Gunther, who lamented that Edwardian architects disapproved of it, maintained, not without truth, that the ivy was a protection against the acid rain from the industrial areas. His own Magdalen College apparently had long and heated governing body debates about the ivy which completely covered the tower. In 1892 the bursar proposed that it should be removed but was outvoted. In 1904 he tried again but the ivy was still saved by nine votes to four. Finally in 1908 the two Waynflete Professors of Botany and Physiology put the case scientifically and this time sealed the fate of the ivy by fifteen votes to eleven. Another factor may well have influenced the decision, as news had just reached them that the ivy's roots had penetrated the vault of the wine cellar under the tower and after branching about in the sawdust had entered and drunk up a bottle of vintage port.[26] Dr Gunther still stuck up for its innocence, maintaining that the plant only makes for moisture and so long as the walls remained dry would not penetrate.

Ivy-coloured colleges were lovingly illustrated by C.L. Rundt, the King of Prussia's painter, in his *Views of the Most Picturesque Colleges in the University of Oxford* of 1852. He admired the romantic terrace garden at Exeter looking on to the Divinity School with its 'crown of ivy' and the ivy-grown bastions in the New College garden enhancing Oxford's picturesque past. The real splendours of Victorian horticulture passed Oxford and Cambridge by. The colleges did not have the country-house

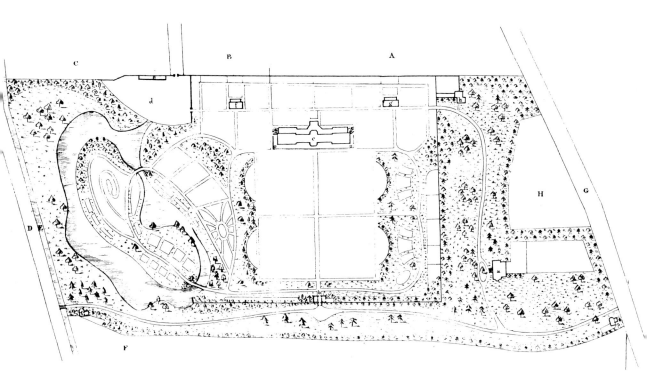

One of the original plans for the Cambridge Botanic Garden in 1840

back up of glasshouses, armies of gardeners and stableyard manure to support the Nesfield type elaborate baroque parterres or the popular bedding out displays: nor did they have the right terrain for the architectural hillside terrace gardens with flights of steps and stone balustrades and ornaments advocated by Barry. Ivy-clad buildings, exotic climbers on walls, modest strips of bedding and the odd mounded flower bed was the extent of college participation in Victorian gardening.

Clear spaces were needed on the lawns of fellows' gardens when croquet became the rage in the late 1850s. One famous garden where croquet was played was the Deanery garden at Christ Church, immortalized in *Alice's Adventures in Wonderland*.[27] In 1856 the Revd Charles Dodgson, alias Lewis Carroll, had first seen Dean Liddell's children playing in the garden from the library windows and later invented a game called Croquet Castles for them. The stories he told them with the Cheshire Cat, Alice's pet tabby cat, looking down from the horizontal bough of the Deanery chestnut tree have become famous all over the world. Walks to the Botanic Garden to admire Daubeny's giant water lilies, to feed the ducks on Worcester lake and see the Magdalen deer all contributed to the magic moments of Wonderland fantasy. It is not clear who ordered the wrong roses for the Dean's garden and was so soundly reprimanded or if the rabbit hole was in the garden or on the river banks, but it was undeniably at Christ Church, through the Alice books, that Lewis Carroll captured for all time the wonder of childhood and its 'unending happy summer days'.

Lawn tennis followed croquet in the 1870s and provisions for tennis courts and college cricket grounds had to be made. In Cambridge the Camside colleges could spread across to the area west of Queen's Road, which had belonged to the university since the middle ages,[28] for this purpose. In the case of Trinity College this land had been rented from the university as early as 1803 for extending walks into the rural environs. Loggan shows the area cultivated in strip farming and traces of ridge and furrow survive in the part of today's fellows' garden nearest the Queen's Road as a reminder of its original purpose. Perimeter walks, known as the Roundabout, were laid out in the manner of the walks round Christ Church Meadow in Oxford and reminiscent of Addison's Walk at Magdalen, where that distinguished alumnus had first observed that 'a cornfield makes a pleasant sight'. In 1871 when Trinity College purchased the freehold from the university, it was decided that the cornfield should be made into a pleasure ground and the whole area then became known as the Roundabout.

Trinity was the only college which called in a well-known professional to lay out a Victorian garden.[29] The royal foundation went for a royal garden designer. This was William Broderick Thomas, who had advised the Queen at Buckingham Palace and had laid out the Prince of Wales's new garden at Sandringham. He also worked at such notable Victorian gardens as Thoresby Hall, Holker Hall and Castle Ashby.[30] For good measure the college pensioned off its head gardener and brought in a new one who had worked at Sandringham. The number of gardeners was increased and there was a considerable expenditure on plants and equipment, hothouses, tool sheds, forcing pits and mowers. It would have taken much time and effort harrowing, levelling and cleansing the ridge and furrow before gardening could begin.[31] At Sandringham W.B. Thomas had introduced colourful parterres broken by small trees of clipped golden holly and yew,[32] but the late nineteenth-century engraving of Trinity's Roundabout shows the influence of the 1870s reaction to what William Morris called 'the nightmare of horticulture'[33] in the carpet bedding era. William Robinson's *Wild Garden* encouraged the naturalizing of bulbs in long grass and hardy exotics grown naturally in a 'home landscape'. The Roundabout retained its original perimeter walk backed by a circle of trees, yew, holly, box and other evergreens, and the central garden was made of bordering irregular island beds of herbaceous plants and shrubs with spring bulbs and scattered specimen trees on the open lawn.

14 Arts and Crafts

Victorian gardens reflected the eclecticism of the age when a 'Battle of Styles' raged in gardening as well as in architecture; picturesque versus Loudon gardenesque, Robinsonian wild gardening versus the Italianate and formal bedding out schemes of Barry and Nesfield. Ripples of this were felt in Oxford and Cambridge colleges and none more so than in the women's colleges, that startling new phenomenon of the 1870s. The Ruskin and Morris inspired Arts and Crafts Movement, which sought to promote craft and the unity of the arts rather than styles, coincided with the arrival of the women. The Arts and Crafts lady gardener, of whom Gertrude Jekyll was the most famous example, transformed Victorian gardens. Gardening became part of the decorative arts of home-making and was clearly seen this way in the new women's colleges.

Even though Oxford had a woman as a patron saint and many of the Cambridge colleges had foundresses, there was no recognized place for women in the universities, other than as wives of heads of houses, professors and the canons of Christ Church. A number of wives and daughters of those permitted to marry, and the mothers, sisters and aunts of those who were not, became increasingly anxious to partake of what Oxford and Cambridge had to offer intellectually and obtained permission to attend lectures and even to have some special classes for women. Ruskin who, for all his progressive ideas, had a nasty habit of referring to young women as girlies, excluded them from some of his art lectures. In no time at all, however, there were committees campaigning for higher education for women, not only for those resident in Oxford and Cambridge, but for those outside, desirous of availing themselves of the special advantages of what the ancient universities had to offer.

If Oxford had a short lead on Cambridge in the foundation of a male mediaeval university, Cambridge can claim to be first in the field with a college for women students. There were, however, only two such colleges founded in Cambridge: Newnham in 1871 and Girton in 1873, as

The wild gardens at St Hilda's, Oxford, a watercolour by Beatrice Parsons

opposed to five in Oxford: Lady Margaret Hall and Somerville in 1879, St Hugh's in 1886, St Hilda's in 1893, and St Anne's, which only became a college in 1938, although it was the successor of the Society of Oxford Home Students, formed in 1878. Cambridge's promotion of women's education was largely due to the single-minded efforts of a man, Henry Sidgwick, the philosopher, fellow of Trinity College. In June 1871 he wrote: 'I am choosing a house for our young women......The work takes up my time rather, but it is very entertaining. And I am growing fond of women, I like working with them.' Five years later, having resigned his fellowship on religious grounds, he married one of the most earnest campaigners for women's education, Nora Balfour, the sister of Alfred Balfour, who was later to become Principal of Newnham College. Students at the incipient Newnham had first taken up residence in 74 Regent Street, acquired and furnished by Henry Sidgwick in 1871, and presided over by the dedicated Miss Clough, sister of Arthur Hugh Clough. Miss Clough found it too noisy and deplored its lack of garden and set to work to find something else. The next year they moved to a rambling old house called Merton Hall buried among apple trees in a large garden on the edge of town.[1]

The garden made up for all the picturersque deficiencies of the house and the poor accommodation of the students, several of whom had to share rooms. 'We were shut in from Cambridge in a corner among trees and shrubs and creeping plants, which bowered us all around', wrote Miss Clough, 'our sitting rooms opened on the garden. What did it matter, if now and then, in very heavy rains, there came a rush of water through the dining room?'[2] She encouraged the students to hold debates under the medlar tree following up the university lectures which she had herself attended as their chaperon. In 1873 a lease was obtained from St John's in the district called Newnham, and Newnham Hall, now forming part of the Old Hall of Newnham College, was opened for thirty students in 1875. In 1880 the new Mrs Sidgwick joined forces with Miss Clough as Vice-Principal and her husband moved in with her to New Hall, now called Sidgwick Hall. She became Principal in 1892 on the death of Miss Clough.

The Cambridge women's colleges look more like country houses than institutions. Girton, which began life as a college in Hitchin in 1869, moved in to its purpose-built premises in 1873 having employed Waterhouse, who had been active in Cambridge for some time. Newnham chose the Arts and Crafts architect, Basil Champneys, who had been educated at Sidgwick's Trinity College and became a member of the Art Workers' Guild, which was formed in 1884 with William Morris's backing. Neither college thought it necessary to adopt the traditional staircase principle of the men's colleges and so without quadrangles and the multiplicity of staircase entrances, were able to achieve a more Arts and Crafts domestic building with a complementary manor house garden setting. The new male Selwyn College, on the other hand, built by Sir Arthur Blomfield in 1884, was on the staircase principle and followed the time-honoured pattern of the second court of St John's. Selwyn arrived on the scene at the same time as the other great feminist victory, the abolition of celibacy as a requirement for a college fellowship, and lost many of its fellows to the new Arts and Crafts suburb going up beyond the Backs.

Oxford's dons' suburb grew up in the extended Banbury Road area beyond the University Parks, which was given the opprobious name of the Parks system by the fellows who did not succumb to matrimony. Tea parties, amateur theatricals, croquet and other respectable dissipations flourished, perambulators increased and cats stalked out their territories as brick wall after brick wall went up in the fashionable suburb. As the Alices, Mauds, Enids and Beatrices grew into children, Lewis Carroll, who himself preferred not to forsake the Christ Church Common Room for the permanent matrimonial delights of North Oxford, was constantly called in to entertain with Mad Hatter tea parties and readings of *The Hunting of the Snark*. On receiving an At Home card with Tea 4–6 p.m. written in the corner, he hastened to reply that even an inveterate tea drinker could not drink tea from 4–6 p.m.[3]

Many of the Wilkinson houses on the Norham Manor estate which accommodated the married dons still looked like convents and parsonage houses but in the words of Mrs Humphry Ward, the great campaigner for women's education, niece of Matthew Arnold and wife of a Brasenose don, 'most of us were very anxious to be up-to-date and in the fashion, whether in aesthetics, in housekeeping or education'.[4] They furnished their houses with Morris wallpapers, spindle-legged chairs, and old chests and cabinets in handworked oak on which they stood blue pots. They arranged a very few well-chosen flowers in vases with a simple and newly self-conscious oriental art. Pampas grass, only recently introduced into the country, was particularly favoured in tall vases against a green wall or de Morgan tiles. The Oxford City Museum has a splendid replica of such a room. It was Walter Pater and his sisters of 2 Bradmore Road who were the first to have Morris wallpapers in Oxford, but the Humphry Wards at No. 17 soon followed and there were soon few North Oxford houses without walls covered with his flower designs of marigolds, blackthorn, honeysuckle, willows, corncockles, snakes' heads or sunflowers. House and garden were united as never before. The garden came into the house with the Morris papers and fabrics and, in fact often, with the ubiquitous creepers. The dining room led into a cool fernery and the drawing room opened on to a wisteria-covered verandah or flower-filled conservatory, tended by the lady of the house herself in a Liberty gown.

The first women's college in Oxford, Lady Margaret Hall, called after Henry VII's mother, 'a scholar, a gentlewoman and a saint', was founded in the midst of the aesthetic dons' suburb. The previous year the university had consented to examinations for women and, as in Cambridge, hostel accommodation became necessary for those working for them from outside. A society, which later became St Anne's, catered for home students. Lady Margaret Hall started life in a house at the end of Norham Gardens with the obligatory Gothic portal, but in 1881 Basil Champneys, fresh from his early success in building for women at Newnham College in Cambridge, erected a small red brick Queen Anne

Girton College students taking tea in the Jekyll-inspired Honeysuckle Walk

style building, and Reginald Blomfield continued the work in 1896 with the Wordsworth Building, named after the first Principal, Miss Wordsworth. Now that Gothic had run its course and Queen Anne lived again, a traditional, old-fashioned yew-hedged style was demanded for the garden.

William Morris had already pleaded for the unity of house and garden with a return to straight walks and clipped yew hedges if appropriate and divided his own garden into compartments hedged with sweet brier and wild roses. Ruskin had condemned hybridization and the bigger and better horticultural cult and saw some Victorian gardens as 'an assembly of unfortunate beings, pampered and bloated above their natural size, stewed and heated into diseased growth, corrupted by evil communication into speckled and inharmonious colours; torn from the soil which they loved, and of which they were the spirit and glory, to glare away this term of tormented life among the mixed and incongruous essences of each other, in earth they know not, and in air that is prison to them'.[5] Ruskin-instructed artists were taught to study native plants and paint flowers as they grew in the wild or in cottage gardens and many of the Pre-Raphaelite paintings have backgrounds of Oxfordshire flowers, drawn with great detail and accuracy. The flowers described by Tennyson in *Maud*, the roses, larkspur, woodbine, jessamine and lilies were much in demand in old-fashioned gardens. Tennyson's 'lilies and roses were all awake' in Alice's garden of live flowers and nobody seemed to mind that the lilies were depicted as tiger lilies, which had only been introduced from China in the beginning of the nineteenth century but, *pace* Ruskin, had settled in as though they belonged to Queen Anne gardens.

The bible for Queen Anne gardeners was Reginald Blomfield's *The Formal Garden in England*, published in 1892. He used his principles of modest seventeenth-century formality when designing the terrace, sunken garden clipped yews and aligned paths to harmonize with his Wordsworth building at Lady Margaret Hall. Blomfield felt very strongly, as Butterfield had done at Balliol, that with new buildings the architect and not the gardener should be responsible for the main lines of the garden design. This was anathema to William Robinson, the authoritative editor of *The Garden* and author of *The Flower Garden* and *The Wild Garden*, who immediately took up the cudgels in *Garden Design and Architects' Gardens* in 1892 and thundered in Ruskinian prose that it was 'barbarous, needless and inartistic' to make gardens harmonize with architecture. He also pointed to the Art Workers' Guild principle that a knowledge of the craft was fundamental for a designer and accused Blomfield of being a garden designer who knew nothing about the materials of his craft, namely plants. John Sedding, as architect and gardener and member of the Arts Workers' Guild, tried to bring the two sides together but the battle was not resolved until the partnership of Lutyens and Jekyll brought a new concept of the unity of house and garden. Meanwhile Sedding advocated 'gardencraft'[6] in a decorative picturesque style, which did away with the Victorian carpet bedding schemes, which Robinson, Morris and Ruskin all abhorred, but favoured Blomfield's traditional formality. He approved of a garden that 'curtseys to the house' and this seemed to strike the right note for the women's colleges built in the sweetness and light Queen Anne style.[7]

Arts and Crafts gardening was also tried by Mrs Daniel, artist wife of the Provost of Worcester College, to provide the Lodgings, which at the back sprang straight out of the eighteenth-century landscape, with an old-fashioned secluded garden. Her cousin, Alfred Parsons R.A., a founder member of the Art Workers' Guild, was noted for the Kate Greenaway look of his gardens, which Henry James referred to as having a 'nook quality'. There was a sundial in the centre of the Worcester garden and round it beds of roses, pinks and snapdragons. The garden later acquired one of the Emperors' heads discarded in a restoration scheme. All the flowers beloved of cottage gardeners, the delphiniums, larkspur, peonies, wallflowers, irises and sweet peas grew happily in the shelter of the high stone wall that separated the Provost's Lodgings from the main quadrangle. Alfred Parsons was one of the Broadway set, consisting of Edmund Gosse, Henry James, Edwin Abbey, John Sargent and Mary Anderson, who were the original promoters of Cotswold charm. The Daniels had their own cottage in the Cotswolds and the cult soon spilled over to Oxford. Not content with bringing the charm of Cotswold cottage gardening to the garden concealed behind the wall of the

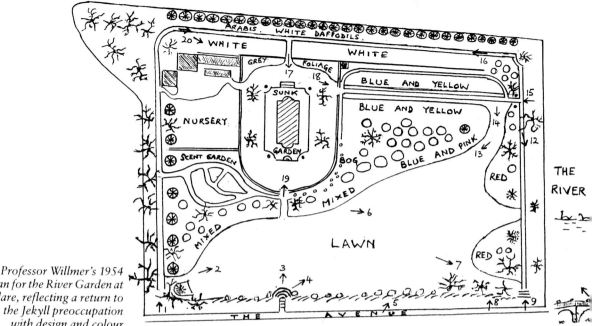

Professor Willmer's 1954 plan for the River Garden at Clare, reflecting a return to the Jekyll preoccupation with design and colour

Provost's Lodgings, the Daniels extended the roses round the door image to Henry Keene's classical buildings on the north side of the quad, and the fan-lighted door of the Lodgings at the end of the terrace was embowered with flowery creepers. The effect today is viewed with mixed feelings.

Rhodes House by Sir Henry Baker was the first Oxford building to be built to look like a Cotswold manor house, as opposed to the Daniel treatment of giving an eighteenth-century college the Cotswold look through rampant planting. While it is true that the entrance from South Parks Road, with its pillars and copper-domed rotunda, is too imperial-looking to reflect Cotswold charm, Baker, who had worked with Lutyens on grand public buildings in Delhi, wanted the entrance front to be a fitting tribute to Cecil Rhodes. On the garden side Rhodes House is seen as a seventeenth-century manor house with hipped roof of stone slates and mullioned windows. It represents the 'traditional craftsmanship of the stone-building shires of Oxford and Gloucester' and inside Morris fabrics and honest Arts and Crafts furniture were used. On one of the walls hangs the Morris tapestry of the Romance of the Rose bequeathed by the architect as a Kelmscott finishing touch. Somerville College in 1933 was the next college to acquire a Cotswold look. Like the other women's colleges Somerville started with an older house, in their case Walton House on Walton Street, and developed piecemeal as benefactors appeared. The entrance from the Woodstock Road through a round-arched gateway leads to a small squared-rubble Cotswold stone quadrangle, which is a contrast to the rest of the college through the next archway. Campion Hall, built by Edwin Lutyens in 1936, fits into Pembroke Street in the shadow of Tom Tower in a masterly and reticent way, making use of the old Micklem Hall and old materials. The courtyard within reveals a Cotswold manor looking on to a masonry-edged pond, all contained in a small area. There is no evidence that Lutyens's partner, Gertrude Jekyll, was ever consulted in Oxford, but as a friend of Herbert Baker, who had asked her advice about the laying out of Groote Schuur, the house he designed for Cecil Rhodes in South Africa, and also for his own garden at Owletts in Kent, she may well have discussed the layout of the garden at Rhodes House with him. There is a unity between the house and garden by the matching of the stone steps with the stone used in the surrounds of the windows in the Lutyens manner, and the broad herbaceous border in front of the Wadham stone wall certainly has a Jekyll character today.

Baker maintained that the early work of Lutyens was inspired by Gertrude Jekyll's sense of the 'harmony of Art and Life'. She was a designer craftsman in the Morris mould, who brought gardening into the Arts and Crafts movement. Not that the Art Workers' Guild recognized gardening as a craft skill qualifying for membership, nor had they any provision for women members, but Miss Jekyll had attended the school of art attached to the South Kensington Museum, heard Ruskin's lectures and knew Morris. For her, the Arts and Crafts creed of the unity of the arts was not just an artistic concept but fundamental to her special art and skills in home-making. She was a painter, interior decorator, gardener, embroiderer and metal worker. It was only when her eyesight began to fade that she devoted herself whole-heartedly to gardening. Herbert Baker said her 'outstanding possession was the power to see, as a poet, the art and creation of home-making as a whole in relation to life'.[8] It was this ideal of the artistic unity of the house which she passed on to Lutyens inspiring him to build not just houses but homes in harmony with their surroundings.

Home-making in the Jekyll manner was very dear to the heart of Miss Clough at Newnham College. Her students were encouraged to furnish their rooms, help in the garden and have their own window-boxes. Although she hoped they would greatly benefit by their academic studies, Miss Clough did not see her students as proceeding to a career, but rather as being better fitted for the 'embellishment of home life'. Her parting words to them were; 'We hope that when the time comes, some of you will be heads of families and that you will apply your power to what you have to do.'[9] Barbara Leigh Smith (Madame Bodichon), one of the founders of Girton, was a great friend of Miss Jekyll's.[10] Madame Bodichon was a cousin of Florence Nightingale and a friend of Rossetti and George Eliot, who portrayed her in Romola. She herself was an artist and gave £1,000 from the sale of her work towards the foundation of the college. Miss Jekyll went over to help advise her on interior decoration at Girton and probably also discussed ideas for the forty-six acre garden. Madame Bodichon, who became ill in 1877, did not return to Girton, however, and the garden was said to be bleak and uninviting in 1879. It was Miss Welsh, the garden steward, who planned the garden from the top of the tower in 1883. The Honeysuckle Walk, in which the ladies delighted to relax and take non-alcoholic drinks, has a particularly Jekyllish character. St Hilda's in Oxford, which was fortunate in being built on meadowland by the river Cherwell also had a wild garden, which

Following page: Reginald Blomfield's formal terraces and sunken garden are still evident at Lady Margaret Hall

161

was delicately painted by Beatrice Parsons who, more than any other artist, caught the feminine spirit of the Arts and Crafts gardens. Lady Margaret Hall later acquired the Cherwell meadows on its North Oxford site and planted a wild garden by the river, full of daffodils, fritillaries and cowslips.

Oxford produced its own Miss Jekyll in the shape of Miss Annie Rogers, *Custos Hortulorum* of St Hugh's College. Annie Rogers spent her life in Oxford and had had no contact with country craft, as Gertrude Jekyll had in her West Surrey retreat, but she was a follower of Morris and Arts and Crafts, and had attended Ruskin's lectures on art. She was the daughter of the Drummond Professor of Political Economy, a child friend of Lewis Carroll's,[11] and one of the chief protagonists of women's education.[12] In 1873, when she was seventeen, she entered for and won an exhibition to Balliol College, whose dons were dismayed to find that the initials A.M.A.H. stood for Annie Mary Anne Henley. The Professor's daughter had to be rejected but she started her campaign for the education of home students like herself. She always took an interest in the resulting St Anne's Society even when she became a tutor at St Hugh's College and assumed responsibility for its gardens. Normally committees supervise college gardens but Miss Rogers, like Miss Jekyll, was a formidable law unto herself. Nobody objected to what was seen as enlightened despotism in the post-war garden as it grew yearly in beauty under her guidance. She owned all the Robinson and Jekyll books, read up on pruning shrubs from the *R.H.S. Journal* and kept copious cuttings from the *Gardener's Chronicle* and *Gardening Illustrated* begun by William Robinson in 1879. The magazine *Country Life*, for which Gertrude Jekyll was gardens adviser, was dedicated to Arts and Crafts ideas and their *Century Book of Gardening* was Annie Rogers' bible. She left her copy in her will to Mr George Harris, the head gardener of St Hugh's, who had been her greatly valued helpmate in the creation of the gardens.

Annie Rogers acquired plants for the garden from friends with or without their knowledge. A fat green book belonging to the *Custos Hortulorum* preserved at St Hugh's has alphabetical lists of addresses and garden plants on the same page. It seems that all the surnames in the book were of gardening enthusiasts from whom cuttings could be obtained at the period indicated and, it is sometimes difficult to see whether 'very sweet — thin out late summer' refers to a rock rose or a North Oxford don beginning with R. Mr Harris, the college gardener, was often taken along with her on garden visits and walked behind her along the herbaceous border filling his pockets with cuttings from plants surreptitiously indicated by Miss Rogers. The artificial rock garden at St John's, one of the first of its kind, was her special delight. This had been made by Dr Bidder, Bursar and Keeper of the Groves, in 1893 and was greatly admired by lovers of the minutiae of nature in Pre-Raphaelite art. The dainty, mainly Alpine, flowers nestling in the local coral ragstone had a bejewelled effect which was seen as a new garden art. Reginald Farrer, who became famous for his book *My Rock Garden*, written in 1908, used to visit the St John's garden regularly when he was an undergraduate at

Balliol and later sent Dr Bidder a root of *Potentilla farreri* to add to his collection. In 1913 the Keeper of the Groves was able to publish a list of nearly 700 plants in his rock garden.[13] The widely-travelled fellows had brought back rock plants from Albania, the Himalayas and New Zealand. The Vice-President contributed a little double campanula from Iceland and the President of Trinity added a gentian from Monte Generoso. Miss Rogers's interest in Dr Bidder's rock garden was not entirely welcome, and college porters were warned that although a blind eye might be turned on an odd snip here and there, if the *Custos Hortulorum* of St Hugh's appeared with her umbrella, a favourite receptacle for cuttings, she must on no account be left on her own.

The St Hugh's garden may now look as though it had been planned as a whole, but it was made up from a number of existing gardens belonging to houses in the Banbury Road, acquired over a period of thirty-five years. The college had only been able to move to new premises from its original cramped quarters in Norham gardens in 1916. The garden was given over to wartime food production, including the keeping of pigs, but Miss Rogers's thoughts were always on the planning of a college garden which would bring together the old gardens that had been inherited. The head gardener from one of the houses, the Mount, was taken into the college's service and was warned that it was Miss Rogers's instructions that were to be carried out in future. He returned from a visit to the dell to announce that the old tramp working there had better be thrown out. 'That *is* Miss Rogers', he was calmly told. Annie Rogers, like Gertrude Jekyll, believed that gardening ladies should be weather-proof and prepared for anything. She always wore boots, an old mackintosh and a kind of trilby hat when working in the garden. Although the actual mount, which had given the Banbury Road house its name, was demolished with the building, Miss Rogers kept many of the features of the inherited gardens or adapted them to form a unified scheme. This part of Oxford had been used extensively for gravel, leaving land pitted with holes and trenches, which had been made into ornamental dells. The overall effect of orchards, dells, shrubberies, and mature trees was of a Jekyll garden, especially the nutwalk underplanted with drifts of daffodils and other spring flowers and the wild garden with violets and periwinkle growing along the winding paths.

Annie Rogers's striking new contribution was the flagged terrace to the redbrick neo-Georgian college's garden front, 60 yards long and 20 yards wide. The south front was covered with wall shrubs and climbers, and, sheltered by the shallow wings from wind and frost, tender plants such as passion flowers and pomegranate survived. The terrace itself was laid out, not as a Bidder rock garden (although many of the plants may well have come from it), but as a tapestry of low-growing plants in beds raised slightly above the paving. When Eleanour Sinclair Rohde, who gave pride of place to St Hugh's in her book on *Oxford's College Gardens* in 1932, visited Miss Rogers, she found the various colours of the helianthemums (nearly forty varieties), alpine phloxes, saxifrages, sedums, thymes and potentillas suggested 'the charming phrase in the Paradisus "the place will seem like a peece of tapestry of many glorious colours to encrease every one's delight" '. Inset in the terrace beds were Italian cypresses and pots of agapanthus and at the western end of the stone path a sundial and rose pergola. Annie Rogers was killed in St Giles in 1937 in the way that many people had felt she would one day end her life as she appeared to have a total disregard for motorized traffic. A sundial was erected at the entrance to the terrace in memory of the *Custos Hortulorum* with the inscription by Professor Myres: 'Floribus Anna tuis faveat sol luce perenni.'

The Jekyll ideas had a lasting effect on planting in England and her books, especially *Colour in the Garden*, are still widely read and have recently been reprinted. When Gertrude Jekyll was a student there were new and exciting ideas about impressionism and the realizing of sensations through colour, particularly in painting. Hitherto, picturesque had implied composition, but now painters were obsessed by colour which blended in the eye to make an impression. Gertrude Jekyll copied Turner's paintings as a student and later drew on what Ruskin called 'the Turner picturesque'[14] for her gardening ideas. She was also influenced by the theories of Michel Chevreul, the Director of Tints at Gobelins, who in his *The Principles of Harmony and Contrast of Colours and their Application to the Arts*, translated into English in 1854, produced a theory of optic mixtures, based on his experience of tapestry tints and suggested that there were horticultural implications for his colour harmony theory.[15] Here are to be found many of Miss Jekyll's ideas for the arrangement of colour in her borders – no one colour is seen alone, colour is affected by colours around it, white flowers are the only ones that possess the advantage of heightening the tone of flowers which have only a light tint of colour, grey helps all colours gain in purity and brilliance.

A notable garden with similar preoccupation with colour perception was designed by the physiologist Professor Nevill Willmer, and laid out by the head gardener Walter Barlow across the Cam at Clare College, Cambridge in 1946. Professor Willmer, who has designed his own artistic garden at Granchester, combined, as Miss Jekyll did, the skills of a painter who understands colour and a gardener who knows plants, where to grow them and how they would flower in colour schemes. His grandfather was John Thomas Willmer, who owned the Sunbury Nursery gardens and was the founder of the Gardeners' Benevolent Institution. At Clare there is a blue garden where delphiniums are offset with yellow privet for, as Gertrude Jekyll said, blues will be more purely blue by the juxtaposition of rightly placed complementary colour. Also in the Jekyll manner the sense of distance in the red border is increased by putting the more orange reds at one end and the more crimson reds at the other. The garden has all the year interest as it is held together by the kind of strong design element which Lutyens supplied to accompany Jekyll planting, a formal pool garden planted with irises, reeds and water-lilies, the vertical form of cypresses and a curved yew hedge. The new Clare garden must have been a wonderful tonic for Cambridge after the war years when air-raid shelters and static tanks disfigured college lawns and most of the gardens were devoted to 'Dig for Victory' vegetable growing.

15 Modern Oxford and Cambridge

After the Second World War and the destruction of so much of the country's heritage, statutory measures were introduced to preserve historic buildings and areas. The listing of buildings began with the Town and Country Planning Act of 1947, which helped to prevent the demolition and alteration of listed buildings. Previously, governing bodies in Oxford and Cambridge could do what they liked with their buildings (in 1720 Merton College library was saved from demolition by one vote). Many of the eighteenth-century buildings in Oxford and Cambridge by Hawksmoor and others had necessitated the removal of ancient buildings, but are today themselves listed as of historic importance; likewise the notorious Victorian restorations. Listed building protection only covered the historic buildings, of course, and had little control over the modern extensions and new buildings in the universities, some of which are seen by many as little less than a disaster, and by others as important twentieth-century contributions to architectural heritage.

In the 1960s there was pressure, largely from the Civic Trust, that the statutory protection of individual buildings was insufficient to stem the erosion of our historic heritage, and that further measures were needed to protect groups of buildings, their settings, and the character of whole historic areas. The result was the Civic Amenities Act of 1967 in which the local planning authorities were enjoined to designate conservation areas of 'special architectural or historic interest, the character or appearance of which it is desirable to preserve or enhance'. It had long been obvious that the whole central areas of Oxford and Cambridge needed protection and under the terms of the new Act these were soon designated to be of outstanding historic and architectural importance. In future the planning authorities were to adopt policies which would control development, including roads, restrict high buildings and office use, and tighten the control of listed buildings, and on the positive side, encourage the enhancement of these designated conservation areas.

A return to the Picturesque at Worcester College. The new Sainsbury building sited over the landscaped lake

Queens' College, Cambridge, its historic wooden bridge and the island where Erasmus used to walk, now the site of the new Cripps Building

Green belts were established around Oxford and Cambridge which helped to prevent urban sprawl and safeguard the background of the historic towns and the views of them from the surrounding countryside. It was Oxford's Professor of Poetry, Matthew Arnold, who first produced the 'dreaming spires' image, which was enthusiastically taken up, not only by contemporary romantics but today by every tourist agent. In his legend of *The Scholar Gypsy* in 1853 Arnold captured the magic of Oxford as seen from the surrounding hills. Literary pilgrims set off in search of the actual spot on the Hinksey ridge whence could be seen 'the festal light in Christ Church Hall'. Unfortunately, when the land came up for sale in the 1920s speculative builders lost no time in catering for those who wanted houses built in the very landscape of the 'loved hillside'. There was then no legislation for the protection of rural amenities and the Arnold haunts, 'spiritual associations which must live wherever the English language is spoken'[1], would have been built over but for the vision and determination of Sir Arthur Evans, Keeper of the Ashmolean Museum, who in 1928 persuaded the newly-founded Oxford Preservation Trust to purchase Matthew Arnold's field and other land to safeguard the 'Scholar Gypsy' views. While negotiations were going on he erected 14-foot high fir poles to stave off the builders and finally, when the garden walls and trees went up, the excavator of Knossos erected a great mound which would enable people to see the immemorial view over the treetops. The Oxford Preservation Trust went on to buy more land and at the most sensitive spot where 'the eye travels down' to that 'sweet city with its dreaming spires' it later paid for the offending electric pylons to go underground. Discussions were then begun which led to the Government's approval in principle, in 1956, of a green belt for Oxford, varying in breadth from four to twelve miles.[2]

In 1962 Cambridge City Council, alarmed at the current trend for high-rise buildings, had commissioned Thomas Sharp to prepare a report on the character and scale of the centre of Cambridge with a view to controlling future development. His report, with its sub-title of *Dreaming Spires and Teeming Towers*, was very influential in both Oxford and Cambridge. Thomas Sharp's conjectural illustrations of what King's College chapel and the Backs would look like with a background of teeming towers did more than anything else to bring in the successful high buildings policy. Nothing above four storeys would in future be accepted for buildings in Oxford and Cambridge. This was too late to spare Oxford from the eight-storeyed Biochemistry and Department of Engineering buildings which jar the dreaming spires image badly. It was the university itself which overturned the preposterous proposal for a zoological tower in the University Parks, which is best described in the manner of John Aubrey in *The Letters of Mercurius*, published in 1970. 'This Tower was to be of prodigious height, dwarfing all other towers, but slender, like a gigantique stone beanstalk, with twenty-nine storeys, and each storey packed with animals, superimposed after their kind, as: moles in the basement, bats in the belfry, and voles, weasels, dormice, squirrels, etc. suspended between 'em', and the tower 'once built, and stacked with animals, would grow mightily and pierce the boundaries of knowledge, revealing new truths for the salvation of mankind'.

Oxford's most controversial issue was the proposal to build a road through Christ Church meadow, put forward in 1923 and last quashed in 1974. Already in 1948 Thomas Sharp had written in his *Oxford Replanned*:

'The quietness of Broad Walk is a very lovely thing. If there were any possible way of avoiding its destruction while at the same time solving the enormous traffic problem of the city, it should certainly be taken. But there is no other way. In face of difficulties like these in Oxford, some sacrifice must be made somewhere...in place of these losses there can be created one of the most beautiful roads in the world – as well as one of the most necessary.'[3]

Undoubtedly the motorist would have had an unequalled architectural experience as he drove down the Sharp mall and saw laid out before him 'that sweet city with her dreaming spires', but Oxonians were more interested in the timeless peace of the meadow, which had never been considered as the garden environs of the college but as the city's green lung held in trust for the citizens. One of those, a nineteenth-century tanner of St Ebbe's, claimed that he had walked round the meadow ten

thousand times in his life. 'I feel thankful' he wrote, 'for the opportunities I have had, from boyhood to old age, of spending some of the most pleasant hours of my life in walking round this delightful meadow.'[4]

The fight against the meadow road became something of a saga, and made news all over the world wherever there were men who had been to Oxford. A *Punch* cartoon showed one of two sheikhs sitting cross-legged in the middle of the desert saying to the other, 'I see they want to put a road through the Meadow'. At one crucial stage in the debate it was found that five members of the Cabinet, including the Prime Minister, had been educated at Christ Church (usually referred to by members as the House) and a report appearing in the Oxford Mail of 25 September, 1956, told the story current in the university that the agenda of a recent Cabinet meeting had read: 1) Oxford Roads 2) Seizure of the Suez Canal.[5] Geoffrey Jellicoe[6] was asked to prepare a report on landscaping the road, were it agreed to be the only solution to the inner relief road. He proposed a sunken road, further away from the meadow colleges but nearer the river. No scheme involving heavy traffic would, however, have compensated for the loss of the ancient peace of Christ Church meadow and finally the Buchanan view prevailed: unless the High Street was closed, traffic would continue to use it, but if it was compulsorily closed, a relief road could be placed anywhere and did not have to be so convenient and attractive to motorists. The meadow remains, still grazed by cattle, as green countryside in the heart of a city. In the words of W.H. Auden of Christ Church:

> May the Meadows be only frequented
> By scholars and couples and cows:
> God save us from all these demented
> Plans for a road Through the House.[7]

One of the areas which would have been swallowed up, together with Broad Walk, in the proposed mall, was the memorial garden flanked with an iron grille and stone piers on St Aldate's, and laid out axially with Broad Walk with steps leading up to it over the Trill mill stream. This garden was created in 1925 as a War Memorial and on the ground is an inscription from *The Pilgrim's Progress*. 'My sword I give to him that shall succeed me in my pilgrimage.' An unintentional reminder for future road planners of what has been called the 'bloodiest battle' over an environmental issue.

A much happier involvement for Thomas Sharp was his Cambridge plan for St John's College for replanting their part of the communal landscape of the Backs. As early as 1949 the Master had written: 'Many of the trees were planted in the late eighteenth century, and, owing to disease, storm, age and other causes, we have lost so large a number that we are faced with the problem of replanning and replanting the grounds...We feel that we can no longer be satisfied to replant in a piecemeal way as we lose trees, but that we need a plan, both of removal

Landscape architecture at St Catherine's College, Oxford, with the Hepworth sculpture and water garden

and replanting, to be carried out perhaps over a period of years.'[8] The subsequent survey made by forestry and geography departments was the basis for a far-sighted landscape management policy, which has now become standard practice for landscaped parks. Hitherto the professional advice given to St John's had been for specific areas. Their Conclusion Book contains instructions to Mr Miller, the newly appointed Curator of Dr Walker's Botanic Garden, to make a plan for improving the gardens in 1765, and in 1778 the record of Capability Brown's 'services in improving the walks'. There was scope for real landscape improvement after the Inclosure Award for the Parish of St Giles added three new areas in 1805. The ditches and fishponds were filled in before the building of the Gothic New Court in 1825, which gave the college an entirely new aspect of the Backs, looking southwards towards Queens' rather than westwards across the Cam. Thomas Sharp was to look at the whole new area including the surroundings of the Master's lodge, built in 1867, and the new Benson Court, built by Lutyens in 1930 for Magdalene adjoining St John's land. Although the whole landscape should be made to flow, Thomas Sharp recommended that a new garden, hitherto an orchard on the opposite side of the avenue from the wilderness, should be enclosed, as complementary to the wilderness and to the feel of the enclosed gardens of Queens' at the other end of the Backs. Sylvia Crowe designed this on broad simple formal lines, one part having a central lawn, the other a parterre.

Christ Church had to face the devastation of Dutch elm disease in the Broad Walk in 1975. Dean Fell had originally planted English elm, *Ulmus procera*, but at the turn of the century the Huntingdon elm had been chosen to fill the increasing number of gaps. Mr Ken Burras,[9] Superintendent of the Botanic Garden, was asked to advise on the replanting of the Broad Walk by Christ Church. In considering the replacement avenue, a species, tolerant of the soil and high alkaline water table, had to be chosen which at maturity would be in scale with the architecture and landscape. A tree which satisfied all the requirements was the oriental plane, *Platanus orientalis*, a fine specimen of which already existed along the Cherwell walk, and, not forgetting Dr Pococke's huge oriental plane in the Priory garden, could be taken as evidence of its ability to succeed under meadow conditions. The oriental plane has been planted alternately with its hybrid offspring, the London plane, *Platanus acerifolia*. This was a most appropriate tree, since this hybrid was raised originally at Oxford by the first Superintendent of the Physic Garden, Jacob Bobart. A direct propagation from Bobart's original tree can be seen at the entrance to the Deer Park at Magdalen College. As with most seedling-raised trees, the plane is subject to genetic variation which results in forms with different growth habits. A clean trunk, free from side-branching characteristics, was particularly desirable for the Broad Walk and it was decided to look for a good 'avenue clone' for propagation. Material was obtained from a mature oriental plane in a Henley water meadow and from a London plane planted in the 1760s by Lord Harcourt in his landscaped garden at Nuneham.

When the elms in Broad Walk were felled, although the stately avenue, said by William Delamotte to resemble 'the cloisters of a cathedral', was greatly missed, new and breath-taking views of the spires and towers and mediaeval buildings of Oxford were opened up from the river. A few gaps have been left in the new planting so that vistas can be seen across the grazed meadow from viewing bays along the rural Cherwell walks. The views from the Merton terrace and from Deadman's Walk, which had previously terminated at the avenue, are now very extensive and remarkably *rus in urbe* in their prolongation across the meadow and the Thames to the hills beyond.

Science advanced on all fronts from the last decades of the nineteenth century and with it the need for more laboratories and experimental grounds in Oxford and Cambridge. Following a large bequest from Reginald Cory, the Cambridge University Botanic Garden was able to extend its acreage and its researches in 1951. Recently it has undertaken formal commitments to botanical conservation, including the establishment of the British Conservation Section under contract to the Nature Conservancy Council. As a late starter the Cambridge garden had the advantage of being built away from the centre of the town which enable it to have its own modern extensions. In 1951, when the Botany Department left the Oxford Botanic Garden to become part of the Science Area by the University Parks, Professor Darlington decided to establish his new Genetic Garden to demonstrate genetically-controlled breeding systems beside it rather than in the overcrowded original Botanic Garden.[10]

A new ornamental garden was, however, made at the Oxford Botanic Garden in 1953 in the more public area bordering the High Street. This Penicillin Rose Garden, designed by Sylvia Crowe, commemorates Oxford's greatest contribution to medicine, the foundation of the science of antibiotics through the discovery of penicillin. It was donated by the American Lasker Foundation and the inscription at the entrance to the garden reads: 'This Rose Garden was Given in Honour of the Research Workers in this University who discovered the clinical importance of Penicillin. For saving of life, relief of suffering and inspiration to further research all mankind is in their debt.' Penicillin was described and named by Alexander Fleming in 1929 but he had not been able to make the preparation chemically stable. In 1939 Howard Florey and the Oxford team took up the challenge stimulated by the wartime need. They worked with makeshift equipment, milk churns and ironmongery from local shops, and in 1941 used penicillin for the first time on a patient in the Radcliffe Infirmary; a small plaque over a bed in one of the wards commemorates one of the greatest steps forward in medical history. It is fitting that the memorial garden should be at the Physic Garden. The donor had stipulated a rose garden and this had to be fitted in with its

The Penicillin Rose Garden designed by Dame Sylvia Crowe

position on the High directly opposite Magdalen, and the historical tradition of the Botanic Garden. Although some felt that there should be an informal treatment of an area flanking the High, Sylvia Crowe was successful in pressing for formal beds, which would make a firm framework for the informal growth of the roses, and echo the traditional plots associated with the Botanic Garden through the centuries. Yew and box were the obvious choice for the framework and magnolias were introduced within the rosebeds for added interest and effect. There are very pleasant contrasts of green, especially the light whitebeam and the silver tassles of the *Garrya elliptica* against the dark yew foliage. There are stone seats at the western end of the garden under a row of stilted copper beech.

Dame Sylvia Crowe was also responsible for the delightful small garden area for the Goodhart Building at University College, utilizing space which might have been overlooked in such a cramped area. Its raised beds, benches and ever-welling well in a small enclosure have the feeling of the mediaeval pleasance, even though it is backed by concrete cloisters. Another courtyard pleasance of left-over space was contrived by Geoffrey Beard in the new student accommodation, built for Lincoln College on the scale of the surrounding small houses in Bear Lane, Oxford. A pioneering project for the conservation of old town buildings was that undertaken by Magdalene College in Cambridge. As early as 1952, David Roberts, a university lecturer in architecture, who was later responsible for a number of Cambridge buildings, was commissioned to develop the west side of Magdalene Street and to preserve as much as he could. Lack of money, as well as a desire for preservation, apparently played a part in the college's consideration of his brief. Much of the old derelict area had already been cleared for the Lutyens Benson Court, but for Roberts's development cottages and the upper rooms of street shops were utilized. This has resulted in an area of great diversity of old and new buildings with a village feel. It was not until 1966 that Oxford began to bring neighbouring town houses into the college complex. Pembroke College restored a range of old houses in Pembroke Street which belonged to the college, but blocked up their entrance doors, extended their backs and made a delightful quadrangle area with space behind the north range of the chapel quadrangle. More recently this has also been done by Hertford on the south side of Holywell Street and on the north side by Wadham, which has been able to incorporate the back of the handsome Holywell Music Room into its labyrinth of little college courts. St Edmund Hall received an Oxford Preservation Trust environmental award in 1980 for building above shops in the High Street. In 1987 Christ Church built a small new quadrangle behind the St Aldate's town houses leaving the familiar street scene virtually unchanged. These sensitive uses of existing old buildings for college developments are encouraged as part of the conservation area policies in Oxford and Cambridge.

The new Oxbridge post-war colleges, which had to be built from scratch, could not fit into the controlled town schemes and went up outside the central areas. Away from the traditionalism of the old colleges, the new foundations turned their thoughts to Le Corbusier and the international style and, on forty-acre sites, to new landscapes. The new democratic age had called for functionalism in architecture and the new technology for producing pre-cast concrete as a building material gave rise to an entirely new style away from Gothic, classical, Queen Anne, Arts and Crafts or any other historical precedents or prettinesses. The first Cambridge college to strike out into the Modern Movement was New Hall, a women's college whose immediate predecessor had been Newnham with its sweetness and light image. In the early 1960s their gleaming white building with its sculptural effects of dome and minarets on the Huntingdon Road was variously hailed as Byzantine, Moghul and Moorish. Its integral sunken garden with its galleries, pool and water channels is certainly reminiscent of a harem garden, which might not altogether please the militant feminists in the establishment.

The Modern Movement came to Oxford with St Catherine's College, the foundation stone of which was laid in 1960, the same year that Nuffield College, built in the Cotswold style of the pre-war era, was completed. St Catherine's was built by the Danish architect, Arne Jacobsen, and according to Nicholas Pevsner is 'the most perfect piece of architecture of twentieth century Oxford'. It is a severely geometrical concrete structure which allows the frame and beam ends to show. The buildings form one long rectangle, 600-foot long and there is a great deal of glass. One cannot help wondering whether the undergraduates exposed in their projecting glass cubicles sometimes hanker after a cosy Tudor den or a bit of Cotswold nooky charm. Professor Arne Jacobsen designed everything – buildings, furniture, fittings, cutlery, the bicycle shed – in a perfect circle and, like New Hall, the gardens were planned on the drawing board with the building. Obviously St Catherine's could not have a garden of old-fashioned flower borders and in Pevsner's words, 'the geometry is made to tell yet further in the paving of the paths through the garden areas inside and outside the parallelepipid'. Given the building, the garden – or perhaps one should say landscape architecture – is remarkably successful, especially now that the college has largely replaced the architect's original planting, which proved unsuitable for land that had been a corporation rubbish tip.[11] The most successful feature is the moat-like water garden parallel to the entrance front with its water lilies, ornamental grasses and the Hepworth sculpture on the lawn in front of the water.

Modern sculpture has given a new interest to college gardens. In Cambridge there are bronzes by Henry Moore and Barbara Hepworth in the landscape at Churchill College; amongst the cedars at Corpus Christi College there is Henry Moore's bronze of a seated man and at Emmanuel a 'warrior with a shield'. In Oxford there is an abstract bronze by Hubert Dalwood for a fountain in the axial layout of the garden of Nuffield College. Heads of houses are usually celebrated by portraits in college halls but Wadham College has chosen to commemorate Maurice Bowra, who was Warden from 1936 until 1970, by a bronze in the cloister garden. It has never been explained why it was decided to portray this famous Oxford eccentric as though in a wheel chair.

Robinson College, Cambridge.
Top: The view from the college towards Thorneycreek across Bin Brook
Bottom: The college from Thorneycreek

St John's College, Oxford, a new design of gardens and buildings

From the late 1960s onwards Oxford and Cambridge have seen the Powell and Moya monumental era. In Oxford this has produced Wolfson College by the Cherwell water meadows, where the college had 'called in the country', using to advantage the bend in the river and the Oxfordshire landscape as William Kent had done higher up the Cherwell valley at Rousham. To make up for their lack of history and the unpicturesqueness of their building, the fellows put one of the discarded pinnacles from Merton tower in a part of the garden and opened up a vista to it. In Cambridge the two most prominent Powell and Moya buildings are the two Cripps Buildings at each end of the Cam at Queens' and St John's. At Queens' the development across the wooden bridge is virtually a new college with its own dining hall, kitchen, common rooms and accommodation. However useful this may be as a conference centre, one cannnot help regretting the passing of the old garden with its willows and honeysuckle and the rural island walk so loved by Erasmus. Gardens always suffer first when there is pressure for new building. This was particularly true in the seventeenth and eighteenth centuries when the colleges began to expand and some, like All Souls and Oriel, lost virtually all their gardens. In recent years, however, there has been a conscious effort to conserve space, so important to the setting of historic buildings, even if it has meant building new libraries and picture galleries underground. The 1980s have produced not only strengthened conservation attitudes but a reaction to modernism. The entrance lodge to the new Green College in Oxford, built by Jack Lankester, the University Surveyor, looks like an eighteenth-century building and when the clock tower went on it, many people were convinced it was a restored old building and had been there all the time.

College gardens have been included in the English Heritage Register of Historic Gardens[12] and there has been a return to the eighteenth-century ideas of the importance of the relationship between a building and its landscape. The latest Worcester College graduate extension, the Sainsbury Building, has been built by McCormack and Jameson on an extended arm of the lake in a picturesque oriental style framed with willows as though it were an ornamental building in a landscaped park. Each set of rooms has its own sitting out area overlooking the backwaters with delightful sedgy natural planting by the head gardener, Mr Hilborne. So delighted is the college by the intricate appearance of its new building that now further extensions are needed, it has been decided to knock down part of the box-like building, which unforgivably appeared on its lawns in 1960, and to commission in its place a picturesque range to sit more appropriately in the landscaped garden.

Robinson College, the new Cambridge college built on a twelve-acre site on Grange Road, was able to acquire a landscape setting composed of the gardens and mature woodland of a number of large houses in the area. The wayward Bin Brook was tamed and part of its course made into a small pool and island to feature in the landscaped garden, but in one woodland area by the road it is seemingly left to go its own wild way. Viewed from the college is a delightful gabled Arts and Crafts house, Thorneycreek, set in mature trees with the long simple curving wooden bridge crossing the Bin Brook in the foreground. Looking from the aptly named Thorneycreek, Robinson College, built by Gillespie, Kidd and Coia of Glasgow, who in 1971 had built the Wadham additions in Oxford, the view is softened by thickets of shrubs with a bank of predominantly grey planting of tall herbs right up against the red brick building. On the Grange Road side of the building are square-patterned frames for climbers. Henry Woolston, the first bursar of the college, has been responsible for much of the planning with advice from J. St. Bodfan Gruffyd on the landscaping. Robinson in the 1980s was able to take advantage of the new centre of gravity for Cambridge, made when the new library was built in the 1930s. The Bodleian is still the intellectual meeting place for the University of Oxford in the very heart of the town but when the Cambridge University Library was severed from the Senate House area, it created a new focal point across the river, quite apart from the main academic complex.

King's and Trinity, which both had garden areas between Queen's Road and Grange Road, were fortunate in having direct garden walks to the new library. Trinity has recently commissioned Richard Bisgrove of Reading University to replan this whole area which also provides access to the new college hostels on the Burrell's Field site.[13] The original intention was for undergraduates to take the route through Burrell's Walk, but everybody seemed to prefer the walk through the Roundabout garden to their rooms. As shortcuts were being taken through herbaceous

borders, it was wisely decided to make an official access to Burrell's Field by a screened path through the Roundabout, which would retain a sense of seclusion in the fellows' garden. The college wanted to keep the Roundabout more or less unchanged, and Richard Bisgrove's plan ensured that its delightful nineteenth-century restful green character was strengthened with the prudent realignment of the path giving additional perimeter planting. The Bin Brook has been exploited, the unrelated avenue integrated and bolder planting is being introduced to tone down the overpowering effect of the University Library. Wittgenstein[14] who, as a fellow from 1930–36, so disliked his neo-Gothic windows in Whewell's Court that he straightened them with strips of black paper, planned some of the philosophically regular paths, which have been retained.

The college gardens in Oxford and Cambridge have succeeded in retaining their timeless sense of seclusion and peace, notwithstanding their frequent use for conferences, commemoration balls and television programmes. For those who have been privileged to enjoy them they are remembered, in Henry James's words, as green retreats 'from the restless outer world,... places to lie down on the grass in for ever, in the happy faith that life is all a vast old English garden, and time an endless summer afternoon'.[15]

Merton College, Oxford,
the oldest university college
where the gardens exude
that timeless quality
enjoyed by so many
generations of scholars

Notes and References

Chapter I   Introduction

1. Hermann Pückler Muskau, *Tour in England*, 1832.
2. Henry James, *A Passionate Pilgrim*, 1875.
3. Lord Kames, *Elements of Criticism*, 1762.
4. Matthew Arnold, *Essays in Criticism*, 1865.
5. A. Toynbee, *Remains*, 1884; quoted in Jan Morris, *The Oxford Book of Oxford*, 1978 p. 225.
6. English Register of Historic Parks and Gardens compiled by the Historic Buildings and Monuments commission after the National Heritage Act, 1983.
7. R. Willis and J.W. Clark, *The Architectural History of the University of Cambridge*, 1886, Vol. II, p. 409; also for account of commonfields exchange C.P. Hall and J.R. Ravensdale, *The West Fields of Cambridge*, 1976, p. 86.
8. Z. Von Uffenbach, who wrote *Oxford in 1710*, ed. Quarrell, 1928.
9. See H.M. Petter, *The Oxford Almanacks*, 1974.

Chapter 2   Mediaeval Origins

1. Articles on the historical evidence in *Oxoniensia* 53, 1988.
2. Brian Durham, 'The Thames Crosing at Oxford', *Oxoniensia* 49, 1984.
3. Daniel Defoe, *Tour through the Whole Island of Great Britain*, 1724. Letter 6.
4. *V.C.H. Oxfordshire* Vol. 2 on Religious Houses.
5. Evelyn Brown-Grant, 'The Gardeners of Paradise', *Oxfordshire Family History*, Vol. 3. No. 7.
6. Geoffrey Chaucer, *The Canterbury Tales*, line 308.
7. H. Salter, *Survey of Oxford*, Oxf. Hist. Soc. New Series XIV, 1960.
8. Chaucer, op. cit., line 3203.
9. A.E. Emden, *An Oxford Hall in Mediaeval Times*, 1927.
10. Chaucer, op. cit., line 3989.
11. R. Willis, 'Description of the ancient plan of the monastery of St Gall', *Archaeological Journal* V, p.8.
12. Town Council 9 January 1445, quoted by Willis and Clark.
13. *Cambridge Antiquarian Society Publication* 31, 1898.
14. T. Fowler, *The History of Corpus Christi College*, 1893. For full bee quotation from the statutes see Jan Morris p.37.
15. G. Trevelyan, *Trinity College*, An Historical Sketch, 1946, p.10.
16. Holinshed's *Chronicles*, 1577.

Chapter 3   St Frideswide's Cloister Garden

1. Sylvia Landsberg, 'The Recreation of a Mediaeval and a 16th century garden in Hampshire', *Pleasure Grounds, The Gardens and Landscapes of Hampshire*, 1987.
2. Christopher Scull's report on the priory cloister excavation by the Oxford Archaeological Unit, *Oxoniensia* 53, 1988.
3. H.C. Maxwell Lyte, *History of the University of Oxford*, 1886, p. 248.
4. John Blair, 'St Frideswide Reconsidered', *Oxoniensia* 52, 1987. A translation of the text is also to be published under the title of *St Frideswide Patron of Oxford*, 1988.
5. S. Heath, *Pilgrim Life in the Middle Ages*, 1911.
6. Lorna Price, *Plan of St Gall*, 1982.
7. See John Harvey, *Garden History* Vol. 15 No I, p. 78. Dr Harvey attributes the appearance of the Sycamore (*Acer pseudoplatanus*) on the shrine to the copying of foreign naturalistic sculptures, rather than local observation.
8. See D. Pearsall & E. Salter, *Landscapes and Seasons of the Medieval World*, 1973.
9. A. Arber, *Herbals, Their origin and Evolution*, 1986, p. 250.
10. Leslie Gordon, *A Country Herbal*, 1980, p. 23.
11. Ibid., p.23.
12. Letters and Papers Henry VIII. Pace to Wolsey, 12 April 1518.
13. Letters and Papers 995, June 1525.
14. W. Shakespeare, *Henry VIII*, Act VI, Scene 2.
15. *Sussex Archaeological Collections*, Vol, 29, p. 25.
16. Letters and Papers 2457.

Chapter 4   Profit and Pleasure in the College Gardens

1. *Archaeologia*, liv, pt 1, p. 166.
2. A.E. Emden, *An Oxford Hall in Medieval Times*, 1927, p. 213.
3. Alice Coats, *Flowers and their Histories*, 1956, p. 62.
4. Willis and Clark, Vol III, p. 581.
5. Ibid., p. 580.
6. J. Buxton & P. Williams, *New College, Oxford 1379 – 1979*, 1979, p. 202.
7. John Harvey, 'Mediaeval Plantsmanship in England: the Culture of Rosemary', *Garden History*, Vol. I No. I, p. 14.
8. John Harvey, *Mediaeval Gardens*, 1981, p. 127.
9. Ibid., p. 135.
10. Teresa McLean, *Medieval English Gardens*, 1981, p. 33.
11. John Harvey, op. cit., p. 88.
12. D. Erasmus, *Colloquia: Convivium Religiosum*. Translated Sir Roger L'Estrange.
13. T. Fuller, *The History of the University from the Conquest to 1634*, 1840.

Chapter 5   Elizabethan Oxford and Cambridge

1. M. Colthorpe, *Royal Cambridge*, 1977, p. 1.
2. Hugh Platt, *The Art of Preserving and Candying*, 1611.
3. Colthorpe, op. cit., p.22.
4. C.R. Fay, *King's College*, Cambridge, 1907, p.72.
5. *Elizabethan Oxford*, Oxford Historical Society, Vol. VIII, 1886, pp. 123 & 177.
6. William Shakespeare, *Henry VIII*, Act VI, Scene 2.
7. Bodleian Library MS, Top Oxon e. 9.
8. *Elizabethan Oxford*, p. 117.
9. W.G. Hiscock, *A Christ Church Miscellany*, 1946, p. 167.
10. W. Lawson, *A New Orchard and Garden*, 1618, p. 70. Lawson said his book was the result of 48 years experience.
11. K. Thomas, *Man and the Natural World*, 1983, p. 205.

12. Samuel Ward from *Two Elizabethan Puritan Diaries* ed. M. Knappen, 1933, p. 113.
13. St John's Register Coll. I 231.
14. L & F Fowler, *Cambridge Commemorated*, 1984, p. 24.
15. G.M. Trevelyan, *Trinity College*, 1946, p. 16.
16. Fay, op. cit., p. 71.
17. The testimonies of Dr Goade and Dr Whitaker are quoted by Willis and Clark Vol III, p. 337.
18. Anthony Wood, *Athenae Oxonienses*, 1691, p. 107.
19. Ibid.
20. Bodl MS. Wood F 28 (207)
21. Lesley Gordon, *A Country Herbal*, 1984, p. 15.
22. Willis and Clark, Vol III, p. 583.
23. M. Batey, *Oxford Gardens*, 1982, p. 26.

Chapter 6   Botanical Gardening
1. Chaucer, *The Canterbury Tales*, line 411.
2. See entry on Herbals by Sandra Raphael in *The Oxford Companion to Gardens*.
3. BM Lansdowne MSS Vol 107, No 92, fol 155. Quoted in *Cambridge Antiquarian Society Communications* Vol IV, 1876, p.7.
4. See Prudence Leith – Ross, *The John Tradescants, Gardeners to the rose and lily queen*, 1984 and Mea Allen, *The Tradescents, their plants gardens and museum 1570 – 1662*, 1964.
5. Bodleian Library. Ashmole MS. 1461.
6. See A. Macgregor, *Tradescant's Rarities* and *Ark to Ashmolean*, 1983. The Tradescant rarities are now displayed in an arklike setting in the Ashmolean Museum in Beaumont Street. The Old Ashmolean Museum in Broad Street is now the Museum of the History of Science. See also C.H. Josten, *Elias Ashmole F.R.S. Notes and Records of the Royal Society of London*, Vol 15, Tercentenary number, July 1960.
7. Transactions. Medical Society, London, Vol. 14, 1917.
8. James Turner, 'Ralph Austen, an Oxford horticulturist of the 17th century', *Garden History*, Vol. VI, No. 2.
9. Robert Plot, *The Natural History of Oxfordshire*, 1677, p. 265.
10. Worthington, *Life of Mede*, quoted in *Cambridge Commemorated*, p. 71.
11. Revd J.J. Smith, *The Cambridge Folio*, 1839, quoting from an earlier source Cole's MSS Vol. XXXIII, p. 26.
12. John Ray, *Diary and Correspondence* ed J. Crossley, 1847, *Life of Ray*, preface by William Derham, 1760.
13. *Fasciculus Plantarum Circa Cantabrigiam nascentium*, 1660.
14. S.M. Walters, *The Shaping of Cambridge Botany*, 1981.

15. T. Salmon, *The Foreigner's Companion through the Universities of Cambridge and Oxford*, 1748, p. 67.
16. *A Short Account of the late Donation of a Botanic Garden to the University of Cambridge* by the Revd Dr Walker, 1763.

Chapter 7   The Restoration
1. John Barwick, *Querela Cantabrigiensis*, 1646, p. 85.
2. Vivian Green, *The Commonwealth of Lincoln College 1427 – 1977*, 1979, p. 247 n.3
3. Gomme's plan of the defences of Oxford, Bodl Ms Top Oxon. b. 167.
4. Anthony Wood, *Life and Times*, ed A. Clark, Vol II, p. 479.
5. Thomas Sprat, *History of the Royal Society*, 1667.
6. R. Plot, *The Natural History of Oxfordshire*, p. 240.
7. *The Reformed Commonwealth of Bees*, Christopher Wren, A letter concerning that pleasant and profitable invention of a transparent beehive, 1655.
8. *John Evelyn, Diary*, ed. E.S. de Beer, 1955, Vol. III, p. 110.
9. MSS Evelyn, Christ Church.
10. Bishop Gilbert Burnet, *A History of His Own Times*, 1753.
11. Quoted in *Cambridge Commemorated*, p. 93.
12. Pope, *Epitaphs*.
13. W. Wordsworth, *The Prelude* Book III, lines 61–3.
14. Brewster's *Life of Newton*, quoted in *Cambridge Commemorated*, p. 122.
15. W. Stukeley, *Memoirs of Sir Isaac Newton's Life* ed. A.W. White, 1936, p. 19.
16. J. Turner 'Ralph Austen an Oxford horticulturist of the 17th century', *Garden History* Vol. VI, no. 2
17. R. Plot, op. cit., p. 152.
18. J.K. Burras, 'The nature of variegation', *Journal of the R.H.S*, Vol. XCIX, Pt 10.

Chapter 8   The Grand Manner
1. Wren to Gower, 1697. J.B. Mullinger, *St John's College*, 1901, p. 194.
2. J. Summerson, *The Sheldonian in its Time*, An oration delivered to commemorate the Restoration of the Theatre, 16 Nov. 1963.
3. *Cambridge Commemorated*, p. 117.
4. The inscription at the foot of Loggan's plate of Trinity College Library records that his services were rendered gratuitously.
5. Buxton & Williams, *New College*, p. 214.
6. Henry Thompson, *Christ Church*, 1900, p. 87.
7. W.D. Caroe, *'Tom Tower', Christ Church, Oxford*, 1923, p.23.

8. *Hearne's Remarks and Collections*, ed. H.E. Salter, Vol IX, p. 361.
9. See Kerry Downes, *Hawksmoor*, 1959.
10. The present Radcliffe Square was at the time full of small houses and gardens as seen in Loggan's plan. Hawksmoor would have left the square open with a large centred statue. The new round library in his scheme would have been joined to the Bodleian.
    See H. Petter, *The Oxford Almanacks*, p. 49 for an illustration of Hawksmoor's 'Forum Universitatis'. The actual drawing is in Brasenose College Drawings, no. 36 and the Gibbs Collection at the Ashmolean Museum. The drawing for the 'Forum Civitatis' at Carfax is in the Bodleian, Ms. Top Oxon a 26 (R).
11. *Hearne's Collections*, Vol VII, p. 110.
12. K. Downes, op. cit., p. 100.
13. Wren to Gower, J.B. Mullinger, op. cit., p. 194.
14. S. Wren, *Parentalia*, 1750, p 351.

Chapter 9   The Glorious Revolution and Dutch Gardening
1. *The Gardens of William and Mary*, ed. David Jacques and A. van der Horst, 1988.
2. Daniel Defoe, *A Tour Through the Whole Island of Great Britain*, 1724, Letter 2.
3. *The Journeys of Celia Fiennes*, ed. Christopher Morris, 1947, p. 37.
4. Bodl MSS Eng. misc b 73 f7.
5. Thomas Salmon, *The Foreigner's Companion*.
6. Celia Fiennes, op. cit., p. 66.
7. G.M. Trevelyan, *Trinity College*, 1946, p. 52.
8. Conyers Middleton, *A true account of the present state of Trinity College in Cambridge, under the oppressive government of Richard Bentley*, 1720.
9. Z. Von Uffenbach, *Oxford in 1710*, ed. Quarrell, 1928.
10. R. Southey, *Letters of Espriella*, 1807, Vol. II, p. 69.
11. Pope's Essay in the *Guardian* 1713 condemns vegetable sculpture in a witty parody. Echoing Addison he makes a plea for informality in gardens. "There is certainly something in the aimable Simplicity of unadorned Nature, that spreads over the Mind a more noble sort of Tranquillity, and a loftier Sensation of Pleasure, than can be raised from the nicer Scenes of Art".
12. William Mason, *The English Garden*, 1772– 81, Book 1 lines 468 – 72.

Chapter 10   The Pleasures of the Imagination
1. *The Spectator*, no. 411.
2. Ibid., no. 10.
3. Ibid., no. 1.

4. The essays on the Imagination were originally a single essay which was expanded into eleven essays in *The Spectator*, nos 411–421. The original ms Essay came into the possession of J. Dykes Campbell who published it as *Some Portions of Essays contributed to the Spectator by Mr Joseph Addison* limited edition Glasgow 1864. See *The Spectator*, ed Donald Bond, 1965, p. 535.
5. *The Spectator* no. 414.
6. Essay on the *Georgics* in Dryden's translation 1697.
7. See M-S Røstvig, *The Happy Man; Studies in the Metamorphosis of a classical idea*, 1962.
8. Nourse was one of the first to suggest siting a house for prospect.
9. *Dialogues upon Ancient Medals* III. See Joseph Addison, Miscellaneous Works, A.C. Guthkelch, 1914, Vol. II, p. 377.
10. These statements are the only observations relevant to natural gardening in the original Essay. The second part of Essay no. 414 was added later.
11. Addison sought to reconcile the extensive landscape gardening he had seen on the Continent with classical ideas of good husbandry. See M. Batey, 'The Magdalen Meadows and the Pleasures of the Imagination', *Garden History*, Vol. 9, no. 2.
12. *The Spectator*, no 414.
13. *Congratulatory Epistle to the Rt Hon. Addison*, by a Student at Oxford, 1717.
14. S. Wren, *Parentalia*, p. 352.
15. See P. Willis, *Charles Bridgeman and the English landscape garden*, 1977.
16. *The Correspondence of Alexander Pope*, ed. G. Sherburn, 1956, Vol. II, p. 264.
17. *The Spectator*, no. 417.
18. *Letters of William Shenstone*, ed. M. Williams, 1936, p. 400.
19. W. Shenstone, *Essays of Men and Manners*, 1794, Unconnected Thoughts on Gardening, p. 65.
20. Ibid., p. 67.
21. Ibid., p. 69.

Chapter 11   Landscaping in the Age of Taste
1. Shaftesbury, Advice to an Author, *Characteristics* I, 215.
2. Shaftesbury, *Moralists*, 1709.
3. E. Burke, *A Philosophical Enquiry into the Origin of our Ideas of the Sublime and the Beautiful*, 1757, Part IV, Section XX, p. 151.
4. *The Spectator*, no. 387.
5. Burke, op. cit., Part IV Section XXIII, p. 159.
6. W.S. Taylor, *Chatham Correspondence*, Vol IV, p. 430.

7. Dorothy Stroud, *Capability Brown*, 1950, p. 153.
8. *Walpole Letters* ed. W.S. Lewis, Vol 28, p. 429.
9. G. Dyer, *History of the University and Colleges of Cambridge*, 1814, I, p. 231.
10. *Cambridge Commemorated*, p. 207.
11. A. Leigh, *King's College*, 1899, p. 202.
12. G. Dyer, op. cit., Vol. I, p. 230.
13. Dyer was one of Coleridge's Pantisocrats, who planned to live at one with Nature in Virginia.
14. Dyer, op. cit., Vol. II, p. 162.
15. Ibid., Vol. I, p. 233.
16. Evelyn Brown-Grant, 'The Gardeners of Paradise', *Oxfordshire Family History*, Vol. 3, No. 7.
17. T.F. Dibdin, *Reminiscences of a Literary Life*, 1836, Vol. I, p. 87.
18. Dyer, op. cit., Vol. II, p. 439.
19. Ibid., Vol II, p. 162.
20. W. Wordsworth, *The Prelude* Book VI, lines 66–68.
21. A. Tennyson, 'In Memoriam', 1833, Lxxxvii, 15.
22. Dyer, op. cit., Vol. I, p. vii.
23. T. Salmon, *The Foreigner's Companion*, p. 55.
24. R. Southey, *The Doctor*, 1834.

Chapter 12   The Picturesque
1. Keith Thomas, *Man and the Natural World*, 1983, p. 261.
2. G.M. Trevelyan, *Trinity College*, p. 90.
3. Gray's Correspondence to Mason, 1765, ed. Toynbee & Whibley, Vol. II, p. 899.
4. *Memoirs of Dr Richard Gilpin*, written by W. Gilpin, ed. W. Jackson, 1879.
5. See W.D. Templeman, *The Life and Work of William Gilpin*, 1939, and Carl Paul Barbier, *William Gilpin. His Drawings, Teaching and Theory of the Picturesque*, 1963.
6. Bodl MSS. Eng. misc. b. 73, f.7.
7. Ibid.
8. Bodl MSS. Eng. misc. c. 388 f.137 and Mavis Batey, 'Gilpin and the Schoolboy Picturesque', *Garden History*, Vol. II, No. 2, p. 24.
9. See *Pleasure Grounds, the Gardens and Landscapes of Hampshire*, 1987, p. 41.
10. See *British and American Gardens in the 18th century* ed. R. Maccubbin & P. Martin, p.44.
11. M. Batey, 'William Mason, English Gardener', *Garden History*, Vol. I, No. 2.
12. Mavis Batey 'Oliver Goldsmith: An Indictment of Landscape Gardening', *Furor Hortensis*, ed. P. Willis, 1974.
13. *Nuneham Courtenay*, 1797 and 1806 (Simon Harcourt).
14. W. Wordsworth, 'The River Duddon'.
15. Magdalen Red Book at the College dated January 1st, 1801.
16. Magd. MS. cII. 3, 4.

17. T.S.R. Boase, 'An Oxford College and the Gothic Revival', *Journal of the Warburg and Courtauld Institutes*, Vol. 18, 1955.

Chapter 13   Horticulture in Victorian Oxford and Cambridge
1. J.C. Loudon, *Gardener's Magazine*, Vol. 8, 1832, p. 700.
2. Ibid., April 1834.
3. Loudon, *The Modern and Approaching style of Rural Improvement*, 1807, p. 12.
4. Hazel Le Rougetel, 'Early Chelsea/Cambridge Associations in Botany', *Garden History* Vol. VII, No. 3, p. 49.
5. *A Short Account.....by the Revd Dr Walker*, 1763.
6. Blanche Henrey, *British Botanical and Horticultural Literature before 1800*, 1975, Vol. II, p. 238.
7. Royal Botanic Gardens Kew Record Book, 1793– 1809.
8. *Vertumnus*, an Epistle to Mr Jacob Bobart, Botany Professor to the University of Oxford and Keeper of the Physick Garden, 1713.
9. J.C. Loudon, *Magazine for Natural History*, 1833.
10. Loudon, *Gardener's Magazine*, April 1834.
11. Loudon's original plan is in the *Gardener's Magazine*, Vol. 8, 1832, p. 414.
12. T. James in *Gardener's Magazine* 1839; quoted in L. Fleming & A. Gore, *The English Garden*, 1979, p. 187.
13. *A Report presented to the Visitors of the Oxford Botanic Garden*, 1834.
14. See *Guide to the Oxford Botanic Gardens*, 1971, compiled by C.D. Darlington, Emeritus Professor of Botany and J.K. Burras, Superintendent of the Oxford Botanic Garden, p. 24.
15. K.L. Davidson, *Gardens Past and Present*, 1908, p. 19. There are several versions of this story.
16. R.T. Gunther, *Oxford Gardens*, 1912, p. 18.
17. *Autobiographical Recollections*, ed. F. Darwin, 1887, quoted in *Cambridge Commemorated*, p. 186.
18. J.W. Clark & T.M. Hughes, *Life and Letters of A. Sedgwick*, 1890, quoted in *Cambridge Commemorated*, p. 246.
19. See Ruth Duthie, 'Growers and Showers of Florists' Flowers in the Oxford area up to 1820', *Top Oxon*, no. 22, 1978.
20. Ruth Duthie, *Florists' Flowers and Societies*, 1988.
21. R. Ackermann, *History of the University of Cambridge*, quoted in *Cambridge Commemorated*, p. 136.
22. First Report of the University Park

delegates, Oxford University Archives.

23. *Oxford Jackson's Journal*, 2 July, 1887.
24. Mavis Batey, 'First of the Garden Suburbs', *Country Life*, 20 March, 1980.
25. Butterfield's letter of 13 Dec, 1856 is in Balliol College Archives.
26. R.T. Gunther, *Oxford Gardens*, 1912, p. 210.
27. See Mavis Batey, *Alice's Adventures in Oxford*, Pitkin, 1980.
28. Willis & Clark, Vol. II, p. 647 n.1.
29. R. Robinson, The Fellows' Garden; An Historical Note, 1981.
30. B. Elliott, *Victorian Gardens*, 1986, p. 261 n.188.
31. For the removing of ridge and furrow from gardens see M. Symes, 'Charles Hamilton's sowing of grass at Painshill', *Garden History*, Vol. 14, no. 2, p.138.
32. G. Plumptre, *Royal Gardens*, 1981, p. 14.
33. W. Morris, *The Quest*, May 1895.

Chapter 14   Arts and Crafts

1. *Memoir of A.J. Clough*, by B.A. Clough, 1897, p. 156.
2. Ibid., p. 200.
3. *The Letters of Lewis Carroll*, ed. Morton.N. Cohen, 1979, p. 189.
4. Mary Augusta Ward, *A Writer's Recollections*, 1918.
5. *The Works of Ruskin*, ed. E.T. Cook, 1903, Vol. I, p. 156.
6. John Dando Sedding, *Gardencraft Old and New*, 1891.
7. Mark Girouard, *Sweetness and Light, The Queen Anne Movement*, 1983.
8. Herbert Baker, *Architecture and Personalities*, 1944, p. 16.
9. *Clough Memoir*, p. 244.
10. Barbara Stephen, *Girton College, 1869 – 1932*, 1933, p. 146.
11. Annie Rogers, 'Alice in Wonderland', *The Times*, March 29th, 1928.
12. Annie Rogers, *Degrees by Degrees*, 1938.
13. H.J. Bidder, A handlist of Alpine and other plants growing in the rockery of St John's College, Oxford, 1913.
14. Betty Massingham, *Miss Jekyll*, 1966, p. 50.
15. M.E. Chevreul, *The Principles of Harmony and Contrast of Colours and their application to the arts*, translated from the French by Charles Martel, 1854, the last chapter of which applies his colour principles to horticulture.

Chapter 15   Modern Oxford and Cambridge

1. Arthur Evans, *Jarn Mound*, 1933, p. 10.
2. Ian Scargill, *The Preservation of Oxford*, 1973, p. 13.
3. Thomas Sharp, *Oxford Replanned*, 1948, p. 118.
4. E.G.W. Bill, *Christ Church Meadow*, 1965, p. 31.
5. Dr R.J. Newman, *The Road and Christ Church Meadow*, 1980, p. 19.
6. G.A. Jellicoe, *Studies in Landscape Design* Vol. II, 1966, p. 58.
7. E. Bill, op. cit., p. 37. Unpublished poem by W.H. Auden.
8. *The Eagle* Vol. LIV No. 239, 1951, p. 314.
9. J.K. Burras, *Tree Planting Proposals for Christ Church Meadow*, 1976.
10. See *Guide to Botanic Garden*, 1980, p. 32 for Genetic Garden. See also C.D. Darlington, Inaugural Lecture, 1953.
11. B.E. Juniper, *A Guide to the Gardens of St Catherine's College*.
12. Register of Historic Parks and Gardens. Unlike buildings schedules the register has no statutory powers, but exists to alert owners and planners.
13. Trinity College Fellows' Garden Landscape Report, 1981.
14. Ludwig Wittgenstein, *Personal Recollections*, ed. Rush Rhees, 1981, p. 21.
15. Henry James, *A Passionate Pilgrim*, 1875.

Acknowledgements

I am particularly grateful to Mr Richard Bisgrove, Mrs Audrey Blackman, Dr. John Blair, Mr J.K. Burras, Mrs Catherine Cole, Dame Sylvia Crowe, Mrs Ruth Duthie, Dr. John Harvey, Mr H. Hilborne, Dr. B. Juniper, Dr. Sylvia Landsberg, Mr Christopher Morris, Mr Harry Pitt, Dr. R. Robson, Professor N Willmer, Mr Henry Woolston and the staff of the Bodleian Library, the Oxford City Library, the Cambridgeshire Collection of the City Library, the Cambridgeshire Record Office, Christ Church Library, the Royal Botanic Gardens, Kew and the Archivists of Girton College and Trinity College, Cambridge.

Mavis Batey

Antler Books would additionally like to thank the following who helped with the picture research for this book: the Governing Body of Christ Church College, Nancy Dowson-Weisskopf, A.M Faux, Eileen Goff, Timothy Hobbs, Clive King, J.A Jolowicz, the President and Fellows of Magdalen College, Kate Perry, Michael J Petty, Mary Williams, Michael Willis and the Christopher Wood Gallery.

Picture Credits

Index

Abbey, E   159
Ackermann, R   11
Addison, J   101, 102–113, 115, 116, 117, 118, 128, 140
Addison's Walk   68, 153
Agas Map   10, 40, 46, 51, 78, 107
Aiton, W.T   145
Aldrich, Dr. H   89, 90
Alison, A   125
All Souls   21, 22, 53, 61, 70, 85, 92, 178
Amesbury   108
Anderson, M   159
Aristotle   55
Arnold, M   27, 135, 168
    The Scholar Gypsy   168
Art Workers Guild   156, 159, 161
Ashmolean Museum   168
Aubrey, J   61, 68, 169
    Brief Lives   68
Auden, W.H   171
Aularian Statutes   36
Austen, J   133
Austen, R   63, 73
Ayliffe, J   85

Backs   8, 12, 120–5, 135, 171, 172
Bagley Wood   12
Baker, Sir H   160, 161
Baker, P   49
Balfour, A   156
Balfour, N   156
Balliol College   20, 36, 70, 76, 123, 151, 159, 162, 164
Banks, Sir J   145
Barlow, W   165
Barnwell   15
Barrow, I   65, 72, 84, 93
Barry, Sir C   155
Bateman, J   149, 150
Beaufort, the Lady Margaret   24, 39, 45
Beaumont Palace   15
Bentley, Dr. R   100
Bidder, Dr. H   162, 164

Biddulph Grange   149
Bird, W   85
Birmingham Botanical and Horticultural Soc.   147
Bisgrove, R   179, 181
Black Death   21
Black, M   84
Blenheim   80
Blois   81
Blomfield, Sir A   156
Blomfield, R   158, 159
Bobart, Jacob the Elder   62, 63, 64, 79, 80, 81, 145, 173
Bobart, Jacob the Younger   81, 99, 149
Bobart, Tilleman   79
Bodichon, Mme.   161
Bodleian Library   92, 118
Boldre   129
Bolingbroke, H. St John   108
Bologna   58
Bowra, M   176
Boyle, H   108
Boyle, R   64, 69, 102
Bradley, R   64, 65
Brasenose College   51, 92
Bridgeman, C   110, 111, 113
British Association   149
Broad Walk   171, 173
Brompton Park   96, 111
Broughton Castle   97
Brown, 'Capability'   11, 12, 118–23, 125, 127, 133, 134, 138, 172
Buchanan, C   171
Buckingham, Duke of   45
Buckler, J.C   140, 141
Bunyan, J   171
Burghers, M   85, 88
Burghley, William Cecil   44, 45, 59, 60
Burke, E   118, 125, 127
Burlington, 3rd Earl of   89, 115, 117
Burne-Jones, E   29

Burnet, Bishop   70
Burras, J.K   173
Butterfield, W   150, 151, 159
Byron, Lord G   127

Caius College   75
Cambridge Botanic Garden   173
Cambridge Horticultural Soc.   149
Cambridge Physic Garden   64, 96
Cambridge Platonists   70, 72, 116
Campion Hall, Oxford   160
Canons   80
Cardinal College   22, 25, 27
Carfax   92
Carroll, Lewis   152, 157, 162
Carrow Abbey   32
Cecil, Sir W (see Burghley)
Champneys, B   156, 157
Chandos, 1st Duke of   85
Charles I   45, 67, 68, 113, 125, 149
Charles II   69, 80, 81, 95
Chaucer, G   8, 15, 17, 20, 21, 29, 31, 34, 55
Cheam   129
Chelsea Physic Garden   145
Chevreul, M   165
Chichele, Bishop   22
Chiswick   115
Christ Church   21, 25, 27, 32, 46, 49, 53, 67, 69, 76, 78, 85, 86–89, 95, 125, 141, 143, 152, 155, 168, 171, 173, 175
Christ Church Meadow   8, 15, 17, 20, 21, 31, 34, 55
Christ's College   24, 39, 100, 143, 148
Churchill College   176
Civic Amenities Act, 1967   167
Civic Trust   167
Clare College (formerly Clare Hall)   12, 24, 45, 70, 75, 84, 99, 100, 108, 121, 122, 165
Clare, the Lady of   39

Clarendon, 1st Earl of   69
Clarke, Dr. G   90, 91, 92
Claymond, J   55
Clayton, T   60, 61
Clayton, Lady   75, 76
Clough, A.H   161
Clough, Miss A.J   156, 161
Codrington, J   51
Coghan, T   52
Coke, T   87
Cole, W   96
Coles, W   63
Colet, J   40, 58
Collins, W   106
Colman, M   62
Colvin, H   12
Compton, Bishop   77
Corpus Christi, Cambridge   21,
   23, 24, 34, 176
Corpus Christi, Oxford   25, 67, 99
Cory, R   173
Cothele   22
Country Life   162
Cox, R   49
Cranmer, Archbishop   49
Cromwell, O   67, 68, 69, 84, 93
Crowe, Dame S   172, 174, 175
Cruikshank, G   143
Cudworth, R   70, 75, 116

Dalwood, H   176
Daniel, Friar H   38
Daniel, Dr. C.H   160
Daniel, Mrs Emily   159
Danvers, H, Earl of Danby   60, 61
Danvers, Sir J   61
D'Argenville, A.J. Dézallier   99
Darlington, Prof. C.D   173
Darwin, C   145, 148, 149
   Origin of Species   149
Daubeny, Prof. C   148, 149, 152
Dawley   108
Defoe, D   96
Delamotte, W.A   11, 118, 135, 151,
   173
Devorguilla, Lady   151
Dilettanti Society   115, 134
Dillenius, J   81, 148
Dioscorides   58
Doctrine of Signatures   31, 63
D'Oilly, R   12, 14
Domesday Survey   29
Donn, J   145
Dover, Earl of   68
Downing College   24, 141
Druce, Dr. C   31
Dryden, J   88
Du Cerceau, A   53
Du Fresnoy, C   133
Duns Scotus   15
Dutch elm disease   173
Dyer, G   11, 121, 122, 123, 124,
   125, 128, 133

Edgehill   113
Edward I   30
Eglesfield, R   38
Emmanuel College   15, 24, 51, 75,
   84, 100, 176
English Heritage Register   8, 179
Epicurus   39
Erasmus, D   39, 40, 58, 118, 122,
   178
Essex, J   111, 122, 141
Evans, Sir A   168, 169
Evelyn, J   64, 69, 70, 76, 84, 110
   Elysium Britannicum   70
Ewelme   60
Exeter College   21, 117, 118, 151

Farrer, R   162, 164
Fell, Dean J   88, 173
Fiennes, C   97–9
Fisher, J   40
Fleming, A   174
Florey, A   174
Fonthill   141
Fox, Bishop   25
Frewin Hall   16
Friars   15, 38
Fuller, T   40

Gaddesden, J   55
Gardeners' Benevolent
   Institution   165
Gardeners Magazine   143
Gardiner, R   86
Gedde, W   52
Genetic garden, Oxford   174
George III   124, 134
Gerard, J   43, 59, 60, 61
Gesner, K   58
Gibbon, E   107
Gibbs, J   92, 105, 111
Gillespie, Kidd & Coia   179
Gilpin, W   128–135, 144
   Essay on Prints   129; Tours   132;
   Remarks on Forest Scenery   132
Gilpin, W.S   143
Girton College   155, 156
Gloucester College   16, 17, 25
Goade, Dr.   49
Godstow   15, 32
Goldsmith, O   113
   The Deserted Village   134
Gonville Hall   24
Gosse, E   159
Graves, R   113
Gray, T   127
Green Belts   168, 169
Green College   179
Greenaway, K   159
Greyfriars   15, 30, 34
Grocyn, W   40, 58
Groote Schuur   161
Gruffyd, J. St Bodfan   179
Grumbold, R   96

Gunther, R.T   78, 151

Hainault, Countess of   38
Hagley   112
Hallam, A   125
Halley, E   102
Hamond Map   10, 46, 51
Hampton Court   80, 85, 93
Harcourt, 1st Earl of   134, 173
Harcourt, 2nd Earl of   133, 134,
   135
Harley, E, 2nd Earl of Oxford   111
Harris, G   162
Harris, W   95, 98
Harrison, W   47, 59
Hartley, D   118
Hawksmoor, N   12, 85, 90–3, 105,
   111, 121, 167
Hearne, T   81, 91
Henry I   15
Henry III   30
Henry VI   24, 38, 123
Henry VII   41, 155
Henry VIII   24, 25, 27, 32, 49, 51,
   55
Henslow, Prof. J.S   145, 148
Hentzner, P   43
Hepworth, B   176
Hertford College   92
Het Loo   95, 96
Hilborne, H   179
Hill, T   53
Hobbes, T   116
Hogarth, W   117, 118
Holywell Music Room   175
Hooke, R   64, 69, 102
Hopkins, G.M   107
Hortus Conclusus   31
Hovenden, R   53
Hutchinson, H   141
Huxley, T   149

Ipswich School   32

Jacobsen, A   176
James I   60
James II   95
James, Henry   7, 159, 181
James, T   125
Jeffreys, Judge   95
Jekyll, G   155, 159, 161, 162, 165
Jesus College, Cambridge   15, 21,
   24, 32, 53, 99
Jesus College, Oxford   51
Johnson, Dr. S   113
Jones, Inigo   61

Kames, Lord H   7
Keble College   150
Keble, J   150
Keene, H   160
Kelmscott   160
Kent, William   88, 178

King's College   24, 33, 38, 40, 45,
   49, 69, 121, 122, 123, 169, 179
King's Hall   23, 24, 25, 34, 37, 40,
   111
Kip and Knyff   99
Kirby Hall   61

Lady Margaret Hall   156, 157,
   159, 162
Landsberg, Dr. S   27
Langley, B   147
Lankester, J   179
Lapidge, E   147
Latimer, Bishop H   55
Lawes, J. Bennet   148
Lawson, W   47
Leasowes   113
Le Corbusier   176
Le Keux   11
Le Nôtre, A   92, 96, 111
Liddell, Dean H   31, 152
Liddell, Alice   152
Linacre, T   40, 58
Lincoln College   27, 48, 50, 51, 67,
   175
Linnaeus, C   148
Locke, J   95, 102, 104, 111, 115, 128
Loggan, D
   Cantabrigia Illustrata   10, 73,
   75, 79, 109, 121, 153
   Oxonia Illustrata   10, 51, 73,
   75, 76, 78, 80, 85, 86, 91, 99, 107
London, G   96
Loudon, J.C   143, 144, 147, 154
Lutyens, Sir E   159, 160, 161, 165,
   172
Lyons, I   145

McCormack & Jameson   179
Magdalen College, Oxford   12, 15,
   21, 40, 41, 58, 61, 62, 67, 68, 69,
   81, 95, 102, 129, 137, 139, 140,
   141, 151, 152, 167, 173
Magdalene College, Cambridge
   15, 17, 24, 41, 172
Mainwaring, Prof. J   120
Malchair, J.B   11
Malmesbury, William of   29
Martyn, Dr. T   65, 144
Martyr, Canon, P   49, 50
Mason, W   101, 120, 123, 127,
   133, 134, 144
Mede, J   64
Merton College   11, 20, 23, 58, 67,
   76, 167, 178
Michaelhouse   24, 25
Middleton, Dr. C   100
Miller, C   145, 172
Miller, P   93, 145
Miller, Sanderson   111, 112, 113,
   135
Milton, J   75
Modern Movement   176

Mollet, A   79
Montpellier   55, 59
Moore, H   176
More, Sir Thomas   39
Morris, W   153, 155, 156, 157, 158,
   159, 160, 162
Morison, Prof. R   80, 81
Munday, Mr   13
Murray, A   147, 148

Nash, J   137, 139, 141, 147
Nature Conservancy Council   173
Nesfield, W   152, 155
New College   11, 21, 23, 24, 32,
   36, 37, 63, 69, 78, 79, 85, 97, 98,
   129, 151
New Hall, Cambridge   176
Newdigate, Sir R   112
Newnham College   155, 156, 157,
   161, 176
Newton, I   65, 70, 73, 95, 102,
   104, 118
North Oxford suburb   150, 151,
   157
Nourse, T   105, 111
Nuffield College   176
Nuneham   133, 134, 135, 144, 173

Orchards   34, 39, 40, 41, 45, 47,
   51, 63, 67, 70
Oriel College   58, 178
Orleans, Duke of   80
Osney Abbey   28, 86
Owlets   161
Oxford Almancks   11, 88, 133
Oxford Archaeological Unit   28
Oxford Botanic Garden   148, 152,
   174, 175
Oxford City Museum   157
Oxford Physic Garden   60–64, 80,
   81
Oxford Movement   150
Oxford Preservation Trust   168,
   169, 175
Oxfordshire Horticultural
   Soc.   149

Padua   58, 59
Palladio, A   90, 117
Paradise Nursery, Oxford   15,
   100, 123
Paris   58
Parker's Piece   8
Parsons, A   159
Parsons, B   162
Pater, Walter   157
Pembroke College,
   Cambridge   37, 47, 75, 84
Pembroke College, Oxford   76,
   113, 175
Pembroke, Countess of   39
Penicillin rose garden   174
Penson's gardens   123

Peterhouse   15, 20, 23, 24, 37, 99,
   100, 127
Petersham   108
Pevsner, N   176
Pinck, Dr.   63
Pisa   59
Platt, Sir Hugh   47
Pliny   32, 58, 97
Plot, Dr. R   63, 70, 81
Pococke, Dr.E   78, 173
Pope, A   72, 102, 111, 117, 128
Powell & Moya   178
Powell, Dr. W   120
Pre-Raphaelites   158, 162
Price, Sir U   128
Prior, M   111
Pückler Muskau, H   7
Pugin, A   13

Queen Catherine of Aragon   32, 33
Queens' College, Cambridge   23,
   25, 38, 40, 48, 75, 99, 121, 122,
   124, 178
The Queen's College, Oxford   37,
   38, 69, 84, 85, 92, 102, 128
Queen Eleanor of Castille   27, 38
Queen Eleanor of Provence   27, 38
Queen Elizabeth I   43, 44–56, 59
Queen Elizabeth Woodville   38
Queen Henrietta Maria   67, 79,
   125
Queen Katherine Parr   25
Queen Margaret of Anjou   38
Queen Mary   49
Queen Philippa   37, 38, 39
Queen Victoria   121, 159

Radcliffe Camera   92
Radcliffe, Canon A   86
Radcliffe Infirmary   174
Radway   113
Ray, J   65, 72, 77
Redman, H   88
Repton, Humphry   11, 12, 137,
   138, 139, 140, 141
Repton, John Adey   137
Rhodes House   160
Rickman, T   141
Ridley, N   47, 55
Riskins   108
Roberts, D   175
Robin, V   80
Robinson College   179
Robinson, W   153, 154, 159, 162
Rogers, A   162, 164, 165
Rohde, E.S   164
Romance of the Rose   31
Rome   58, 92
Rooker, M.A   134
Rothamsted   148
Rousham   108, 178
Roubiliac, L   72
Routh, Dr. M   41

Royal Horticultural Society   143
Royal Society   64, 65, 84, 88, 102, 115
Rundt, C.L   151
Ruskin, J   155, 158, 159, 161, 162, 165

St Anne's College   156, 157, 162
St Augustine's Abbey, Canterbury   21
St Catherine's College   176
St Edmund Hall   17, 175
St Frideswide   14, 25, 49
St Gall   22, 30
St Hilda's College   156, 161
St Hugh's College   152, 162, 164
St John's College, Cambridge   15, 21, 23, 24, 39, 58, 75, 92–3, 99, 100, 120, 121, 141, 156, 171, 172, 178
St John's College, Oxford   12, 16, 25, 48, 98, 101, 105, 123, 124, 125, 134, 162
St Mary's, Oxford   92
Salisbury, 1st Earl of   61
Salmon, T   98, 99, 109, 111, 125
Sandringham   153
Sargent, J   159
Scaleby Castle   128
Scott, Gilbert   28
Sedding, J   159
Sedgwick, A   149
Selwyn College   156
Shaftesbury, 1st Earl of   95
Shaftesbury, 3rd Earl of   102, 115, 116, 117, 127, 128
Sharp, T   169, 171, 172
Sharrock, R   64
Sheldon, Archbishop   84
Sheldonian Theatre   84, 92
Shenstone, W   111, 113
Sherard, W   81
Sherborne, Bishop   33
Sidgwick, H   156
Sidney Sussex   15, 24, 34, 39, 47, 51, 75, 124
Sixtus V   91
Smith, Dr. T   25
Somerville College   156, 160
Southcote   108

Southey, R   101, 125, 128
Spenser, E   43
Sprat, T   69
Sterne, Dr. R   70, 72
Stone, N   61
Stourbridge Fair   14
Stukeley, W   73
Sussex, Countess of   39
Switzer, S   110, 111, 113
Switzerland   127

Tennyson, A   125, 158, 159
Thomas, W.B   153
Thomson, J   105, 113
Thorneycreek   179
Tijou, J   85
Tottie, Dr.   11, 49
Town and Country Planning Act, 1947   167
Townesend, W   85, 90, 92
Toynbee, A   7
Tradescant, J   61, 62
Trevelyan, G.M   100
Trinity College, Cambridge   8, 15, 20, 23, 24, 25, 40, 45, 49, 53, 65, 72, 75, 84, 85, 93, 100, 121, 122, 127, 153, 156, 179, 181
Trinity College, Oxford   16, 68, 85, 99, 101
Trinity Hall   21, 24, 36, 75
Turner, J.M.W   11, 165
Turner, W   58, 59
Tusser, T   51

University College, Oxford   20, 175
University Hall, Cambridge   24
University Parks   149, 150

Vanbrugh, J   105, 111
Venice   121
Versailles   85, 92
Virgil   105, 110, 129
    Aeneid   129
    Georgics   105
Vitruvius   90
Von Uffenbach, Z   10, 100

Wadham College   25, 68, 69, 73, 84, 99, 123, 161, 175, 176, 179

Walker, Dr.   144, 145, 149, 172
Walker, R   65
Walpole, H   113
Ward, J   63
Ward, Mrs H   157
Ward, Seth   69, 84
Ware, I   117
Waterhouse, A   151
Waynflete, William of   22, 41
Welsh, Miss   161
Whitaker, Dr.   49
Wilberforce, Bishop   149
Wilkins, Dr. J   69, 70, 73, 84, 102
Wilkins, W   123
Wilkinson, W   157
William III   93, 95, 97, 98, 99, 117
Williams, W   Oxonia Depicta   10, 90, 97, 98, 99, 117
Willis, R   11
Willis, T   69
Willmer, Prof. N   12, 165
Willughby, F   65
Wimpole   111, 112
Winchester College   22
Winchester Great Hall   27
Wise, H   96, 111
Wittgenstein, L   181
Wolfson College   178
Wolsey, Cardinal   22, 25, 28, 32, 33, 46, 58, 85
Wooburn farm   105
Wood, Anthony   11, 49, 51, 60, 62, 63, 69, 75, 76, 78, 79, 107
Woodstock   41
Woodward, Warden   78
Woolston, H   179
Worcester College   12, 15, 17, 25, 91, 135, 159, 179
Wordsworth, Miss   158
Wordsworth, W   123, 125, 128, 135
Worthington, J   70, 72
Wren, Sir Christopher   64, 69, 70, 84–90, 92, 93, 97, 102, 111, 117, 122
Wren, Matthew   69, 84
Wroxton   80
Wyatt, J   90, 141
Wykeham, William of   22